Envisioning Process as Content

This series of books is dedicated to all children whose natural giftedness is not recognized under our current educational structure. Within each one of them lie the beauty and wisdom of the whole world, and so we are choosing to honor their unique and diverse strengths—their spiritual essence. They have touched our hearts and filled us with love. They are the individual stars that together form the galaxies. We invite them to fill our lives with their special light and help us learn from and appreciate the kaleidoscopic world in which we live.

Envisioning Process as Content

Toward a Renaissance Curriculum

Editors

Arthur L. Costa
Rosemarie M. Liebmann

CORWIN PRESS, INC.
A Sage Publications Company
Thousand Oaks, California

For information address:

Corwin Press, Inc.
A Sage Publications Company
2455 Teller Road
Thousand Oaks, California 91320
E-mail: order@corwin.sagepub.com

SAGE Publications Ltd.
6 Bonhill Street
London EC2A 4PU
United Kingdom

SAGE Publications India Pvt. Ltd.
M-32 Market
Greater Kailash I
New Delhi 110 048 India

Printed in the United States of America

Library of Congress Cataloging-in-Publication Data

Main entry under title:

Envisioning process as content: Toward a renaissance curriculum /
  editors, Arthur L. Costa, Rosemarie M. Liebmann.
      p.   cm.
  Includes bibliographical references and index.
    ISBN 0-8039-6309-2 (alk. paper).—ISBN 0-8039-6310-6 (pbk.:
  alk. paper)
    1. Curriculum planning—United States.   2. Curriculum change—
  United States.   3. Total quality management—United States.
  I. Costa, Arthur L.   II. Liebmann, Rosemarie M.
  LB2806.15.E55   1996
  375′.001—dc20   96-9985

This book is printed on acid-free paper.

97 98 99 00 01 02 10 9 8 7 6 5 4 3 2 1

Editorial Assistant:	Kristen L. Green
Production Editor:	Michèle Lingre
Production Assistant:	Sherrise Purdum
Typesetter & Designer:	Andrea D. Swanson
Cover Designer:	Marcia R. Finlayson

Contents

Foreword

Peter M. Senge

The Tragedy of Our Times

Gordon Brown, former dean of the MIT School of Engineering, used to say, "To be a great teacher is to be a prophet—for you need to prepare young people not for today, but for 30 years into the future."

At few times in history has this admonition been more true than today. Yet if we look at the process, content, and achievements of public education, can any of us be confident that we are preparing young people well for the future in which they will live? Are we contributing to the capabilities of a 21st-century society to govern itself wisely, to prosper economically and culturally, and to generate insight into pressing problems and build consensus for change?

We stand poised at a turning point in history, with unprecedented challenges, some of which are literally unique in our history as a species. For the first time in our evolution, human beings have the power to fundamentally alter the natural environment within which we all live. No generation has ever had to face problems such as global warming (or cooling) and deterioration of the ozone layer. We are now the first species in the history of life on this planet that systematically destroys other species. No generation has ever had to confront the prospect of human activities that literally alter the gene pool and the evolutionary process. The nuclear arms race, now 50 years old, has entered a new, potentially more dangerous stage, with many nations involved. No generation before has ever had to live with the prospect of nuclear terrorism.

Within the United States, we are faced with uncontrollable government deficits and an unprecedented breakdown of the traditional family structure. No generation in America has ever had to confront such wholesale mortgaging of the future—simultaneously borrowing from future generations to support our current standard of living and leaving "no one at home" to raise that generation.

The common denominator of all the problems above is that they are *systemic* problems. The destruction of the environment, the arms race, and the erosion of community and family structures are not isolated problems with singular causes. They arise from the interactions, often during long periods, of diverse forces of change worldwide—forces such as technological progress, shifting societal values, global economics, and continuing population growth. Such problems cannot be understood by breaking them apart into components, and they will only be exacerbated by the "business as usual" politics of polarization and special interest groups. There are no villains to blame, no simple problems to fix. As the cartoon character "Pogo"—the first systems thinker in popular U.S. culture— said, "We have met the enemy and he is us."

A system of public education inevitably rests on public consensus regarding the skills, knowledge, and attitudes that will be needed by future citizens. Today, I believe our traditional consensus regarding the goals and process of public education leaves us dangerously vulnerable in a world of expanding interdependence. We have all been taught to analyze complex problems and to fix the pieces. Our traditional education process—indeed our theory of knowledge in the West—is based on reductionism, fragmenting complex phenomena into components and building up specialized knowledge of the parts. Moreover, our traditional educational process is based on competition and individual learning. This educational process, founded on fragmentation and rivalry, starts in elementary school and continues right through university, getting worse and worse the further one "progresses" in higher education. Literally, to be an "expert" in our society is to know a lot about a little. Such an educational process can never lay a solid foundation for understanding interdependency and for fostering genuine dialogue that integrates diverse points of view.

Concerns today with public education focus on achievement relative to traditional standards. But the real problem lies with the relevance of the traditional standards themselves. Preparing citizens for the future with the skills of the past has always been the bane of public education. Today, it could be the tragedy of our times.

A Leading Edge of Change

Given the profound changes that are unfolding all about us, it is not surprising that we are witnessing a massive deterioration of traditional institutions worldwide. In a world of rapid change and growing interdependence, large, centrally controlled organizations have become virtually ungovernable. The former Soviet Union, General Motors, and IBM, one-time paragons of power and control, all suffered massive breakdowns of their central nervous systems in the 1980s. The fundamental problem became the management system itself—the inability to effectively coordinate and adapt in an increasingly dynamic world, the inability to push decision making to "front lines," and the inability to neutralize traditional political power blocks committed to self-interest over common interest.

The failure in our traditional system of management is driving extraordinary change in the institution in which I spend most of my time—large business enterprises. Perhaps no sector has been forced to confront the startling changes of an interdependent world more rapidly than business. Because businesses literally compete against one another around the world, if one company or one part of the world makes significant headway in developing new skills and capabilities for a dynamic, interdependent world, it quickly gains advantage. Others will have to play catch-up or go out of business.

This is precisely what began to happen in the 1960s and 1970s, first with the Japanese, followed in rapid succession by the Koreans, Taiwanese, Singaporeans, and the other "Asian tigers"—what eventually became known as the total quality management (TQM) revolution. TQM represented, in the words of the Japanese TQM pioneer Ishikawa, "a thought revolution in management," based on such "radical" notions as "continuous improvement" (i.e., continuous learning) and focusing on "processes," not just products—how we are doing things, not just measuring the results of what we have done. TQM included a principle that everyone is part of a larger system, and the question should be not "What is my job description?" but "Who do I serve?" Extended to the enterprise as a whole, this principle implied that everyone in the enterprise needs to understand who the enterprise intends to serve—its "customers."

But TQM was merely the first wave of far more sweeping changes in traditional, centrally controlled bureaucratic organizations. Today, process-oriented management is being extended beyond basic manufacturing processes, the traditional focus of TQM, to thinking of everything an organization does as processes and to considering major reengineering of processes as well as continuous improvement. This is leading to new ideas about organization design—decentralization and network organizations, and even "virtual corporations," in which large numbers of highly autonomous operators interact, in effect, to create the scale of a large enterprise. Clearly, effective knowledge workers, whether they operate in networks of smaller enterprises or "networked," process-oriented larger enterprises, will need new skills and capabilities to understand complexity, communicate in ways that integrate diverse points of view, and build shared aspirations and mental models. In fact, without such new skills and capabilities, these new organizational forms may never come into being because they rely as much on the "soft technologies" of reflective conversation and systems thinking as they do on the "hard technologies" of information systems and telecommunications. In addition, in my view, running below the surface of these diverse changes may be a return to some guiding ideas from traditional management wisdom, ideas lost in the drive to reduce the art of management to a purely rational, quantifiable, mechanical model. These include ideas such as that an enterprise should exist to serve society, to contribute in some important way, and that this alone is their basis for sustaining a profit; that there is no substitute for passion, personal vision, excitement, and belief in what one is doing; and that profits when they are earned are more like oxygen than an end in and of themselves—they enable the enterprise to stay in the game and continue to generate and contribute.[1]

This whole cluster of changes in guiding ideas, core capabilities, management focus, and organization design represents a fundamental shift in our entire system of management and the overarching ethos of organizations, from "controlling organizations" to "learning organizations." This is the only ethos that seems compatible with organizational health in a world of growing interdependence and change.

The basic problem with all of this is that it is not easy. It takes years to develop the skills and knowledge to understand complex human systems, to learn how to think and learn together across cultural boundaries, to reverse years of conditioning in authoritarian organizations in which everyone "looks upward" for direction, and to build genuinely shared visions and promote "looking sideways" to see the larger systems of which each is a part. Equally challenging are the patience, perseverance, and extraordinary commitment required to develop these skills and understandings in the context of corporate environments still dominated by authoritarian, control-oriented cultures.

A Lagging Edge of Change

The more we understand the skills, knowledge, and beliefs needed to succeed in an interdependent world, the more we see the folly of thinking that we can focus exclusively on our system of management and ignore our system of education. Probably no one became more identified with the early stages of the quality management revolution than the American Dr. W. Edwards Deming. Shortly before Dr. Deming passed away in December 1993, I had an opportunity to ask him, "Dr. Deming, could the system of management you propound ever be widely implemented in the United States in our business enterprises if it is not implemented in our schools?" His simple answer was "No."

Having worked now for 20 years at developing the particular capabilities that seem vital to "learning organizations" in business organizations, it becomes clear that Deming was right. Isn't it silly to begin developing systems thinking capabilities in 35-year-olds who have spent the preceding 30 years becoming master reductionists? Isn't it grossly inefficient to begin developing reflectiveness, the ability to recognize and challenge one's own mental models, with successful adults—who to be successful in school and work had to become masters at solving problems rather than thinking about the thinking that generated the problems? Isn't it naive to think that we as adults can suddenly master collaborative learning, when so much of our lives has been devoted to win-lose competition and proving that we are better than each other? Shouldn't *personal mastery*, the discipline of fostering personal vision and working with "creative tension," be a cornerstone of schooling? Educators often speak of the ideal of lifelong learners—people with a keen sense of purposefulness, who are self-directed and good at objective self-assessment. Isn't it hypocritical to espouse personal vision and mature self-assessment when so much of traditional schooling is devoted to learning what *someone else* says we should learn and then convincing *them* we've learned it?

Increasingly, business people are recognizing the tragic neglect of fundamental innovation in public education. And they are moving from corporate contributions and public relations to action. For example, Electronic Data Systems (EDS) has a corporate policy that allows any employee to take time off each week with pay to volunteer in public schools. Intel employees have worked to start new public schools in Arizona and in statewide educational reform movements in Oregon and New Mexico. Ford employees are teaching systems thinking and mental models in community colleges in Detroit. Motorola has started its own "summer camp," teaching basic science and technology for children of Motorola employees.

But little is likely to take hold, spread, and grow from such isolated experiments until there is a widespread revolution in professional *and* public thinking about the nature and goals of public education for the 21st century. How will the traditional skill set of the industrial era have to be expanded for successful workers and citizens in the knowledge era? How must the traditional education process be transformed? How must traditional ideas of what constitutes "school" give way as more and more of the content of traditional education becomes available over the Internet? What will educational institutions commensurate with the knowledge era actually look like?

There will be no easy answers to such questions. My guess is that two cornerstones to the new system of education will be elevating the learning process to comparable standing with the content of what is learned and making high-level thinking and learning skills, such as systems thinking and collaborative learning, as important as traditional skills of reductionistic thinking and individual problem solving. These could indeed be two elements of a thought revolution in education.

Who Will Lead the Transformation?

Recently, my wife and I attended an awards assembly at our teenage son's school. Our 5-year old son, Ian, was with us. When the winner of the first award was announced, Ian turned to Diane and asked, "Mommy, is only one child getting an award? So, the other kids don't get a reward?"

What does a 5-year-old see that the sophisticated educators do not see? Why can he see the system as a whole—all the kids—and the educators see only the pieces, the "exceptional" kids? Maybe it's simply because the professional educators have spent their whole lives in schools. Maybe, despite their knowledge about learning theory and research, they also have the hardest time seeing beyond "the way it's always been done." Maybe the leadership that will be needed must come from all of us.

In 1994-1995, I participated in a series of satellite broadcasts on learning organizations.[2] One of these shows involved three kids from the Orange Grove Middle School in Tucson, Arizona, a school that has been integrating systems thinking and learner-directed learning throughout its curriculum and management practices for more than 5 years. The clarity, articulateness, and composure of these young people (ages 13 and 14) deeply impressed the other participants, mostly corporate managers doing the same types of work within their businesses. As the program went on, many of the most penetrating insights were offered by the young people. When the moderator asked who would like to offer any closing remarks, Kristi Jipson, an eighth-grade student at Orange Grove, said,

> I'd really like to say to those parents who say that "a book and a ruler is what it's all about," that you really need to talk to kids. If you talk to us, you'll see that we are really excited about what we are learning now. Before, you only needed to learn the "book and ruler" stuff. But now, as this program shows, businesses are changing, and by the time we get there this is what will be going on, and we'll need to know it.

One of the most forceful voices for innovation in the Catalina Foothills District, in which Orange Grove is located, has been a group of senior "citizen champions," many in their 70s and older, who in the words of Luise Hayden, became "enrolled in a revolution." They formed the Ideals Foundation with a vision of "entire curricula" organized around

> demonstrating how the parts relate to the whole. The foundation should benefit all children who are capable of learning, quickening their academic growth and enlarging their future aspirations and opportunities for school and career success, regardless of their present level of achievement. It should be a search for methods whereby students can use their own learning advances to help another, in a sustained and mutually supportive relationship.

The profound rethinking of public education required today cannot be led by any one constituency or professional group. The future is the responsibility of us all. And *all* includes those who have seen most of the past and those who will see the most of the future. All must participate, and all must lead.

Notes

1. Such ideas may seem naively idealistic, but that is only because of widely shared mental models about business, not because of any careful study of successful enterprises historically. For example, Royal-Dutch Shell's study of long-lived companies—business enterprises that have survived for more than 100 years—found virtually exactly these characteristics (see deGeus, 1995).

2. The broadcasts were a series of three programs on *Applying the Principles of the Learning Organization* (1994-1995), sponsored by a learning partnership of the Associated Equipment Distributors (AED) Foundation, the Association for Supervision and Curriculum Development (ASCD), The Learning Circle (TLC), and the PBS Adult Learning Services. The programs were coproduced by The Learning Circle and N.A.K. Production Associates.

References

deGues, A. P. (1995, January). *Companies: What are they?* [Speech delivered to the Royal Society of the Arts]. Available from the MIT Center for Organizational Learning, Cambridge.

The Learning Circle and N.A.K. Production Associates (Coproducers). (1994-1995). *Applying the principles of the learning organization* [Satellite broadcasts]. Sudbury, MA: The Learning Circle.

Preface to the Trilogy

Arthur L. Costa
Rosemarie M. Liebmann

When we no longer know what to do we have come to our real work and when we no longer know which way to go we have begun our real journey. The mind that is not baffled is not employed. The impeded stream is the one that sings.

Wendell Berry

Each new journey begins with a quest, a yearning to move beyond present limits. As we tried to envision the future needs of our learners, we were taken aback by how little we actually know about the world in which they will live. Numerous studies guided our way, but in reality, these are only predictions of a time we cannot fathom. Change is with us, and it seems to be invading our lives at an ever more rapid rate. Not only are we feeling the personal transitions, but organizational change, which has been traditionally slow, is responding to a faster and more demanding society.

This set of books provides educators with a bold but responsive perspective on curriculum intended to serve learners well into the 21st century. In today's complex and intelligence-intensive world economy, organizations can no longer rely exclusively on the intelligence of those few at the top of the pyramid. The amount of clear thinking required to meet the demands for speed, flexibility, quality, service, and innovation means that everyone in the organization must be involved. The organization must engage the acumen, business judgment, and systemwide responsibility of all its members.

Processes for the Workplace

Students entering the marketplace must come fully equipped with the skills that enable them to be lifelong learners. They must bring into the workplace their ability to think for themselves—to be self-initiating, self-modifying, and self-directing. They must acquire the capacity to learn and change consciously, continuously, and quickly.

The members of future organizations will require skills beyond that of content knowledge. The new employees must possess process skills. As Peter Senge addresses in the foreword, community members will be and are expected to go beyond just fixing problems to anticipating what might happen and to searching continuously for more creative solutions.

Societal Processes

The development of such a learning society depends on people's willingness to define the relationships between the individual and the community. The collective nurturing and understanding of our interdependence is essential if we wish to ensure our survival on this earth. More and more facets of society are beginning to challenge the traditionally held views of reductionist thinking. We are recognizing the need to see the world not only through the eyes of the individual but also as a part of a greater system in which connections are as important as differences.

Our society further recognizes a growing need for informed, skilled, and compassionate citizens who value truth, openness, creativity, and love, as well as the search for personal and spiritual freedom. We hear statements about community, interdependence, a balance in all areas of one's life, and making work an arena for self-discovery. This implies that the school's curriculum must be open enough to accept an androgynous perspective.

In an age in which self outweighs all other considerations, popular society is responding to the media because they appeal to their senses, not their thoughts. The advertising industry is geared to selling the sizzle to the senses and not the steak to the cerebrum. An Anheuser-Busch commercial delivers the following message: "Why ask why? Drink Bud dry." Or simply put, don't think, just drink! The media deliver the message that image is everything and substance is nothing. A recent Mazda commercial advocates, "Buy the car because it feels right." And Nike T-shirts are emblazoned with the statement, "Just Do It," which sends a message that impulsivity, rather than deliberation, is valued in this popular society.

Many persons are currently concerned with the increasing violence in schools, communities, and the world. Yet the media send a message that rules are unacceptable—"On Planet Reebok there are no rules!" The effect of the media as forces in learning cannot be underestimated. Education, therefore, must begin to help learners understand that not every opinion is worthwhile and that experts should be consulted. Educators must assist the young in moving away from the episodic grasp of reality created by the media.

These are not new thoughts but rather part of the continual quest for meaning as humans increase their knowledge base. Our desire to improve the current educational system has been founded on the erroneous belief that more of the same techniques and strategies will make all the difference. Yet if we consider the following quotes and their accompanying dates (from *Newsletter of the Curriculum and Supervisors Association*, 1994), one is left thinking that more of the same may in fact not hold the answers:

> More than eleven-twelfths of all the children in the reading classes in our schools do not understand the meaning of the words they read. —Horace Mann, 1838
>
> It is the opinion of high school teachers that from one fourth to one half the pupils are not greatly benefited by their course of study. These students lack interest, industry, effort, purpose, and are feebly endowed. —A Boston School Official, 1874
>
> A "despairing teacher" sent the *New York Times* samples of students' atrocious writing. —1911
>
> The president of the Carnegie Foundation complained, "In a large number of institutions the teaching has become enormously diluted." —1923
>
> The *Elementary School Journal* reported a "chronic problem facing American schools: a significant proportion of children were practically unable to learn to read under the prevailing methods of instruction." —1929
>
> The New York Committee on Delinquency in the Secondary Schools reported a "wide array of reckless, irresponsible, and anti-social behavior, with instances of violence, extortion, gang fights, and threats of bodily harm. There was vandalism against school property, private property, and pupils' personal possessions; there was theft, forgery, obscenity and vulgarity." —Early 1950s (p. 1)

The current education problems are the result of business as usual.

The revisioning of education now required is so profound that it reaches far beyond the questions of budget, class size, teacher pay, and the traditional conflicts over the curriculum. In truth, the current industrial model of education is largely obsolete.

Processes of Meaning Making

Educators, in conjunction with other stakeholders, must begin to address the purpose behind the content. They must ask themselves the question, "Why do we do what we do at all?"

The exploding array of information makes it more impractical than ever to cover content at the expense of in-depth treatment. We are on the verge of a paradigm shift—content will become the mechanism by which we teach process. This shift will embrace the child's natural love of learning. As Senge (1990) has stated,

> Children come fully equipped with an insatiable drive to explore and experiment. Unfortunately the primary institutions of our society are oriented predominantly toward controlling rather than learning,

rewarding individuals for performing for others rather than cultivating
their natural curiosity and impulse to learn. (p. 7)

Content can no longer be the end in and of itself but the tool by which people
learn to make meaning for themselves or to solve the problems for which they
do not have answers.

In the past, educators have considered knowledge as static. This concept
has influenced how we view a student's ability to learn. Valued is the possession
of information, thus excluding the dynamic processes by which information is
acquired and applied to authentic challenges. In the words of Deepak Chopra
(1994), we "have become obsessed with the child's weaknesses, hiring tutors to
make up for his [her] deficiencies, instead of looking at his [her] strengths and
nurturing the natural talents." Not all children can be mathematicians, scientists, artists, authors, poets, musicians, historians, and so forth. Children come
for a purpose unique to who they are, a purpose appropriate to the overall
mosaic of life. It is time educators value individuals for their natural skills and
talents, instead of trying to create clones, all possessing the same abilities.

Each human being has an inestimable potential for higher-order thought.
As a result, we believe processes should be at the center of education. According
to Chopra (1994),

> We think of the human body basically as a physical machine that has
> learned to think. Consciousness becomes the by-product of matter. The
> reality is that your physical body is not a frozen anatomical structure,
> but literally a river of intelligence and energy that's constantly renewing
> itself every second of your existence.
>
>   I'd like to propose that we are not physical machines that have learned
> how to think. Perhaps it's the other way around: We are thoughts (and
> impulses, consciousness, feelings, emotions, desires, and dreams) that
> have learned how to create physical bodies; that what we call our physical
> body is just a place that our memories call home for the time being.
>
>   Understanding that consciousness is the creator of the mind and
> body, I think, is really necessary for us to survive and create a new
> reality. Not only is the body a field of ideas, but so is the physical
> universe we inhabit.

Curriculum: A Shared Purpose

All institutions are changing as the relationships between employee and
employer, woman and man, offspring and parent, and student and teacher alter
in deep and permanent ways in response to the need for all to contribute their
intelligence, creativity, and responsibility to society.

The dilemma of what to teach and how best to teach dates from early
colonial times. In the present controversy, educators and those outside education wrestle with basic skills, which can be seen as quantifiable measures of the
success of education, versus intellectual skills, which are essentially qualitative
and require authentic forms of assessment.

The importance of establishing a shared purpose for education in a culturally diverse country needs to be understood. As one corporate executive stated,

> Schools have no alignment on purpose. It is as if someone blows the whistle and starts the football game but forgets the goalposts and the markings on the ground. The players are simply running around and the game keeps going on, but we have no idea if we are winning.

To be effective, an organization must have a clear vision or shared purpose, clear insights into current reality, and a willingness to work at closing the gap between the two. Until schools begin to recognize the changes in society, focus on new visions for students that are congruent with these changes, and come to grips with the current state of reality, the industrial model of education will be perpetuated in an intellectual, community-modeled learning society. As the old smokestacks of the industrial era vanish from the horizon, so must the industrial model of education. We need to reawaken in our students the joy of learning to use and develop their intellects.

Toward a Process Curriculum

Tomorrow's workplaces will require the following characteristics: flexible and customized production that meets the needs of the consumer, decentralized control, flexible automation, on-line quality control, work teams of multiskilled workers, delegation of authority to workers, labor-management cooperation, a screening procedure for basic skills abilities, a realization that the workforce is an investment, a limited internal labor market, advancement by certified skills rather than by seniority, a recognition that everyone requires continuing training, and employees with broader skills as opposed to specialists. Therefore, education needs to focus on

- The development of thinking skills
- Self-assessment integral to learning
- Opportunities for students to actively construct knowledge for themselves
- Learning environments that develop cooperative problem solving
- Skills that are learned in the context of real problems
- Learner-centered, teacher-directed management
- Outcomes that ensure all students have learned to think

Anthony Gregorc (1985) expresses this focus well:

> The intent of education is to aid the student in realizing that he/she is a thinking person equipped with a personal knowledge bank and a decision-making instrument called a mind. Each student is expected to realize that he/she has a personal set of truths, opinions, biases, and blind spots which guide attitudes and actions. The educational process is intended to demonstrate how the student uses his/her thinking mind,

how he/she learns from others and how he/she is affected by the environment. (pp. 98-99)

Ernest Boyer (1993) of the Carnegie Foundation saw the need for the following outcomes for students: being well-informed, acting wisely, continuing to learn, going beyond isolated facts to larger context and thereby discovering the connection of things, and seeing patterns and relationships that bring intellectual or aesthetic satisfaction.

We believe that the purpose of education is to enhance and develop the natural tendency of human beings as meaning makers. Humans' curiosity is aroused as we search for the meaning behind ambiguous principles and concepts. It is this continual search that promotes technological as well as personal advancements. When engaged in this search, we experience moments of illumination and moments of total change of heart. Educators need to return to learners their willingness to be playful, courageous, trusting, and risk taking. We need to invite them to reach for their outermost limits at all times. We need to create environments that allow students to practice freely without fear. We need to build not only strength of body but strength of character and strength of mind.

Where are we now? Csikszentmihalyi (1990) states,

> In the past few thousand years—a mere split second in evolutionary time—humanity has achieved incredible advances in the differentiation of consciousness. We have developed a realization that mankind is separate from other forms of life. We have conceived of individual human beings as separate from one another. We have invented abstraction and analysis—the ability to separate dimensions of objects and processes from each other, such as the velocity of a falling object from its weight and its mass. It is this differentiation that has produced science, technology, and the unprecedented power of mankind to build up and to destroy its environment.
>
> But complexity consists of integration as well as differentiation. The task of the next decades and centuries is to realize this under-developed component of the mind. Just as we have learned to separate ourselves from each other and from the environment, we now need to learn how to reunite ourselves with other entities around us without losing our hard-won individuality. The most promising faith for the future might be based on the realization that the entire universe is a system related by common laws and that it makes no sense to impose our dreams and desires on nature without taking them into account. Recognizing the limitations of human will, accepting a cooperative rather than a ruling role in the universe, we should feel the relief of the exile who is finally returning home. The problem of meaning will then be resolved as the individual's purpose merges with the universal flow. (p. 41)

For what should educators strive? Many of the answers lie in the chapters of these books. We need to develop holonomous thinkers—people who understand their individuality as well as their interdependence. We need to equip every member of society with the skills to survive in and contribute to a chaotic universe that is in constant change. All members need the strength and courage to live their lives to the fullest by giving their unique gifts back to the universe. Perhaps it is time that we as educators found the courage to open Pandora's box and release the butterfly inside.

> The solution which I am urging is to eradicate the fatal disconnection of subject which kills the vitality of our modern curriculum. There is only one subject-matter for education, and that is Life in all its manifestations.
>
> *Alfred North Whitehead (1929)*

References

Boyer, E. (1993, March). *Keynote address.* Address presented at the national conference of the Association for Supervision and Curriculum Development, Washington, DC.

Chopra, D. (1994, September). *Ageless body, timeless mind.* Presentation given at the Boundless Energy Retreat, Somerset, NJ.

Csikszentmihalyi, M. (1990). *Flow: The psychology of optimal experience.* New York: Harper & Row.

Gregorc, A. (1985, Fall/Winter). Toward a redefinition of teaching, instructing, educating, and training. *Curriculum in Context*, 97-100.

Newsletter of the Curriculum and Supervisors Association. (1994, June). p. 1.

Senge, P. (1990). The leader's new work: Building learning organizations. *Sloan Management Review*, 32(1), 7-22.

Preface to
Envisioning Process as Content

Arthur L. Costa
Rosemarie M. Liebmann

New frameworks are like climbing a mountain—the larger view encompasses, rather than rejects the earlier more restricted view.

Albert Einstein

The trilogy *Process as Content* invites a new vision of education and literacy. As humans enter a world in which knowledge doubles in less than 5 years (the projection is that by the year 2020, knowledge will double every 73 days), it is no longer feasible to anticipate the future information requirements of individuals. Educators must look differently and with greater depth at what learning is of most worth. We need, in the words of Michael Fullan (1993), to take a "quantum leap" (p. 5) in how we think about and develop curriculum.

The intent of this book, *Envisioning Process as Content: Toward a Renaissance Curriculum*, is to lay a foundation for our argument that the time has come to adopt process outcomes for education. We will provide definitions and theoretical constructs derived from the quantum sciences and the needs of students entering the information era. Implications will be drawn for curriculum planners. Readers will form an image of what education would be like if process were content by examining the contributions that various school-taught subjects could make if they were viewed as vehicles for developing the intellectual processes of learning rather than being taught as ends in themselves.

Because of increased knowledge on how the brain learns, because of paradigm shifts from the new sciences, and because of societal needs to engage in systems thinking, the time has come to shift our focus from the *what* of knowledge (content) to the *how* of learning (processes)—from, as Seymour Papert (1991) states, "instructionism to constructionism" (p. 24). We need to nurture the skills, operations, and dispositions that will enable individuals to solve problems when answers are *not* readily known. Educators need to embark on radical reforms that shift away from content to process and to value the collective intelligence of the group, as well as the intelligence of each learner.

We are not suggesting that content be devalued. We are suggesting that content be viewed from the perspective of how it enhances and accomplishes the development of processes. As Parker and Rubin (1966) wrote,

> Process—the cluster of diverse procedures which surround the acquisition of knowledge—is, in fact, the highest form of content and the most appropriate base for curriculum change. It is in the teaching of process that we can best portray learning as a perpetual endeavor and not something which terminates with the end of school. Through process, we can employ knowledge, not merely as a composite of information but, as a system for learning. (p. 1)

If we accept that the industrial model of society is currently shifting to a learning model of society, then the focus of education must also shift. The change will require a movement away from a content-driven curriculum toward a curriculum that provides individuals with the skills necessary to engage in lifelong learning.

Simultaneously, the role of the educator needs to shift from the information provider to that of a catalyst, coach, innovator, researcher, and collaborator with the learner throughout the learning process. The development of the learner's unique abilities becomes the central focus of the learning environment.

The intent of the book is to influence curriculum decision makers at all levels—teachers, administrators, school board members, test constructors, textbook authors, legislators, and parents—and to support them in thinking anew about the role of restructuring the curriculum in the school. We believe that the most critical, but least understood, component of the school reform movement is the restructuring of curriculum—which drives everything else. Curriculum is the pulse of the school; it is the currency through which educators exchange thoughts and ideas with students and the school community. It is the passion that binds the organization together. Curriculum, in the broadest sense, is everything that influences the learning of the students both overtly and covertly, inside and outside the school.

Current reform movements are being propelled by national, state, and local mandates; reorganization of time concerning the school day or the school year; redistributing the power of decision-making processes; investing in technology; and recombining interdisciplinary teams and subjects. These and other such reforms constitute the *how* of delivery, not the sum and substance of what we are all about. When we begin to address the heart of the organization, the driving component—curriculum—then all other reform efforts will fall into place. We have been building new reform structures around old-fashioned curriculum. Therefore, this book offers a bold proposal: Redesign the curriculum as the main component of revisioning the school.

Such radical shifts in current thinking require a clear articulation of process education. The first section of this book addresses what is meant by process and what some of these processes are. This is not a definitive list, but it serves to open the doors to new ways of thinking about what is worth learning.

We draw from supportive literature to underscore why the time is right for such a shift in thinking about how we educate. The concepts are assembled from current research and theory in education, findings from the new sciences, and expectations of performance from U.S. corporations.

Included are the ideas of expert theoreticians, researchers, and practitioners concerning curricular issues about the implementation of process education. We begin by considering curriculum itself as a process and present a case for why curriculum based on content and the disciplines has become outmoded and obsolete.

The chapter authors draw on their research, theoretical, and practical experiences to examine several curricular areas from a process orientation: Reading, writing, mathematics, foreign languages, and creativity are described as the processes they incorporate. Science, history, and aesthetics are presented as modes of inquiry.

The second book in this set, *Supporting the Spirit of Learning: When Process Is Content*, explores questions about curriculum and instruction such as these: What would instruction, assessment, teacher education, and staff development be like if process were content? How would we view human variability if process were content?

Numerous changes and shifts in paradigms are offered to those who embark on the journey. The third book of this set, *The Process Centered School: Sustaining a Renaissance Community*, offers leadership techniques and change strategies designed to help the adventuresome get started.

We invite you, as readers, to play with these visions, thoughts, and ideas— to elaborate, change, or modify them in ways that best meet the needs of your learning organizations. These concepts are offered to you as a way to stimulate your own growth and continued learning. Process, by its very nature, enables a dynamic response to the environment that surrounds us.

As people continue to recognize that knowledge speaks to us not in a single voice but with many voices, we will simultaneously accept the multiple ways of thinking and understanding. As Marvin Minsky (1987) has stated,

> Everyone can benefit from multiple ways of thinking about things. Understanding something in just one way is a rather fragile kind of understanding. You need to understand something at least two different ways in order to really understand it. Each way of thinking about something strengthens and deepens each of the other ways of thinking about it. Understanding something in several different ways produces an overall understanding that is richer and of a different nature than any one way of understanding. (p. 103)

We invite you to consider curriculum in a different way—to enter a world of learning that permits greater freedom, greater control, and, in the end, more thoughtful learners. From this increased freedom, we will generate eager, autonomous, interdependent, lifelong learners.

References

Fullan, M. (1993). *Change forces: Probing the depths of educational reform.* Bristol, PA: Falmer.

Minsky, M. (1987). *The society of mind.* New York: Simon & Schuster.

Papert, S. (1991). Situating constructionism. In I. Harel & S. Papert (Eds.), *Constructionism.* Norwood, NJ: Ablex.

Parker, J. C., & Rubin, L. J. (1966). *Process as content: Curriculum design and the application of knowledge.* Chicago: Rand McNally.

Acknowledgments

We wish to acknowledge the valuable contributions of each of the contributors to this volume and this series. Their contributions represent a vast and diverse range of points of view while at the same time a common focus, dedication and commitment to promoting process-oriented education. They have been patient with our prodding, agreeable to our edits, and supportive of our mission. For their time, energies, and talents we are forever grateful.

We also wish to acknowledge Alice Foster of Corwin Press whose encouragement and support sustained us over the 3 year duration of this project. We also wish to express our thanks to the editors at Corwin Press who assisted us greatly with refining the manuscript. And finally, we wish to acknowledge the high-school students in Mrs. McCann's Word Processing Center, Basking Ridge, NJ, who helped with the production of the graphics.

Arthur L. Costa
Rosemarie M. Liebmann

About the Authors

Merv Akin is Executive Director of Curriculum and Instruction for the Marysville Joint Unified School District in California. With more than 25 years of teaching experience, he has contributed to numerous curriculum and staff development projects. He has also taught methods classes for the California State University teacher education programs at Sacramento and Chico.

Louis T. Coulson serves on the faculty of the Creative Problem Solving Institute, Buffalo, New York, and is a Colleague of The Creative Education Foundation. He has spent 15 years in public education and 15 years as a creativity and innovation consultant in business and industry. He is one of the cofounders of Applied Creativity, Inc., a consulting firm dedicated to helping individuals and organizations reach their creative potential. He and cofounder Alison Strickland have designed and led hundreds of creative process workshops and problem-solving meetings for corporations including American Express, Chase Manhattan Bank, Du Pont, General Electric, and IBM. He holds a PhD in human development from the University of Maryland. His graduate work focused on creativity, adult learning theory, and idea development. Before establishing his own business, he was Director of Human Relations for Prince George's County Schools in Maryland.

Arthur L. Costa is Emeritus Professor of Education at California State University at Sacramento and Co-Director of the Institute for Intelligent Behavior in Berkeley, California. He has served as a classroom teacher, a curriculum consultant, and an assistant superintendent for instruction and as the Director of Educational Programs for the National Aeronautics and Space Administration. He has made presentations and conducted workshops in all 50 states and in Mexico, Central and South America, Canada, Australia, New Zealand, Africa, Europe, Asia, and the islands of the South Pacific. Author of numerous journal articles, he edited *Developing Minds: A Resource Book for Teaching Thinking* and authored *The Enabling Behaviors, Teaching for Intelligent Behaviors,* and *The School as a Home for the Mind.* He is coauthor of *Cognitive Coaching: A Foundation for Renaissance Schools* and coeditor of *The Role of Assessment in the Learning Organization: Shifting the Paradigm* and *If Minds Matter.* Active in many professional organizations, he served as President of the California Association for Supervision and Curriculum Development and was the National President of ASCD from 1988 to 1989.

David M. Dees is a Teaching Fellow in cultural foundations at Kent State University, Ohio. Since receiving an MA in theater from the University of Kentucky in 1989, his research, dissertation interests, and community involvement have centered on the ways in which aesthetic knowing can inform the art of teaching.

John Dyer is Senior Associate with the Institute for Intelligent Behavior and works as an international trainer in educationally related programs. Previously, he was an educator with the Calgary Board of Education, Alberta. His 28 years of experience with the board include positions of teacher, assistant principal, principal, assistant superintendent, and coordinator of staff development. He makes numerous presentations in both the private and the public sector. A frequent keynote convention speaker, he has worked in all Canadian provinces and territories and in numerous states in the United States. His specialities include cognitive coaching, supervision for reflective practice, regenerative work environments, the power of laughter and play in professional wellness, staff cohesion and collaborative leadership, and managing by agreement. More recently, he has been extensively involved with issues relating to strategic learning: core human systems that support change, learning, and innovation.

James G. Henderson is Associate Professor of Curriculum and Teaching at Kent State University, Ohio. His work focuses on curriculum and teacher education reform. He has been actively involved in the Holmes Group, a broad network of universities dedicated to fundamental changes in the preparation of teachers and the reform of schools. His publications include *Transformative Curriculum Leadership* (coauthored with Richard Hawthorne) and *Reflective Teaching: The Study of Your Constructivist Practices.*

Rosemarie M. Liebmann is Director of the Institute for Continuous Learning Systems, a private consulting firm; Director of Curriculum and Instruction, Livingston School District, Livingston, New Jersey; and Adjunct Professor at Seton Hall University, South Orange, New Jersey. She attained her Ed.D. from Seton Hall University and has done extensive work in the field of human resource development. Her doctoral thesis probed the holonomous skills required of a literate society. This research has led her to a recognition of the need for society to return to valuing personal and interpersonal spirituality. She has extensively researched the ancient art of shamanism as well as feminist spirituality. Having served in the educational field for 25 years as a teacher and administrator, she seeks to help others through the use of cognitive coaching. In her work as lecturer, workshop leader, educator, and author, she aspires to model for others that our minds will blossom only when we permit the buds to open. The richness of learning and experiencing the world around us is the nutrient for the soil of our spirits.

Carol T. Lloyd is a secondary mathematics teacher for the Cumberland County Schools in Fayetteville, North Carolina, and has conducted staff development in thinking skills for her school system for the last 3 years. Although she holds an M.A. in teaching from Duke University in social studies, she has taught high school mathematics for 18 years. During a time of major change in her school system, she served as a member of the Strategic Planning Committee for Thinking Skills and was chosen as one of 10 teachers charged with developing and implementing a training program on thinking skills for a system of 2,500 teachers. She has also conducted workshops on SAT preparation, computer use, and instructional alignment for Cumberland County Schools and on mathematics for regional and state conferences. Her major current interests are the continued infusion of thinking skills across the curriculum and the implementation of Costa and Garmston's cognitive coaching model in Cumberland County.

Ruth M. Loring is an educational consultant with more than 20 years of experience at the elementary through graduate levels as a classroom teacher, reading supervisor, and teacher educator. She earned a bachelor's in elementary education from Baylor University and a master's and a PhD in reading from the University of North Texas. The primary emphases in her professional development consultation are the direct teaching of thinking, teaching reading as a thinking process, motivation to read and learn, and skillful communication. She received recognition for outstanding research in reading from the International Reading Association and is a regular presenter at conferences around the United States on thinking and reading. She conducts Professional Development Institutes for the Association for Supervision and Curriculum Development and is a faculty member of the Greater Boston Institute for the Infusion of Critical Thinking. In 1994, she was a member of the Planning Committee for the Sixth International Conference on Thinking.

Peggy M. Luidens has been an educational consultant since 1985. As a Senior Associate with the Institute for Intelligent Behavior, she has collaborated with Arthur Costa and Robert Garmston on the elaboration of cognitive coaching, a coaching model that supports educators as mediators of critical thinking. She is also codeveloper of Project CRE (Collaboratively Restructuring Education for the 21st Century) to foster collective planning, program design, and implementation involving teachers, administrators, school staff, and parents. Project CRE was featured in the ASCD publication *HRDP Newsletter* (Fall 1994 and Spring 1995). She has developed and widely employed a workbook for use with the Writing Process. Using Writing Process techniques, she has worked with teachers from kindergarten through high school. Trained as an English teacher, she spent 7 years working in middle school classes. Following a graduate degree at Rutgers University, she served on the staffs of intermediate school districts in western Michigan.

Virginia Pauline Rojas is President of Rojas Language Associates, a consulting firm specializing in the teaching of second and foreign languages. She travels extensively to American and international schools around the world to develop language programs and conduct professional training sessions. She also works with stateside foreign language, ESL, and bilingual programs and is recognized for her leadership and her commitment to the development of bilingualism among school populations. Her interests lie in interactive language teaching instruction and performance assessment strategies. She focuses on the need for parents and teachers to unite to dispel myths surrounding second language acquisition to promote the benefit of more than one language for 21st-century citizens. She holds her academic credentials in language education, applied linguistics, and educational philosophy from Ohio State and Rutgers University. She has taught students at every grade level. She was formerly Director of the Office of Language and International Education for the New Jersey Department of Higher Education and Associate Professor of Education at Trenton State College.

Louis Rubin is Professor of Curriculum and Instruction at the University of Illinois, Champaign-Urbana. He has taught at Stanford University, the University of California at Berkeley, the University of Nebraska, and Emery University, as well as at Simon Fraser University and the University of British Columbia in Canada. He has published an extensive array of articles dating from 1960 and is the author-editor of 11 books, including a two-volume *Handbook of Curriculum, Facts and Feelings in the Classroom* and *The Future of Education: Frontiers in Leadership and Artistry in Teaching*. He was formerly the Director of the Communications Coalition for Educational Change in Washington, DC, and Director of the Center for Coordinated Education in Santa Barbara, California. He has served as a consultant to UNESCO, the U.S. Department of Education, the Ford and Kettering Foundations, and numerous state departments of education and several foreign nations. A frequent speaker, he has lectured in Europe, Asia, Africa, and South America.

Peter M. Senge is a faculty member of the Massachusetts Institute of Technology and Director of the Center for Organizational Learning at MIT's Sloan School of Management, a consortium of corporations that work together to advance methods and knowledge for building learning organizations. He is author of *The Fifth Discipline: The Art and Practice of the Learning Organization* and is coauthor (with colleagues Charlotte Roberts, Rock Ross, Bryan Smith, and Art Kleiner) of *The Fifth Discipline Fieldbook: Strategies and Tools for Building a Learning Organization*. He is also a founding partner of the management, consulting, and training firm Innovative Associates. He has lectured extensively throughout the world, translating the abstract ideas of systems theory into tools for better understanding economic and organizational change. His special interests and expertise focus on decentralizing the role of leadership in an organization to enhance the capacity of all people to work productively toward common goals. His work articulates a cornerstone position of human values in the workplace, namely, that vision, purpose, alignment, and systems thinking are essential if organizations are to truly realize their potentials. He has worked with leaders in business, education, health care, and government. He works collaboratively with organizations such as Ford, Federal Express, Motorola, AT&T, Intel, Electronic Data Systems (EDS), Harley-Davidson, Hewlett Packard, and Royal/Dutch Shell. He received a BS in engineering from Stanford University, an MS in social systems modeling, and a PhD in management from MIT.

Nancy Skerritt is Curriculum Director for the Tahoma School District in Maple Valley, Washington. She has designed and published a training model for writing integrated curriculum with thinking skills as the core. Her work includes authoring thinking skills strategy charts and designing graphic organizers for teaching thinking skills. She has conducted numerous workshops in curriculum integration and thinking skills instruction both in and out of Washington State. Her school district is viewed as a state leader in implementing the Washington State Education Reform Act. She is a member of the Washington State Assessment Advisory Committee charged with the design of the new performance-based assessment system. Prior to her work in curriculum development, she was a secondary language arts teacher and a counselor. She received her MA in teaching from Johns Hopkins University in 1971.

Alison G. Strickland has spent 15 years in public education and 15 years as a creativity and innovation consultant in business and industry. She is one of the cofounders of Applied Creativity, Inc., a consulting firm dedicated to helping individuals and organizations reach their creative potential. Alison and cofounder Louis (Ted) Coulson have designed and led hundreds of creative process workshops and problem-solving meetings for corporations including American Express, Chase Manhattan Bank, Du Pont, General Electric, and IBM. Their mission is to teach as many people as possible how to think, work, and live more creatively. She serves on the faculty of the Creative Problem Solving Institute, Buffalo, New York, and is a Colleague of The Creative Education Foundation. She holds a master's in education in curriculum and instructional design from the University of South Florida. She received her specialized training in creative problem solving at the Creative Problem Solving Institute and Synectics, Inc., Cambridge, Massachusetts. Among her published work are several young people's novels. Before cofounding her own business, she served in the Pinellas County Schools in Florida as a middle school classroom teacher, English department chair, countywide resource teacher, and trainer.

Martha I. Turner is Professor of Education at Southern Oregon State College. Her teaching experience includes both secondary and elementary levels in California public schools. She was a Research Fellow for the Ministry of Education in Japan, where she studied the Japanese educational system. In addition, she has conducted research on the computer culture of middle school students and global studies curriculum in secondary schools around the Pacific Circle.

Donald B. Young is Associate Professor of Science Education at the Curriculum Research & Development Group of the University of Hawaii, where he serves as coordinator for science education research. He has been involved for 25 years in the development, dissemination, and evaluation of elementary and secondary science programs. He received his master's degree from the State University of New York at Albany in science education and his EdD from the University of Hawaii. He has many years experience as a science teacher and curriculum developer and has been the coauthor of several science programs now being used nationally and internationally. Through these programs, he has also been active in providing inservice, professional development institutes for teachers nationwide. His recent research activities have been in learning and teaching science, program implementation and maintenance in schools, and multidimensional assessment. Currently, he is the Director of the Foundational Approaches in Science Teaching (FAST) project and the Standards-based Teacher Education through Partnerships (STEP) projects and is Associate Director of the Developmental Approaches in Science, Health and Technology (DASH) program.

1

Toward Renaissance Curriculum

An Idea Whose Time Has Come

Arthur L. Costa
Rosemarie M. Liebmann

Parker and Rubin (1966) elaborate on the distinction between process and content knowledge in education. They describe content as

> the compendium of information which comprises the learning material for a particular course of a given grade. Content, in short, is the rhetoric of conclusions to be transferred to the student.
>
> Process, in contrast, refers to all random or ordered operations which can be associated with knowledge and human activities. There are a wide variety of processes through which knowledge is created. There are also processes for utilizing knowledge and for communicating it. Processes are involved in arriving at decisions, in evaluating consequences, and in acquiring new insights. (p. 2)

Many schools today tend to teach, assess, and reward the acquisition of content and convergent thinking with a limited range of acceptable answers. Life in the real world, however, demands multiple ways to do something well. Understanding the process-content dynamic requires a fundamental shift in perceptions of what learning, teaching, and schooling are about. It is a shift from valuing right answers as the purpose for learning to knowing how to behave when we *don't* know answers—knowing what to do when confronted with those paradoxical, dichotomous, enigmatic, confusing, ambiguous, discrepant, and sometimes overwhelming situations that occur throughout life. It requires a shift from valuing knowledge *acquisition* as an outcome to valuing knowledge *production* as an outcome. The intent is to embark on the human quest for continual improvement—to have a lifelong passion to continue learning, to lend oneself to new experiences, and to greet the necessity for learning a new skill, understanding, or attitude with openness and eager anticipation.

Processes may be thought of at three levels: *skills, operations,* and *dispositions.*

- *Skills* are discrete and include such mental functions as comparing and classifying as well as behaviors such as listening, asking questions, catching a ball, and multiplying fractions.
- *Operations* are larger strategies employed through time. Operations require and include clusters of numerous skills. For example, *communicating* may be considered an operation composed of such verbal and nonverbal skills as attending, paraphrasing, clarifying, questioning, monitoring body language, and making eye contact.
- *Dispositions* are habits of mind, inclinations, proclivities, and characterizations. Unlike skills, they are never fully mastered but rather are attitudes that seem to characterize the human will: having a questioning attitude, persevering when an answer is not immediately known, and being willing to change one's mind in light of new information.

In addition, there are five states of mind: the invisible, internal human energy forces or passions that motivate and drive human will. They give rise to and fuel dispositions, operations, and skills (Costa & Garmston, 1994).

What Are the Processes?

Without getting too hierarchical, we believe that the skills enable the operations, and the operations, performed through time, are habituated into the dispositions. The performance and growth in those dispositions are determined by the balance and strength of internal drives, forces, or passions. Taken together, they constitute what is meant by processes and can become the objectives, outcomes, purposes, and mechanisms of instruction and curriculum. Process skills and behaviors are explained in Resource 1 at the end of this chapter.

According to Barry Beyer (1996), Edward de Bono (1991), and Reuven Feuerstein (1991), these skills may need to be taught directly to students who have not learned how to use them or who do not comprehend the acts of performing these skills. Few people simply go out and observe, compare, and synthesize. These skills, then, are engaged within a larger context. They are the skills used to perform the operations needed to respond to the stimulus.

Therefore, if they are taught directly, they should be transferred, bridged, or linked to life situations that call for their performance (see Swartz & Parks, 1994). For example, the operation of decision making involves the skills of generating alternatives, exploring consequences, making predictions, comparing and contrasting, considering temporal dimensions, prioritizing, considering alternative points of view, and so forth. A more complete, but not final, list of operations can be found in Resource 2 at the end of this chapter.

Dispositions

The dispositions are characteristics that teachers and parents can teach and observe. Following is a list of 13 attributes or character traits (from Costa, 1991) providing the third level of the process goals. As with the previous lists, this list is not meant to be complete.

Persistence: Persevering When the Solution to a Problem Is Not Readily Apparent

Efficacious people stick to a task until it is completed. They don't give up easily. They are able to analyze a problem and develop a system, structure, or strategy to attack a problem. They have a range of alternative strategies for problem solving. They collect evidence to indicate their problem-solving strategy is working; if one strategy doesn't work, they know how to back up and try another. They recognize when a theory or idea must be rejected and another employed. They have systematic methods of analyzing a problem that include knowing how to begin, knowing what steps must be performed, and knowing what data need to be generated or collected.

Decreasing Impulsivity

Effective individuals have a sense of deliberativeness: They think before they act. They intentionally form a vision of a product, plan of action, goal, or a destination before they begin. They strive to clarify and understand directions, develop a strategy for approaching a problem, and withhold immediate value judgments about an idea before fully understanding it. Reflective individuals consider alternatives and consequences of several possible directions prior to taking action. They decrease their need for trial and error by gathering information, taking time to reflect on an answer before giving it, making sure they understand directions, and listening to alternative points of view.

Listening to Others—With Understanding and Empathy

Highly effective people spend an inordinate amount of time and energy listening. Some psychologists believe that the ability to listen to, empathize with, and understand another person's point of view is one of the highest forms of intelligent behavior. Being able to paraphrase another person's ideas, detecting indicators (cues) of the other's feelings or emotional states in oral and body language (empathy), and accurately expressing another person's concepts, emotions, and problems—all are indications of listening behavior (Piaget called it "overcoming egocentrism"). They gently attend to another person, demonstrating their understanding of and empathy for an idea or feeling by paraphrasing it accurately, building on it, clarifying it, and giving an example of it.

Metacognition: Awareness of Our Own Thinking

Metacognition means that humans are conscious of our actions, plans, strategies, behaviors, feelings, and values. It means installing a plan of action before beginning to solve a problem, determining if that plan is working or if it should be discarded and another plan employed, and evaluating the strategy to determine its efficacy or a more efficient approach. It means being able to describe the strategies, steps, and sequences employed in the problem-solving process—transforming into words the visual images held in the mind. Humans plan for, reflect on, and evaluate the quality of their own thinking skills and strategies.

Metacognition means becoming increasingly aware of one's actions and the effect of those actions on others and on the environment, forming internal questions as one searches for information and meaning, developing mental maps or plans of action, mentally rehearsing prior to performance, and monitoring those plans as they are employed. It involves being conscious of the need for midcourse correction if the plan is not meeting expectations, reflecting on the plan on completion of the implementation for the purpose of self-evaluation, and editing mental pictures for improved performance.

Striving for Accuracy and Precision

People who value accuracy, precision, and competence take time to check over their products, review the rule by which they are to abide, review the models and visions they are to follow, review the criteria they are to employ, and confirm that their finished product matches the criteria exactly. They take pride in being craftspersons and have a desire for accuracy as they take time to check over their work. They are concerned with precision, clarity, and perfection.

Craftspeople communicate accurately in both written and oral form—taking care to use precise language, defining terms, and using correct names and universal labels and analogies. They spontaneously develop criteria for their own value judgments and describe why they think one product is better than another. They speak in complete sentences, voluntarily provide supporting evidence for their ideas, and can elaborate, clarify, and operationally define their terms in a concise, descriptive, and coherent manner.

Questioning and Problem Posing

One of the distinguishing characteristics between humans and other forms of life is our inclination and ability to *find* problems to solve. Effective problem solvers know how to ask questions to fill in the gaps between what they know and what they don't know. Effective questioners are inclined to ask a range of questions, for example, requests for data to support others' conclusions and assumptions—such questions as, "What evidence do you have?" or "How do you know that's true?"

They pose hypothetical problems characterized by iffy questions: "What do you think would happen *if*. . ?" or "*If* that is true, then what might happen if . . ?"

Inquirers recognize discrepancies and phenomena in their environment and probe into their causes: "Why do cats purr?" "How high can birds fly?" "Why does the hair on my head grow so fast, while the hair on my arms and legs grows so slowly?" "What would happen if we put the saltwater fish in a freshwater aquarium?" "What are some alternative solutions to international conflicts other than wars?"

Drawing on Past Knowledge and Applying It to New Situations

Intelligent human beings learn from experience. They are able to abstract meaning from one experience, carry it forth, and apply it in a new situation. They can often be heard to say, "This reminds me of . . " or "This is just like the time when I . . " They explain what they are doing now with analogies or references to previous experiences. They call on their store of knowledge and experience as sources of data to support, theories to explain, or processes to solve each new challenge.

Displaying a Sense of Humor

Laughter links all human beings. Its positive effects on physiological functions include a drop in the pulse rate, the secretion of endorphins, and increased oxygen in the blood. Laughter has been found to liberate creativity and provoke such higher-level thinking skills as anticipation, finding novel relationships, and visual imagery. Humorous people have the ability to perceive situations from an original and often interesting vantage point. They tend to initiate humor more often, to place greater value on having a sense of humor, to appreciate and understand others' humor, and to be verbally playful when interacting with others. Those with a whimsical frame of mind thrive on finding incongruities and discontinuities; perceiving absurdities, ironies, and satire; and being able to laugh at situations and themselves. As creative problem solvers, they characteristically can distinguish between situations of human frailty and fallibility that are in need of compassion and those situations that are truly funny (see Dyer, Chapter 15 in this volume).

Cooperative Thinking

Human beings are social beings. We congregate in groups, find it therapeutic to be listened to, draw energy from one another, and seek reciprocity. In groups, we contribute our time and energy to tasks that we would quickly tire of when working alone. In fact, one of the cruelest forms of punishment that can be inflicted on an individual is solitary confinement.

Cooperative humans realize that all of us together are more powerful, intellectually and/or physically, than any one individual. Probably the foremost disposition in the postindustrial society is the heightened ability to think in concert with others, to be more interdependent and sensitive to the needs of others. Problem solving has become so complex that no one person can go it alone. No one has access to all the data needed to make critical decisions; no one person can consider as many alternatives as can several people. Working in groups requires the ability to justify ideas and to test the feasibility of solution strategies on others. It also requires the development of a willingness and openness to accept the feedback from critical friends. Through this interaction, the group and the individual continue to grow. Listening, consensus seeking, giving up an idea to work with someone else's, empathy, compassion, group leadership, knowing how to support group efforts, and altruism—all are behaviors indicative of cooperative human beings.

Using All the Senses

All information gets into the brain through the sensory pathways: visual, tactile, kinesthetic, auditory, olfactory, and gustatory. Most linguistic, cultural, and physical learning is derived from the environment by observing or intaking through the senses. To know a wine, it must be drunk; to know a role, it must be acted; to know a game, it must be played; to know a dance, it must be moved; to know a goal, it must be envisioned. Those whose sensory pathways are open, alert, and acute absorb more information from the environment than those whose pathways are withered, immune, and oblivious to sensory stimuli. Effective learners use all the senses as they encounter various objects in their environment. (Young children may put things in their mouths.) Children will request a story or rhyme to be read again and again. They will act out roles and "be" the thing: a father, a flatbed, or a fish. "Let me see, let me see." "I want to feel it." "Let me try it." "Let me hold it," they will plead. They conceive and express many ways of solving problems by use of the senses: making observations, gathering data, experimenting, role playing, simulating, manipulating, scrutinizing, identifying variables, interviewing, breaking problems into components, visualizing, imitating, illustrating, and model building.

Ingenuity, Originality, Insight: Creativity

"I can't draw." "I was never very good at art." "I can't sing a note." Some people think creative humans are just born that way—that it's in their genes and chromosomes. Increasingly, people are coming to realize that all human beings have the capacity to generate original, clever, and ingenious products, solutions, and techniques—if that capacity is developed.

Creative human beings often try to conceive problem solutions differently, examining alternative possibilities from many angles. They tend to project themselves into different roles using analogies, starting with a vision and working backward, and imagining they are the object being considered. Creative people take risks and frequently push the boundaries of their perceived limits (Perkins, 1989). They are intrinsically rather than extrinsically motivated, working on the task because of the aesthetic challenge rather than the material rewards. Creative people are open to criticism. They hold up their products for others to judge and seek feedback in an ever increasing effort to refine their technique. They are uneasy with the status quo. They constantly strive for

greater fluency, elaboration, novelty, parsimony, simplicity, competence, perfection, beauty, harmony, and balance.

Risk Taking

Flexible people seem to have an almost uncontrollable urge to go beyond
established limits. They are uneasy about comfort; they "live on the edge" of
their competence. They seem compelled to place themselves in situations in
which they do not know what the outcome will be. They accept confusion,
uncertainty, and the higher risks of failure as part of the normal process, and
they learn to view setbacks as interesting, challenging, and growth producing.

Wonderment, Inquisitiveness, Curiosity, and the Enjoyment of Problem Solving

Inquisitive people have not only an "I can" attitude but also an "I enjoy"
feeling. They seek problems to solve for themselves and to submit to others.
They delight in making up problems to solve on their own and request enigmas
from others. They enjoy figuring things out by themselves and continue to learn
throughout their lifetimes.

Curious persons commune with the world around them. They reflect on the
changing formations of a cloud, are charmed by the opening of a bud, and sense
the logical simplicity of mathematical order. They find beauty in a sunset,
intrigue in the geometrics of a spider web, and exhilaration at the iridescence of
a hummingbird's wings. They see the congruity and intricacies in the derivation
of a mathematical formula, recognize the orderliness and adroitness of a chemical change, and commune with the serenity of a distant constellation.

They are curious and derive pleasure from thinking. Their environment
attracts their inquiry as their senses capture the rhythm, patterns, shapes, colors,
and harmonies of the universe. They display cognizant and compassionate
behavior toward other life forms because they are able to understand the need
for protecting their environment, respecting the roles and values of other human
beings, and perceiving the delicate worth, uniqueness, and relationships of
everything and everyone they encounter.

States of Mind

Five states of mind (Costa & Garmston, 1994), described below, may be
thought of as catalysts—the energy sources and the passions fueling human
behaviors. Taken together, they are forces directing one toward increasingly
authentic, congruent, and ethical behavior—the touchstones of integrity. They
are the tools of disciplined choice making that guide human action. They are
the primary vehicles in the lifelong journey toward integration.

> There is a dimension of the universe unavailable to the senses. (Joseph
> Campbell)

We know there are invisible forces in the universe: Gravitational, electro-magnetic, and electrostatic fields; inertia; and centrifugal forces are some common examples. Although they cannot be observed directly, they are known through their effects. We believe unseen forces affect humans as well. These basic human forces are the passions that drive, influence, motivate, and inspire our intellectual capacities and high performance. They also are known by their effects: productive human thought and action. We categorize and define the five human passions as follows (Costa & Garmston, 1994):

1. *The Passion for Efficacy:* Humans quest for continuous, lifelong learning, self-empowerment, mastery, and control.
2. *The Passion for Flexibility:* Humans perceive from multiple perspectives and endeavor to change, adapt, and expand their repertoire of response patterns.
3. *The Passion for Craftspersonship:* Humans yearn to become clearer, more elegant, precise, congruent, and integrated.
4. *The Passion for Consciousness:* Humans strive to monitor and reflect on their own thoughts and actions.
5. *The Passion for Interdependence:* Humans need reciprocity, belonging, and connectedness and are inclined to become one with the larger system and community of which they are a part.

We believe these five passions to be the generators of effective thought and action. We will elaborate each, describe their intellectual manifestations, and draw educational implications for their continuous development.

Efficacy

Efficacious people have internal loci of control. They produce new knowledge. They engage in causal thinking. They pose problems and search for problems to solve. They are optimistic and resourceful. They are self-actualizing and self-modifying. They are able to operationalize concepts and translate them into deliberate actions. They establish feedback spirals and continue to learn how to learn.

Efficacy means knowing one has the capacity to make a difference and being willing and able to do so. Efficacy is a particularly catalytic state of mind because the sense of efficacy is a determining factor in the resolution of complex problems.

If a person feels little efficacy, then blame, withdrawal, and rigidity are likely to follow. With robust efficacy, people are likely to expend more energy in their work, persevere longer, set more challenging goals, and continue in the face of barriers or failure. Efficacious people regard events as opportunities for learning. They believe that personal action produces outcomes, they control performance anxiety by accessing personal resources, and they recognize and draw on previous experiences. They are aware of what is not known and actively seek other resources to complement and enhance their knowledge.

One value of efficacy and its by-product, self-confidence, is that they free up common sense. The more efficacious we feel, the more flexibly we can engage in critical and creative work. Developing efficacious thinking, therefore, requires becoming increasingly self-referencing, self-evaluating, self-initiating, and self-modifying.

Flexibility

Flexible thinkers are empathic. They are able to see through the diverse perspectives of others. They are open and comfortable with ambiguity. They create and seek novel approaches and have well-developed senses of humor. They envision a range of consequences. They have the capacity to change their minds as they receive additional data. They engage in multiple and simultaneous outcomes and activities, draw on a repertoire of problem-solving strategies, and can practice style flexibility—knowing when it is appropriate to be broad and global in their thinking and when a situation requires detailed precision.

Flexible people can approach a problem from a new angle using a novel approach (de Bono, 1994, refers to this as *lateral thinking*). They consider alternative points of view and deal with several sources of information simultaneously. They are able to sustain a process of problem solving through time and therefore can tolerate ambiguous situations. Their minds are open to change on the basis of additional information or reasoning that contradicts their beliefs. They can state several ways of solving the same problem and can evaluate the merits and consequences of alternate courses of action. When making decisions, they will often use such phrases as "however," "on the other hand," and "if you look at it another way." They develop a well-formulated set of moral principles to govern their own behavior. When working in groups, they often resolve conflicts through dialogue, express willingness to experiment with another person's idea, and strive for consensus.

Flexible people know that they have and can develop options to consider about their work and are willing to acknowledge and demonstrate respect and empathy for diverse perspectives. They understand means-ends relationships. They are able to work within rules, criteria, and regulations, and they can predict the consequences of flouting them. They not only understand the immediate reactions but also are able to perceive the bigger purposes that such constraints serve. Thus, flexibility of mind is essential for working with social diversity, enabling individuals to recognize the wholeness and distinctness of other people's ways of experiencing and making meaning.

Flexible thinkers display an ability for flexible attention, being able to shift, at will, through multiple perceptual positions. One perceptual orientation is what Piaget called *egocentrism*—perceiving from one's own point of view. By contrast, *allocentrism* is the position in which we perceive through another person's orientation. We operate from this second position when we empathize with other's feelings, predict how others are thinking, and anticipate potential misunderstandings.

Another perceptual position is *macrocentrism*. This is similar to looking down from a balcony at ourselves and our interactions with others. Macroattention, the bird's-eye view, is useful for discerning themes and patterns from assortments of information. It is intuitive, holistic, and conceptual. Because humans often need to solve problems with incomplete information, we need the capacity to perceive general patterns and jump across gaps in present knowledge. Macrocentric thinking is necessary for bridging the gaps and enabling us to perceive a pattern even when some of the pieces are missing.

Yet another perceptual orientation is *microcentrism,* the examination of the individual and sometimes minute parts that make up the whole. A micromode is the worm's-eye view without which science, technology, and any complex enterprise could not function. Microattention involves logical, analytical computation and searching for causality in methodical steps. It encompasses attention to detail, precision, and orderly progressions.

Flexible thinkers display confidence in their intuitions. They tolerate confusion and ambiguity up to a point and are willing to let go of a problem, trusting their subconscious to continue creative and productive work on it. Flexibility is the cradle of humor, creativity, and repertoire. Flexibility is interrelated with consciousness. Although there are many possible perceptual positions—for example, past, present, future, egocentric, allocentric, macrocentric, visual, auditory, and kinesthetic—the flexible mind is activated by knowing when to shift perceptual positions. Because the most flexible person is the one with most control, developing effective thinking requires the continuous expansion of repertoire.

Craftsmanship

Craftsmen seek perfection and take pride in their artistry. They seek precision and mastery. They seek refinement and specificity in communications. They generate and hold clear visions and goals. They strive for exactness of critical thought processes. They use precise language for describing their work. They make thorough and rational decisions about actions to be taken. They test and revise, constantly honing strategies to reach goals.

Craftsmanship is about striving for mastery, grace, and economy of energy to produce exceptional results. It means knowing that we can continually perfect our craft by working to attain our own high standards and by pursuing learning.

Craftsmanship includes exactness, precision, accuracy, correctness, flawlessness, faithfulness, and fidelity—but not in all things. The craftsperson also works flexibly. Craftsmanship without flexibility is perfectionism.

Because language and thinking are closely entwined, precision of language is an important characteristic of the craftsperson. Language acquisition plays a critical role in enhancing a person's cognitive maps, the ability to think critically, and the knowledge base for efficacious action. Precision and mastery across six temporal dimensions are also the mark of effective thinkers. Every thought, event, occurrence, and situation is definable in these ways:

1. *Sequence:* how events are ordered—first, second, third
2. *Duration:* how long the event will last
3. *Rhythm:* how often the event will occur
4. *Simultaneity:* what other events are happening at the same time
5. *Synchronization:* how several events can be coordinated with other events

6. *Time perspectives (temporal logic):* keeping both the short-range—moment to moment—and long-range future events in mind

As humans acquire more exact language for describing their work, they begin to recognize concepts, identify key attributes, distinguish similarities and differences, and make more thorough and rational decisions. Developing crafts-manship, therefore, enriches the complexity and specificity of language and simultaneously produces effective thinking.

Consciousness

Conscious thinkers metacogitate. They monitor their own values, inten-tions, thoughts, and behaviors and their effects on others and the environment. They are aware of their own and others' progress toward goals. They articulate well-defined value systems. They generate, hold, and apply internal criteria for their decisions. They practice mental rehearsal and the editing of mental pic-tures in the process of seeking improved performance.

Conscious thinkers know what and how they are thinking about their work in the moment. It is being aware of their actions and how they affect others as well as the environment.

Consciousness is the central clearinghouse in which varied events pro-cessed by different senses can be represented and compared and, therefore, has particular catalytic properties for the other passions. It is *the* state of mind that is prerequisite to self-control and self-direction. Consciousness means being aware that certain events are occurring and being able to direct response to the events.

Csikszentmihalyi (1993) defines consciousness as states of enjoyment, con-centration, and deep involvement. He uses the term *flow* for a special state of concentration so focused that it amounts to absolute absorption in an activity, making the experience genuinely enjoyable.

The function of consciousness is to represent information about what is happening outside and inside the organism in such a way that it can be evaluated and acted on. Without consciousness, people would still "know" what is going on, but we would have to react to it in a reflexive, instinctive way. Because we have consciousness, we can daydream, change our perceptual position, write beautiful poems, and develop elegant scientific theories.

Consciousness provides a distinctive characteristic of the human nervous system in that we are able to affect our own emotional or mental states. We can make ourselves happy or miserable regardless of what is actually happening "outside," just by changing the contents of our consciousness.

Intentionality keeps information in consciousness ordered. Intentions arise whenever we have a goal or we become aware of desiring or wanting to accomplish something. Intentions are also bits of information, shaped either by biological needs or by internalized social goals. The intentions we inherit or acquire are organized in hierarchies of goals and values, which specify the priorities among them.

Attention is psychic energy. What we allow into consciousness determines the quality of our lives. Human beings can attend to seven (plus or minus two)

bits of information, such as differentiated sounds, visual stimuli, and recognizable nuances of emotion or thought, at any one time (Miller, 1963). Information enters consciousness either because we intend to focus attention on it or as a result of attentional habits based on biological or social instructions. It is attention that selects the relevant bits of information from the potential millions of bits available.

The mark of a person who is in control of consciousness is the ability to focus attention at will, to be oblivious to distractions, to concentrate for as long as it takes to achieve a goal. Developing effective thinking, therefore requires the development of this priceless resource, consciousness.

Interdependence

Interdependent people have a sense of community: "we-ness" as much as "me-ness." They are altruistic. They value consensus and are able to hold their own beliefs and actions in abeyance to lend their energies and resources to the achievement of group goals. They contribute themselves to a common good, seek collegiality, and draw on the resources of others. They regard conflict as valuable, trusting their abilities to manage group differences in productive ways. They continue to learn on the basis of feedback from others and from their conscious attending to their own actions and their effects on others. They seek engagement in holonomous part-whole relationships, knowing that *all of us* are more efficient than any one of us.

Interdependence means knowing that we will benefit from participating in, contributing to, and receiving from professional relationships and being willing to create and change relationships to benefit our work. The human intellect grows in reciprocity with others. The Russian psycholinguist Lev Vygotsky reports, "Every function in cultural development appears twice. First, in the social level and later on the individual level. First, between people and then inside. All the higher functions originate as actual relations between individuals" (cited in Costa & Garmston, 1994, p. 140).

Vygotsky suggests that intelligence grows in two ways. One is the intelligence that develops through individual experience. But intelligence also gets shaped through reciprocity with others. Justifying reasons, resolving differences, actively listening to another person's point of view, achieving consensus, and receiving feedback actually increase intelligence.

As humans develop cognitively, they value and, with increasing consistency, view situations from multiple perspectives. As stated earlier, flexibility is prerequisite to the state of mind of interdependence because flexibility allows one to see others' points of view and to be able to change and adapt on the basis of feedback from others.

Interdependent people interpret conflict as valuable, with the potential benefits of solving problems and finding new ways of solving problems. Persons endowed with the passion for interdependence can focus on ways to let a conflictual relationship transform the parties rather than focusing on the parties resolving the conflict.

As individuals become more interdependent, they may experience a sense of interconnectedness and kinship that comes from a unity of being, a sense of sharing a common community (e.g., class, school, and neighborhood) and a mutual bonding to common goals and shared values. An interdependent individual's sense of self is enlarged from a conception of *me* to a sense of *us* (Sergiovanni, 1994). Interdependent persons understand that as they transcend the self and become part of the whole, they do not lose their individuality but rather their egocentricity.

As interdependence develops, it is characterized by altruism, collegiality, and the giving of self to group goals and needs. Just as interdependent persons contribute to a common good, they also genuinely value and draw on the resources of others. They value dialogue and lend their energies to the achievement of group goals. Interdependent people envision the expanding capacities of the group and its members.

Interdependence facilitates systems thinking in which many variables are constantly interacting. Each variable affects another, which affects another, and so on. Families, weather systems, and national economies are examples of systems. In these dynamic systems, tiny inputs can reverberate throughout the system, producing dramatically large consequences. Because of this, interdependent thinkers realize the potential to significantly influence the direction of the community of which they are a part.

Interdependence, along with the other four passions of efficacy, flexibility, craftspersonship, and consciousness, makes possible more complete and effective intellectual functioning of human beings.

Implications for Education

These five passions may serve as mental disciplines. When confronted with problematic situations, students and teachers might habitually employ these five habits of mind:

What is the most *efficacious* thing I can do right now? How can I learn from this? How can I draw on my past successes with similar problems? What do I already know about the problem? What resources do I have available or need to generate?

How can I approach this problem *flexibly*? How might I look at the situation in another way? How can I draw on my repertoire of problem-solving strategies? How can I look at this problem from a fresh perspective (lateral thinking)?

What is the most *craftsman-like* thing I can do? How can I illuminate this problem to make it clearer, more precise? Do I need to check my data sources? How might I break this problem into its parts and develop a strategy for understanding and accomplishing each step?

The *conscious* person asks, what do I know or not know? What questions do I need to ask? What strategies are in my mind now? What am I aware of regarding my own beliefs, values, and goals with this problem? What feelings or emotions am I aware of that might be blocking or enhancing my progress?

The *interdependent* person might turn to others for help. How does this problem affect others? How can we solve it together? What can I learn from others that would help me become a better problem solver?

These five passions also may serve as diagnostic tools—constructs through which to assess the cognitive development of ourselves, other individuals, and groups and to plan interventions for their continual refinement. For an individual, they represent the continuing tensions and resources for acting holonomously. For an organization, they form an invisible energy field, in which all parties are affected as surely as a strong magnetic field affects a compass.

The goal of education, therefore, should be to support ourselves and others in unleashing and developing these passions more fully. Taken together, they are a force directing us toward increasingly authentic, congruent, and ethical behavior, the touchstone of integrity. They are the tools of disciplined choice making. They are the primary vehicles in the lifelong journey toward integration.

Selecting Content for Process Outcomes

> I think that only daring speculation can lead us further and not accumulation of facts. (Albert Einstein)

Process, in its most basic sense, comprises those life activities that take one or more types of inputs and create meaningful outputs. Process requires processing something. The learning of processes, therefore, does not deny content. Each piece of subject matter is a way of knowing, a way of representing, or a way of solving problems. Each has some unique form and way of thinking that should become the subject of instruction.

We are not suggesting, therefore, that content be devalued. We still want students to be able to read, write, spell, and compute. We are suggesting, however, that content be rethought of as means, not ends—that students learn *from* the content instead of learning *of* the content. We are suggesting that content be viewed from the perspective of how it enhances and accomplishes the development of processes. Content should be selected because of its generative qualities—because it produces fecund opportunities for experiencing the euphoria of knowledge production, the revelation of one's efficacy as a continual learner, the applicability and transference of learning to other settings, and the expansion of one's repertoire of response patterns.

Teachers continually make decisions about the outcomes of their instruction (see Costa, Chapter 4 in this volume). Those decisions include a variety of levels, diagrammed in Figure 1.1.

Figure 1.1 illustrates several levels of decision making in which teachers engage as lessons are planned, as students' needs are considered, as the immediate and long-range goals of the curriculum are kept in mind, and as the environment of the school and classroom are considered. These levels are cumulative, hierarchical, and complex. As a result, expert teachers operate at multiple levels of outcomes simultaneously.

Activity Level. At the most basic level, the teacher plans learning activities. An activity-level planner might describe the outcome as, "Today, I'm going to show a videotape about Mexico." The plan is episodic. The teacher may be satisfied with accomplishing the activity for that period or day. Success is measured as

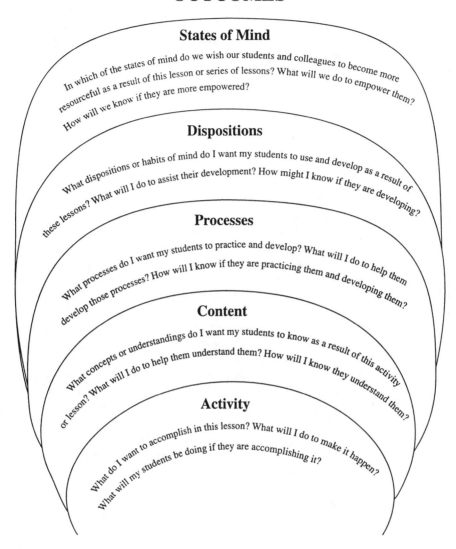

Figure 1.1. Maturing Outcomes

"survival": Did I make it through okay? Did it come out all right? Was my timing too far off? Do the students like me?

Content Level. The teacher is interested not only in the activity but also in whether the activity is enabling the understanding of the concepts or content to be learned. For example, a foreign language teacher might ask students to role-play or to put on a skit in which the students must practice some vocabulary to master the language they are learning.

Process Level. The teacher is interested not only in the activity and in mastering the content but also in the processes of thinking, collaboration, creativity, and so forth that are involved. For example, the teacher might have the students learn the processes of collaboration by having the students plan a project related to finding patterns in the environment. Students not only must present an exhibit demonstrating the understanding of patterns but also must develop criteria for effectively working together. On the basis of these preestablished criteria of cooperative group work, students are expected to reflect on and evaluate themselves both individually and collectively.

Dispositions Level. The teacher is interested in internalizing or habituating the goal for all students. For example, the teacher may try to build students' consciousness of their own behaviors and the effects of those behaviors on others. During the project on finding patterns in the environment, students will be expected to attempt to consciously employ listening skills: paraphrasing, clarifying, and empathizing with each other. An observer will be designated to collect evidence of group members' performance. On completion of the project, the observer will give the participants feedback as to individuals' performances. Students will assess themselves on the effects of their listening skills while collaborating within a group and on whether the task was achieved.

States of Mind. The teacher is also interested in using these concepts to conduct a meta-observation of group work—to draw implications and applications to the larger environment or universe. For example, an outcome might be to have students analyze functional and dysfunctional groups—to be able to look down on group functioning and observe it from a detached position. From these learnings about group interaction and listening abilities, the students will draw implications and generalizations about the effects of cooperation and listening in life situations. Changing patterns of interaction will be identified and de-scribed as groups develop and mature from initial task understanding through becoming task oriented to task completion.

We advocate that the metacurriculum described by Perkins (1989) no longer lurk in the background but rather become the public curriculum: that processes are stated as the explicit goals of education and become the purpose of instruction and the subject of assessment.

Process education, by its very nature, enables a dynamic response to the surrounding environment. Organizing the curriculum around processes allows increased freedom, greater control, wider transfer, and, in the end, more thoughtful learners. The intent, therefore, is to embark on the human quest for continual improvement—having a lifelong passion to continue learning, lending oneself to new experiences, and greeting the necessity for learning a new skill, understanding, or attitude with openness and eager anticipation.

Resource 1

Skills

Described below are some discrete process skills and behaviors. This list is intended not to be a finite list but rather to be illustrative of what is meant by skills.

Analyzing: Separating or breaking up a whole into its parts according to some plan or reason.

Brainstorming: Spontaneously generating numerous alternative ideas while deferring judgment.

Categorizing: Arranging items that possess the same properties according to a predetermined scheme, criterion, or rule.

Finding cause-and-effect relationships: Investigating and stating the reasons for a set of results that is produced.

Classifying: Adding ideas or objects to a group according to an established or invented scheme, criterion, or rule.

Comparing: Examining the attributes of two or more objects to discover resemblances or similarities.

Contrasting: Examining objects, ideas, or situations to discover their dissimilar qualities and examining the differences.

Deductive reasoning: Deriving the unknown from the known; drawing from general information to a specific conclusion that necessarily follows from the premise.

Generalizing: Formulating a rule, principle, or formula that governs or explains a number of related situations.

Generating criteria: Creating standards, rules, or tests for judging ways in which one event, item, or person may be differentiated from another.

Hypothesizing: Formulating statements of "if-then"; making a statement of experimentation.

Inferring: Drawing tentative conclusions that evidence points to but does not absolutely establish. Inferring takes place whenever data is reviewed, an evaluation or judgment is required, and relevant facts are unknown.

Using metaphor: Forming linguistic comparisons from similarities between things that are basically dissimilar.

Observing: Using all appropriate senses to gather information.

Ordering: Arranging conditions, objects, events, and ideas according to an established schema or criterion in relationship to one another.

Patterning: Grouping objects, conditions, events, or ideas according to a repeated schema or recognizing repeated schemas.

Prioritizing: Ranking objects, ideas, persons, conditions, or events in order of importance or personal preference.

Questioning: Making relevant inquiries to find information and to fill in the gaps between what is known and what is not known.

Finding relationships: Detecting regularity between two or more operations: temporal, causal, syllogistic, transitive, spatial, mathematical, and so forth.

Sequencing: Arranging items in relation to one or more ordering criteria.

Summarizing: Presenting the substance of complex ideas in a condensed or concise form.

Syllogistic reasoning: Drawing a logical conclusion from two statements or premises; using deductive logic to reason from the general to the particular.

Synthesizing: Putting information together in a new way.

Transforming: Relating known to unknown characteristics, thus creating new meanings.

Resource 2

Operations

The following are descriptions of several types of operations. Again, this is not meant to be a complete list. The descriptions are illustrative of processes in which humans engage when confronted with puzzling life situations. The reader may not necessarily agree with these descriptions or may wish to define them differently. We welcome the differences in interpretation and believe the process of defining these desirable operations is vastly more important than agreeing with and adopting these descriptions.

Collaborating: Knowing how to reciprocate and work with others on a common endeavor in ways that are mutually productive by aligning personal goals with larger group goals, seeking consensus, resolving conflicts and disagreements with dignity and respect, valuing and protecting the common good, volunteering, and being of service to and feeling compassion for others.

Communicating: Engaging in productive discussions, discourse, debate, and dialogue in their multiple forms (Schein, 1994; linguistic, visual, technological, kinesthetic, musical, etc.) by including such skills as listening with understanding and empathy; speaking and writing with clarity; using precision and accuracy; and knowing how to behave when value, language, belief, cultural, gender, or religious differences may cause misunderstanding, confusion, or difficulties in interpersonal interactions.

Consulting: Lending one's knowledge, experiences, and expertise in assisting others to understand situations, explore alternative solutions, and develop the most productive courses of action.

Creating and inventing: Generating new ideas and products of interest and value to others; accepting that each human being has a large capacity and potential for creative thought and action; learning how to access inner resources to cause the creative juices to flow when a situation demands it.

Decision making: Considering alternative outcomes and courses of actions by prioritizing and selecting among the options; knowing how to evoke and trust one's intuitive powers—recognizing there are matches and/or mismatches between the logic of the brain and the emotions of the heart.

Facilitating: Conducting and managing group decisions including planning for outcomes, building agendas, allocating time, maximizing participation, resolving differences, striving for consensus, summarizing decisions, planning next steps, and so forth.

Forming, testing, and revising concepts and generalizations: Finding, making, and testing relationships among events and experiences and from them making and testing broader generalizations (inductive reasoning); revising and expanding concepts, conclusions, and generalizations as additional data, evidence, and experience are obtained and the adequacy of data sources is revealed.

Imagining: Forming visions and mental images of situations, events, and conditions that could exist beyond the senses—being able to envision end products, big picture universals, microscopic details, and allocentric as well as egocentric views.

Inquiring: Playfully "messing about" with things and ideas to satisfy curiosity and wonderment, becoming more and more intrigued and curious; formulating questions and questioning strategies to fill in gaps between what is known and what is unknown; designing plans of action to gather data, to experiment, and to test theories and hypotheses.

Intuiting: Listening and attending to quick and ready insights or convictions that lack rational thought or inference; contemplating perceptions based on feelings or other sensory stimuli; knowing without knowing the source of the knowledge. Intuitive experiences include discovery and invention, inspiration, creative problem solving, perceptions of patterns and possibilities, extrasensory perception, clairvoyance, telepathy, precognition, retrocognition, hunches, premonitions, feelings of attraction and aversion, picking up "vibes," and knowing or perceiving throughout the body rather than only through the rational mind.

Investigating: Knowing how to persist and conduct extended research to a satisfactory completion; drawing on multiple resources, organizing and synthesizing into a coherent whole, and presenting the results in a succinct manner.

Meaning making: Reflecting on experiences and deriving relevance and learning from them—having the inclination to observe the synchronicity in life experiences; analyzing and abstracting meaning from experiences that can then be carried forth to future situations so that each new experience may be encountered with greater efficacy.

Mediating and coaching: Serving as a critical friend and mentor; assisting others in clarifying goals, anticipating actions, searching for indicators of success, and constructing data-gathering mechanisms; monitoring and collecting data during the activity; mediating meaning through reflecting, analyzing, and planning next steps.

Networking: Making linkages and connections—finding commonalties of interests and dispositions among diverse agencies, individuals, and populations and placing them in contact with each other for endeavors of mutual support.

Operationalizing: Translating concepts and generalizations into actions, details, and particulars (deductive reasoning).

Presenting: Communicating knowledge of concepts, principles, and skills in a coherent manner to a particular audience in a manner that produces and enhances the audience's understanding.

Problem solving and problem posing: Being aware that a problem exists; defining, refining, and clarifying a problematic situation; analyzing a situation, describing the inherent problems in that situation, and designing and conducting a plan of action to resolve some discrepancy between an existing state and a desired state.

Researching: Defining criteria for assessment; knowing how to control variables; designing short-term and long-range strategies to gather evidence of results in a variety of modes including interviews, observations, tests, and interpreting the evidence in light of the established criteria.

Self-evaluating: Generating, holding in mind, and applying a set of internal and external criteria as a guide to one's thoughts and actions; having the flexibility to change one's mind on the basis of new or additional data.

Transferring: Applying what was learned in one situation to other similar, as well as to distant, dissimilar situations; finding opportunities to use what is known; drawing from previous knowledge and applying it to new and novel situations.

References

Beyer, B. (1996). *Improving student thinking: A comprehensive approach.* Needham Heights, MA: Allyn & Bacon.

Costa, A. (Ed.). (1991). *Developing minds: Programs for teaching thinking.* Alexandria, VA: Association for Supervision and Curriculum Development.

Costa, A., & Garmston, R. (1994). *Cognitive coaching: A foundation for renaissance schools.* Norwood, MA: Christopher-Gordon.

Csikszentmihalyi, M. (1993). *The evolving self: A psychology for the third millennium.* New York: HarperCollins.

de Bono, E. (1991). *The CoRT thinking program.* In A. Costa (Ed.), *Developing minds: Programs for teaching thinking.* Alexandria, VA: Association for Supervision and Curriculum Development.

de Bono, E. (1994, July). *Keynote address*. Address presented at the International Conference on Thinking, Massachusetts Institute of Technology, Cambridge.

Feuerstein, R. (1991). Instrumental enrichment. As described by F. Link, in A. Costa (Ed.), *Developing minds: Programs for teaching thinking*. Alexandria, VA: Association for Supervision and Curriculum Development.

Miller, G. A. (1963, March). The magical number seven, plus or minus two: Some limits to our capacity for processing information. *Psychological Review, 2*, 81-97.

Parker, J. C., & Rubin, L. J. (1966). *Process as content: Curriculum design and the application of knowledge.* Chicago: Rand McNally.

Perkins, D. (1989). Selecting fertile themes for integrated learning. In H. Jacobs (Ed.), *Interdisciplinary curriculum: Design and implementation*. Alexandria, VA: Association for Supervision and Curriculum Development.

Schein, E. (1994). On dialogue, culture and organizational learning. In *The learning organization in action* (pp. 56-67). New York: American Management Association.

Sergiovanni, T. J. (1994). *Building community in schools*. San Francisco: Jossey-Bass.

Swartz, R., & Parks, S. (1994). *Infusing the teaching of critical and creative thinking in elementary instruction*. Pacific Grove, CA: Critical Thinking Press and Software.

2

Difficulties With the Disciplines

Arthur L. Costa
Rosemarie M. Liebmann

In recognition that the basic heart of education, the reductionist curriculum, is being challenged by the shifting paradigms, we contemplated the answer to the question, "How strong are we?" Years and years and years of beliefs and values are being confronted by our continually evolving society. For instance, more than 350 years ago, René Descartes (1596-1650) conceived of the separation and classification of knowledge into discrete compartments. He separated the mathematics of algebra from the study of geometry, distinguished meteorology from astronomy, and initiated the concept of hematology within the domain of physiology. From those beginnings, the classification of the natural sciences grew to include biology, physics, geology, chemistry, and astronomy; the social sciences to include economics, geography, history, and anthropology; and the arts and humanities to include music, painting, sculpture, dance, drama, and so on.

Educators are still living with and operating under this archaic and obsolete rubric. The organization of the curriculum into these static compartments, although a helpful classification system for allocating time, writing textbooks, hiring and training teachers, managing testing, and organizing university departments, has probably produced more problems than benefits. The time has come to think anew about how schools and curriculum should be organized. Following is an identification of some of the inherent constraints in organizing the curriculum around the traditional Cartesian disciplines and a proposition for alternative concepts and criteria for curriculum selection and organization.

Separation of the Disciplines Separates the School Staff

Organizing schools around the disciplines separates schools, grades, and teachers and prevents communicating and finding connections.

Art was invited to make a presentation to a high school staff on thinking across the curriculum. When he entered the room in which the presentation was to be given, he immediately apprehended a problem. In the far back, seated around a table, were the men in sweats. At the next table, were the women in sweats. To the middle and right were teachers in blue coats; on the left were teachers in white coats. From the table at Art's immediate right came a cacophony of languages. There, seated separately, were the men's P.E. department, the women's P.E. department, the industrial arts department, the science department, and the foreign language department.

Our obsession with the boundaries of content is what keeps school staffs separated. Until we find the strength to consider process as the core of the curriculum and content is selectively abandoned and judiciously selected because of its contributions to the thinking-learning process, we shall continue to endure this dilemma.

Limitations of time and communication in school settings often prevent teachers from different departments, grade levels, and disciplines from meeting together. The mutual support, continuity, reinforcement, and transference of processes throughout the grade levels and across the subject areas have yet to be accomplished. As with the trend of reengineering organizations, however, the shift is from functional departments to process teams (Hammer & Champy, 1993).

Separation of the Disciplines Alienates Intuitive Ways of Knowing

According to some curriculum theorists, the existing view of curriculum and its development has emerged from a largely male and Western way of thinking. As we learn to respect the female voice (Gilligan, 1982), as we gain greater understanding of the perspectives of indigenous peoples, and as we become more global and encounter Eastern philosophies, other modes of learning, and more multicultural thought and history, curriculum may need to be strengthened to reflect richer and more diverse views of how humans construct meaning (Pinar, Reynolds, Slattery, & Taubman, 1994).

The disciplines, shaped and directed from a masculine perspective, are grounded in visual, analytical, and reductionist metaphors. They have served well the intellectual capacities of Western man rather than identifying aspects of intellectual thought more common and highly developed in women and in other cultures. The disciplines were narrowly designed around attributes associated with didacticism, autonomy, independence, and critical thought. Neglected, however, are those who prefer interdependent, interpersonal, contextual, and synthetic thinking. The traditional format of organizing the curriculum around the disciplines may silence women's and some cultures' ways of knowing (Belenky, Clinchy, Goldberger, & Tarule, 1986).

Certain Disciplines Are Perceived to Be of More Worth Than Others

Teachers express concern over the value placed by students on an art course, for example, versus a science program. Schools send covert messages to students and the community concerning which is of greater worth through credit requirements; time allotments; allocation of resources; national, state, and local mandates; college entrance requirements; standards; testing; and so forth. This fractionalization across departments results in incongruent goals among the different people involved.

We need to put back together groups of teachers who have been artificially separated by their departments. Their task needs to be redefined from that of teaching their isolated content to that of developing the various intellectual capacities of students.

Howard Gardner (1993), for example, has helped us understand the multiple forms of intelligences and the need for development of well-rounded, multifaceted individuals who can learn through and employ many ways of thinking and learning—kinesthetically, spatially, logically, musically, visually, interpersonally, and linguistically. Valued equally, together they characterize a more efficacious, flexible, conscious, craftsmanlike, and interdependent individual.

The Disciplines May No Longer Exist

A colleague of Art's, who was dean of the School of Engineering, informed him that in teaching engineering students the principles of bridge building, comparatively little time was spent on mathematical and physical science principles. More time was spent in learning how to conduct and present an environmental impact study; the aesthetic dimensions of bridges so that the public would accept them; understanding the political and social implications of the bridge; and, most important, how to prepare and present the economics of the various aspects of bridge building for contractual and funding purposes.

With the advent of increased technology and the pursuit of knowledge in all quarters of human endeavor, the disciplines are losing their distinctions.

Today, for example, to be an archaeologist requires employment of radar and distant satellite infrared photography as well as understanding radioactive isotopes. We are increasingly aware of specialized professions in which multiple disciplines are combined into unique and ever smaller specialties: space biology, genetic technology, political geography, neurochemistry, and astrohydrology. Today, it is nearly impossible to find simply a biologist. We may more likely find a "hydromicrobiogeochemist" who draws on vast knowledge to spend a lifetime studying the chemical interactions of minute life forms in small bodies of water in subterranean caves.

The disciplines as educators have known them and taught them no longer exist. Rather, they are being replaced by human activities that draw on vast, generalized, and transdisciplinary bodies of knowledge and relationships applied to unique, domain-specific settings.

We are shifting our metaphor from compartments and clocklike mechanisms toward more complex ecosystems—decentralized interactions and feedback spirals. Today, researchers work together to find and forge connections and themes as they search for universal similarities in the behaviors of minds, machines, animals, and societies. The study of self-organizing systems is, in some ways, the "related opposite" of the study of chaos. In self-organizing systems, orderly patterns emerge from lower-level randomness. When one studies a flock of birds, for example, there really is not a lead bird. Each bird flies freely, yet together, they create an exquisite pattern. In chaotic systems, unpredictable behavior emerges from lower-level deterministic rules. For example, an ant seems to have a predisposition for a particular type of work, but a few ants randomly wander off and begin to find new food sources. This randomness eventually leads to a pattern in which all ants go to the new food sources.

Philosophers continue to move away from the notion of single, absolute, unifying conception of knowledge, arguing instead that knowledge is constantly being constructed and reconstructed in a much more centralized way. Waldrop (1992) states,

> The most distressing thing of all was what the fragmentation process had done to science as a whole. The traditional disciplines had become so entrenched and so isolated from one another that they seemed to be strangling themselves . . . the old reductionism approaches were reaching a dead end, and that even some of the hard-core physical scientists were getting fed up with the mathematical abstractions that ignored the real complexities of the world. (pp. 61-62)

George A. Cowan, president of the Santa Fe Institute, observes,

> There is an underlying unity . . . one that would encompass not just physics and chemistry, but biology, information processing, economics, political science, and every other aspect of human affairs. If this unity were real . . . it would be a way of knowing the world that made little distinction between biological science and physical science—or between either of those sciences and history or philosophy. Once, the

whole intellectual fabric was seamless. And maybe it could be that way again. (cited in Waldrop, 1992, p. 67)

Daniel Dennett (1991) proposes a multiple drafts model of consciousness, arguing that there is no single stream of consciousness in the mind. Rather, multiple narratives are simultaneously created and edited in different parts of the mind/brain.

An example of this lies in literature. Traditional theories of literature assumed that meaning was created by the authors and conveyed through their writings. But modern schools of literary criticism adopt a different stance now, focusing on the readers, not the authors, as the main constructors of meaning. In this new view, texts have little or no inherent meaning. Rather, meanings are constantly reconstructed by communities of readers through their interactions with the text. Meaning itself has become decentralized (Resnick, 1994).

Difficulties in Defining the Disciplines

The philosopher Dudley Shaphere (as cited by Ennis, 1989) characterized a discipline as "encompassing a certain set of real-world phenomena, a set of concepts used to represent those phenomena, and the laws and other explanatory mechanisms that constitute an understanding of the domain" (p. 7). However vast or narrow one wishes to draw the boundaries that define a discipline, the discipline remains elusive.

As an example of the vagueness in the distinction of the disciplines, try to decide which of the following three topics is in the same subject matter domain as one or more of the others: (a) the degree to which a straight rod will bend, (b) the degree to which a spring will stretch, and (c) the impact of a sphere that rolls down a ramp. All three examples conceivably could be classified under the same discipline—science. But science itself, as a discipline, may be divided into many areas: physics, chemistry, biology, and so forth. These three phenomena might be classified as problems in physics. So is physics the discipline?

The study of physics as a course taught in school, however, may often include the study of mechanics. The study of mechanics may include the study of the degree to which a straight rod will bend, the degree to which a spring will stretch, and the impact of a sphere that rolls down a ramp. The rod and spring, however, involve the study of statics, whereas the ramp and sphere are considered dynamics.

If we apply Shaphere's definition above, a serious boundary dispute emerges. Should we describe *physics* as a set of concepts and laws and mechanisms or are we talking about the concepts, phenomena, and laws of *mechanics?* Are we considering one discipline to be *statics* and another discipline to be *dynamics?* Or are the organizing principles, phenomena, concepts, laws, and mechanisms unique to the individual problem for study—*springs, rods,* and *ramps?* Do the same sets of principles, phenomena, and mechanisms apply equally to the springs as they do to the rods as they do to the ramps? If we try to amalgamate the study of rods by the concept of a spring being a spiral rod, the concept is not particularly useful in knowing why the rod bends. Indeed, the set of principles

...nd concepts needed to understand inclined planes, inertia, and the impact of spheres is quite different from the set of principles required to understand springs and rods. So how big or small should we draw the boundary of a discipline? (Ennis, 1989).

Deceiving Students

Constructivist classrooms encourage the personal construction of categories rather than imposing existing categorical systems. The process-oriented classroom focuses more on drawing out existing abilities than on precisely measuring a student's success with imposed skills, encourages the personal construction of categories rather than imposing existing categorical systems, and emphasizes the individual personal solutions of an environmental challenge—even if inefficient—more than efficient group manipulations of symbols that merely represent the solution (Sylwester, 1995).

The disciplines, presented as organized bodies of content, may deceive students into thinking they are incapable of constructing meaning. Students have frequently been indirectly taught that they lack the means to create, construct, connect, and classify knowledge. They are taught that organized theories, generalizations, and concepts of a particular discipline of knowledge are the creations of experts. Thus, students may think they are incapable of generating such information for themselves. Although students are challenged to learn the information, the manner in which such information was created and classified often remains mysterious. Students frequently perceive information presented in school as the polished products of minds far removed from them. All they can hope for is to acquire other people's meanings and answers to questions that someone else deems important. An example is when student are asked, "What did the author mean or conclude in the article?" rather than "What do you conclude from this article?" Thus, students, not feeling that something can be known, will resist seeking answers.

> Rosemarie asked her third-grade daughter if she had asked any good question in school that day. Amy's response was, "Mom, in school you don't get to ask questions. The teacher asks the questions and you're supposed to know the answers."

Our challenge as educators is to illuminate for students that what at first might seem impossible to comprehend or not feasible to know may be quite possibly and joyfully understood. For students to intensely desire knowing and participating in knowing, they must realize they do have the skills and the necessary background to engage in knowledge construction. They are not shackled with the responsibility of accepting someone else's content or by only answering questions posed by teachers or textbooks. Students need to accept that what they desire to know can come from within them. There are times when the students must recognize that their ideas and constructs are significant enough to require action. We can do this by inviting students to find connections and to make relationships, to draw on and apply previous information and experiences learned elsewhere, and to share and constantly reorganize their mental maps and constructs of meaning.

What Distinguishes the Disciplines
May Be Their Modes of Inquiry

What makes a discipline a discipline is a disciplined mode of thinking (Paul & Elder, 1994). Consider the terms *biology, anthropology, psychology,* and *cosmology*. Notice that each ends in *-logy*, which comes from a Greek word that means *logic*. Thus, *bio-logy* is the logic of the study of life forms. *Anthropo-logy* is the logic of the study of humans and culture. *Psycho-logy* is the logic of the study of the mind, and so on. All areas of study are topics of interest in which something has to be reasoned out. Mathematics, for example, means being able to figure out a solution to a problem using mathematical reasoning. History means learning how to figure out a reasonable answer to a historical question or problem. Any subject or content must, therefore, be understood as a mode of figuring out correct or reasonable answers to a certain body of questions.

Regardless of the area of endeavor—whether employing historical, psychological, artistic, or any other form of inquiry—all share a set of common principles: (a) There is first a period of confrontation with a problem, a challenge, or a quest that evokes some form of disequilibrium and requires some form of resolution; (b) next, the inquirer forms some theory, vision, or set of principles to guide experimentation, action, or intervention intended to bring the system back into equilibrium; (c) feedback data from the intervention are gathered to test and compare with the vision or theory to see if the theory has been supported, the question answered, the problem resolved, and the equilibrium reestablished.

One content or discipline is distinguished from another by its mode of inquiry—the types of problems it defines and solves. Each content has a logic that is defined by the thinking that produced it: its purposes, problems, information, inferences, concepts, assumptions, implications, points of view, forms of communication, technology, and interrelationships with other disciplines.

Mathematics, for example, is different from other fields because mathematics seeks and employs processes of deductive proof, whereas most fields do not even seek it for the establishment of a final conclusion. In the social sciences, voting, interviewing, and the processes of finding statistical significance are important considerations; in most branches of physics, these processes are largely ignored. In the arts, the processes of arriving at subjective interpretation are valued; in the sciences, they are usually shunned. Replicability, control of variables, and experimentation are the quest in the hard sciences; experimentation with human beings is abhorred in anthropology.

Depending on the area of inquiry, certain constraints or boundaries are placed on its form of experimentation. We cannot, for example, go back and re-create a historical event to determine if it would have turned out differently had we changed some condition or controlled some variable. That form of intervention might suffice in a scientific sense but not in a historical sense. Thus, although all problem solving, regardless of domain, shares some process similarities, the constraints imposed by the nature of the problem itself designate the logic and technology of the processes to be employed. As Paul and Elder (1994) state, "When we master the logic of 'History,' we simultaneously master the logic of historical thought. There is nothing else that remains" (p. 2).

Disciplines Deter Transfer

Although depth of knowledge about a topic is a necessary condition for understanding and thinking critically about the topic, subject matter knowledge alone is not sufficient for good thinking involving application and transfer to novel situations. Experienced persons can be so well informed about and immersed in a discipline that they stop thinking, become inflexible, and are unable to conceive of and consider alternatives. Knowledge, as traditionally taught and tested in school subjects, often consists of a mass of knowledge-level content that is not understood deeply enough to enable students to think critically in the subject and to seek and find relationships with other subjects.

Immersion in a discipline will not necessarily produce learners who have the ability to apply the concepts and principles of the discipline into everyday life situations. To ensure application outside of school, immersion must be accompanied by explicit attention to transfer through the general principles of critical thinking and inquiry.

Students acquire the idea that they learn something for the purpose of passing the test, rather than accumulating wisdom and personal meaning from the content. They perceive learning to be a game of mental gymnastics with little or no application outside the school in everyday living.

Art recently asked his ninth-grade granddaughter, Shaun, what she was learning in social studies. "We're learning about the Constitution," she responded. "Great! Tell me three things you've learned about the Constitution," Art inquired. "I can't. I've forgotten it already," she replied. "Shawn, how could you forget it already?" Art pursued. "Well, we've already had the test!"

Furthermore, the separations of the disciplines produce episodic learning in students. When the biology teachers say, "Today, we're going to learn to spell some biological terms: *stamen, monocot,* and *pistil*," students often respond by saying, "Spelling—in biology? No way!" Their thinking of the subject is confined, compartmentalized, and episodic. Biology has little meaning for physical education, which has no application to literature and has even less connection to algebra. They may be viewed as a series of subjects to be mastered rather than for making meaningful relationships, connections, and applications. Students need to transfer and apply their knowledge from one situation to another—to draw forth from their storehouse of knowledge and apply it in new situations.

Teachers Can't Cover the Content

A friend of ours, a high school history teacher, remarked with great despair, "It's almost Easter, and I'm only up to the Civil War. I don't think I'm going to make it to the present by the end of the school year!" Our friend expressed the frustration felt by myriad teachers who find covering the content difficult, if not impossible. Furthermore, in the sciences and social sciences, the content grows and changes so rapidly that no one can keep current. Cartographers are presently rushing to change their maps of the former Soviet Union and, at this writing, are awaiting the verdict on Yugoslavia. Astronomy textbook authors are reconsidering their presentation of the Big Bang theory, and biology textbook writers are wondering whether to categorize environmental studies as a social, biological, economic, or political issue.

Little Consistency Among Educators as to What Constitutes Their Discipline

There is great variation in the content of what is taught to teachers in their preservice education about the structure of their disciplines. What they were taught is often a far cry from what the curriculum demands in the school setting and is usually vastly different from what typically composes the content of the textbook. From one college course to another, beginning teachers take classes in and are certified as teachers of a certain discipline. There is little similarity, however, between such teacher preparation experiences and even less similarity between preparation and what is actually taught in school. Teachers envision models of their discipline on the basis of how and what they were exposed to in their content and methods courses. These teachers tend to carry forth to their teaching those strategies and content that they were taught. The result is a maintenance of old and familiar models: Because I dissected a frog in my college biology class, I therefore have my biology students dissect frogs. Because I learned to conjugate verbs in my French class, I therefore have my students conjugate verbs.

In some districts, in some states, and in some programs (advanced placement or the international baccalaureate, for example), teachers are constrained by a written curriculum, a set of student proficiencies to be mastered, and a summative evaluation of competencies. Although the degree to which all teachers in that state, district, or program "cover" that curriculum may differ, their freedom to be creative, to allow students to pursue their individual interests, and to diverge from the adopted content is discouraged.

Such mandated content may vary greatly among districts, states, and university teacher education programs. What is learned in preservice courses—American history for example—may be a far cry from what the curriculum demands in a particular school setting.

We know a biology teacher who, by recommendation of the department chair, spends most of the time allocated for the subject on the major unit of instruction—human physiology and anatomy. Students enroll in and are given credit for a semester of biology. No attention is paid, however, to biomes, animal phyla, plants, or environmental issues.

There Is Never an End Point to
Knowing Everything About a Discipline

> The only thing that we can know is that we know nothing and that is the highest flight of human wisdom. (Leo Tolstoy)

The reductionist search seldom leads to a satisfying end. When we study the individual parts and try to understand the curriculum through the disciplines, we inevitably get lost in a meaningless world lacking quality, beauty, and interconnectedness. For example, by introducing the world to the concept of fractals, Benoit Mandelbrot gave us a language for understanding nature and the world around us in a new way. Fractals have taught us that there is no definitive measurement, no smallest unit. Important are complexity, distinguishing characteristics, and differences—quality, not quantity. Fractals remind us of the lessons of wholeness we encounter in holonomous organizations (Wheatley, 1992).

This profound shift is consistent with the findings in the scientific worldview away from things to interrelatedness. For example, we've learned that there is no such thing as a smallest particle—no electron, no proton. There are only electron clouds that are made up of 99% "no-thing." To assist learners in the learning process, the curriculum must capitalize on discovering the natural interdependency and interrelatedness of the disciplines. Peter Senge (1994) contends that we are all natural systems thinkers and that the findings from cognitive research are compatible with and supportive of the need to move from individual to collective intelligence, from disciplines to themes, and from independence to interdependence.

Education Is About Creating Environments in Which
People Can Engage in Fundamental Shifts in Their Thinking

The world community, as evidence by the curriculum established by the International Baccalaureate Program, has recognized that a theory of learning is at the heart of the curriculum. The theory of learning is used as the connecting form that binds all the other disciplines together. Currently, with the exception of North America, the nations involved with this curriculum are looking to redesign the science offerings. Agreement has been reached that a shift away from the separate disciplines of physics, chemistry, biology, and so forth is necessary and that science needs to be taught in a realistic natural setting that emphasizes the connectedness of interrelationships in the world. Theories will be taught when they are connected in meaning and are needed to understand other theories and concepts. As Senge (1994) has said, "There is a shift away from teaching trivia to educating for understanding."

In a manner consistent with cognitive research, humans learn best when we can recognize themes. This approach represents a fundamental shift. For hundreds of years, we've dissected knowledge into smaller and smaller skills and discrete concepts to help make the information more learnable for students. It now appears this position is inconsistent with how the brain actually learns.

In Summary

When educators take all the above into account, the reason for organizing curriculum around the traditional disciplines has dubious merit. Another basis for organization of curriculum is needed. To assist learners in the learning process, the curriculum should capitalize on the natural interdependency and interrelatedness of the disciplines. Senge (1994) contends that we are all natural systems thinkers and that the findings in cognitive research are compatible and supportive of the need to move from individual to collective intelligence, from disciplines to themes, from independence to relationships.

References

Belenky, M., Clinchy, B., Goldberger, N., & Tarule, J. (1986). *Women's ways of knowing: The development of self, voice, and mind.* New York: Basic Books.

Dennett, D. (1991). *Consciousness explained.* Boston: Little, Brown.

Ennis, R. (1989, April). Critical thinking and subject specificity: Clarification and needed research. *Educational Researcher*, 4-10.

Gardner, H. (1993). *Frames of mind: The theory of multiple intelligence.* New York: Basic Books.

Gilligan, C. (1982). *In a different voice.* Cambridge, MA: Harvard University Press.

Hammer, M., & Champy, J. (1993). *Reengineering the corporation.* New York: Harper Business.

Paul, R., & Elder, L. (1994). All content has a logic: That logic is given by a disciplined mode of thinking: Part 1. *Teaching Thinking and Problem Solving, 16*(5), 1-4. (Newsletter of the Research for Better Schools, Philadelphia, PA)

Pinar, W., Reynolds, W., Slattery, P., & Taubman, P. (1994, April 5). *Understanding curriculum: A postscript for the next generation.* Paper presented at the annual meeting of the American Educational Research Association, New Orleans, LA.

Resnick, M. (1994). *Turtles, termites, and traffic jams: Explorations in massively parallel microworlds.* Cambridge: MIT Press.

Senge, P. (1994, July). *Keynote address.* Address presented at the International Conference on Thinking, Massachusetts Institute of Technology, Cambridge.

Sylwester, R. (1995). *A celebration of neurons: An educator's guide to the human brain.* Alexandria, VA: Association for Supervision and Curriculum Development.

Waldrop, M. M. (1992). *Complexity: The emerging science at the edge of order and chaos.* New York: Touchstone.

Wheatley, M. J. (1992). *Leadership and the new science.* San Francisco: Berrett-Koehler.

3

Shifting Paradigms From Either/Or to Both/And

Arthur L. Costa
Rosemarie M. Liebmann

The challenge to education in the coming years will be to develop students for living in a world where trends of the past no longer predict the future.

Costa & Liebmann

The world is borderless when seen from a high enough perspective. A force our senses cannot identify binds humans together. Despite our diversities, humanity shares and is greatly influenced by these invisible forces. One such force of which we are rarely conscious is known as a *paradigm*. A paradigm simply places a hold on our perception of reality so deep that it is hard to imagine any other way of looking at the event, situation, or content.

As we recognize that our world is changing at an ever rapid pace, we need to find new ways of seeing—new paradigms that allow us to develop as human beings and not merely grow, paradigms that allow for growth beyond fixed end points requiring nutrients from the environment. Although growth is a precondition to development, growth alone is not sufficient. "Development," as defined by Charles Krone (cited in Sanford, 1992), "is the process of increasing our scope and power to do *and* to be" (p. 206). Development of the potential held deeply within each individual requires nourishment from without as well as from within.

Paradigm shifts are necessary to support a curriculum that values the interaction of process and content, growth and development. Although Jerome

Bruner and others hold the belief that all children can learn, we believe all children do learn—the questions are what and how.

Shifting Educational Paradigms

Old Paradigm #1: *The school's mission is to produce an educated, literate person—one who has mastered basic skills and acquired significant concepts.*

New Paradigm: *The school's mission is to produce lifelong learners who continue their personal development and who promote the well-being of the larger community.*

As we began to collect the contributors for this trilogy, repeated concern about our vision surfaced, namely, were we reversing the dichotomy from content being highly valued and prized—so much so that process has almost been excluded—to process being the primary emphasis and content being forgotten? The answer to this question is a firm, resounding "No!" We, as editors and authors, believe strongly in the duality that both are required and must be intertwined. It is not a dichotomy of inclusion versus exclusion, but rather an interaction of process and content.

We advocate content being used as the means to develop the processes. People cannot think in a vacuum. People must bring certain expertise to a situation to expect to be heard. And people must have the abilities, skills, and dispositions to be able to productively use this knowledge. It is knowledge production as opposed to knowledge acquisition that is advocated in the new paradigm. As human resource developers across America have stated, "The traditional school will have to shift to a Renaissance school where people can look for meaning in their lives, ask deeper level questions, and become collaborators and interpreters of data" (Liebmann, 1993, p. 237).

In this new paradigm, the individual spirit will be permitted to develop the inner qualities of intuition, joy, compassion, visionary thinking, playfulness, curiosity, and wonderment—the traits of the authentic inner child. Knowledge production brings with it the sense that "I too can create," that "I am not only the receiver of knowledge but also a producer and designer of knowledge," that "I am a teacher and a learner," and that "I am in a continual process of development."

Few people are presently prepared for the frequent and demanding changes in careers. Education needs to broaden its scope of literacy to include those skills that enable people to understand what they can offer in our changing society. Gone are the days when reading, writing, and arithmetic were sufficient. The workforce is transforming into one that requires people to create their own value and marketability.

Old Paradigm #2: *It is the responsibility of the schools to educate the child.*

New Paradigm: *It is the responsibility of all community agencies to contribute to the development of the continued growth and lifelong learning of all members of the community.*

Individuality and Community. The problems facing the world today are so complex that no one person can solve them alone. It takes many individuals working together around a shared vision, contributing their expert knowledge, engaging in dialogue, striving to understand each other, achieving consensus, reflecting on their accomplishments, reviewing their processes, and planning for constant improvement.

In the 1830s, the French social philosopher Alexis de Tocqueville (1969) warned Americans that some aspects of our character—he was one of the first to call it *individualism*—might eventually isolate Americans from one another. As a nation, we have valued individual freedom to the extent that it is woven throughout the very fabric of our society. In recent years, we are coming to recognize that we need to modify the needs of the individual to establish a balance with the needs of the community, the country, the world community, and the planet Earth.

Furthermore, it is through such reciprocity that the individual grows. Humans, as social beings, mature intellectually in reciprocal relationships with other people. Vygotsky (1978) points out that the higher functions actually originate during interaction with others.

> Every function in . . . cultural development appears twice—first, on the social level, and later on the individual level; first between people (inter-psychological), and then inside (intra-psychological). This applies equally to voluntary attention, to logical memory, and to the formation concepts. All the higher functions originate as actual relationships between individuals. (cited in Costa & Garmston, 1994, p. 3)

An old African saying now frequently heard is, "It takes a village to raise a child." We could actually modify this to, "It takes a community to care for a nation." When students are brought together to learn in a community, they experience the increased power of collective intelligence. The shared insights produce not only rapid growth but also learning that is in context and is therefore significant. At the heart of these procedures is the capacity for empathy—the attempted sharing of other persons' experiences to understand their ideas. As a result, appropriate frameworks are discovered for decision making and conflict resolution on the basis of what is best for everyone.

School and Society. Throughout the United States, people are waking up to their responsibility for the quality of their community life. Within our communities, many social, economic, and political forces are rendering students unable to learn when they come to school. Poverty, homelessness, drugs, and abusiveness are not school problems; they are societal problems—but they highly impinge on students' capacities to profit from school. Solving these societal problems is not the sole responsibility of the school even though they have a significant impact on educational organizations. Only through networking with the community (parents, law enforcement, human development, social services, the media, and businesses) can educators create safe communities for continuous learners.

The Greeks had a word for it: *paideia.* This term, popularized by Adler's *Proposal* (1982), is an ideal concept we share: a school in which learning, fulfillment, and becoming more humane are the primary goals for all students, faculty, and support staff. It is the Athenian concept of a learning society in which self-development, intellectual empowerment, and lifelong learning are esteemed core values, and all institutions within the culture are constructed to contribute to those goals.

Independence and Interdependence. The industrial model of schooling, along with the reductionist curriculum, was appropriate for the society in which it was developed. We have learned a great deal about autonomy and independence, abstract critical thought, and the unfolding of a morality of rights and justice in both men and women. We have learned less about the development of interdependence, intimacy, nurturance, and contextual thought. Yet in our pluralistic and intellectually challenging environment, schools must be increasingly dedicated to dislodging the reliance on a single authority and to creating stimulating environments that develop more adequate concepts of knowing.

It isn't finding truth that's so wonderful; it's in the looking for it—the exploring and the searching. When we think that we've finally arrived at the truth, we haven't. *Truth* should be thought of as a verb, a process of construction in which the knowers are active participants and in which their continual passions for learning are unleashed. Seeking the truth opens the mind and the heart to embrace the whole world. Truth is a collaborative phenomenon that requires holistic thinking—viewing knowledge from a systemic perspective.

Together, individuals generate and discuss ideas, eliciting thinking that surpasses individual effort. Together and privately, they express different perspectives, agree and disagree, point out and resolve discrepancies, and weigh alternatives. Because people grow by this process, collegiality is a crucial factor in the fulfillment of the intellectual potential of all human beings.

> Old Paradigm #3: *Learners should check their deepest personal selves on the steps of the school and should be passive recipients of teachers' knowledge.*
>
> New Paradigm: *Learners are active participants in the learning process. Educational settings should be created as arenas in which relationships, creativity, innovation, authenticity, self-expression, and human spirits are valued while embracing diversity in the community.*

Many attempts have been made at changing the nature of traditional classrooms away from student passivity and toward more active engagement. Early education classrooms often have hands-on, student-centered, active learning. Toward the upper levels, however, experiential learning becomes less and less evident.

Yet Seymour Papert (1991) encourages educators to move from instructionism toward constructionism, from simulation to stimulation. Learning, by its nature, is social and is effective when learners share ideas; inquire and problem solve together; reflect and metacogitate on the construction of knowledge and the process of sense making; and consciously mediate these experiences from prior knowledge, values, and beliefs.

In addition, people construct new knowledge with particular effectiveness when they are engaged in constructing products that are personally important to them. Learners need to actively participate in creating something that is significant to themselves or to others around them. Educators need to provide opportunities for students to design and construct knowledge that not only activates their hands but also engages their heads and hearts. This implies that learners be permitted to follow their fantasies and be given the support to make those fantasies come to life.

For process educators, these become essential skills to be modeled for students: sharing the truth with ourselves and others, being open about who we are, bringing new ideas to the classroom, taking risks and getting rewarded or at least supported, expressing our feelings and points of view, and being fully heard while making our individual needs known. These skills, attitudes, and dispositions involve bringing our whole persons into the learning process and creating an arena for creativity and innovation in which the authenticity of the human spirit is valued.

The United States is made up of the richest and most diverse group of people found in any nation. Americans value diversity, dialogue, discussion, and free and open debate—the right to *free speech*. Flexibility in the curriculum is required to meet and honor students' complex and varied needs. When communities of learners convene, the group's understanding is illuminated by the colorful mosaic of voices that can be heard. All members must stretch their own percep-tions to share the perceptions of others. Through mutual sharing, the group achieves an understanding that is deeper and fuller than any individual could achieve alone.

> Old Paradigm #4: *Evaluation of student learning is a summative measurement of how much content students have retained. It is useful for grading and segregating students into ability groups. It is useful in predicting success in later life and indicates aptitude for profiting from more advanced academic instruction.*
>
> New Paradigm: *Evaluation is neither summative nor punitive. Rather, assess-ment is a mechanism for providing feedback to the learner as a necessary part of the spiraling processes of continuous personal development: self-analyzing, self-evaluating, and self-modifying.*

Educators must constantly keep in mind that the ultimate purpose of evalu-ation is to have students become self-evaluative. If students graduate from schools still dependent on others to tell them when they are adequate, good, or excellent, then we've missed the whole point of what education is about. The highest level of Bloom's (1956) taxonomy is generating, holding, and applying a set of internal and external criteria. For too long, adults alone have been practicing that skill. We need to shift that responsibility to students. The goal of process education must be to help students develop the capacity to modify themselves.

> Old Paradigm #5: *The understanding of the whole can be achieved only as a result of studying the smallest unit (reductionism).*
>
> New Paradigm: *Nothing can be truly understood except by studying it in isolation as well as in connection (holonism).*

The scientific revolution brought with it a desire to study concepts in isolation. There was a passion for finding the smallest particle. It was believed that through this knowledge, the universe could be understood. Our curriculum followed this same pattern. Each discipline was split off from the others and studied in isolation.

The new sciences—chaos theory and complexity theory, for example—have begun to revolutionize the world. It is apparent that nothing can be fully understood in isolation. As Sanford (1992) writes,

> Instead of the cool clockwork of an hermetically sealed universe run according to immutable laws and driven by the need for stabilization, we see emerging a view of a constantly changing and dynamic world of interconnected systems in which chaos is a nurturing environment for the spontaneous regeneration of increasingly higher orders of creation. (p. 201)

Learners must acquire the skills, attitudes, dispositions, and passions that enable them to broaden their perspectives, accept and live with ambiguity, and continually challenge the existing paradigm. Learners need to develop creative forces, visionary leadership-followership, and risk-taking skills. Human beings need to reach beyond confining boundaries in anticipation of a new world and to develop processes as guides to traversing new and exciting paths. Students must develop consciousness, as well as capability, flexibility, creativity, and efficacy.

Old Paradigm #6: *The intent of objective, linear, scientific/mechanistic inquiry is to establish causality, laws, truth, and how to control and make accurate predictions.*

New Paradigm: *The quantum paradigm of process intends to continue seeking greater understanding of multiple causalities, non-linear and chaotic systems, interactions, connections, and to continually discover hidden meanings.*

Values:	*Beliefs:*
Right/wrong polarity	Stabilization
Mind/matter dualism	Control
Objectivism	Exploitation
	Steady state
Symbolic Generalizations:	*Puzzle Solutions:*
Predictability	Knowing the whole through its parts
Cause/effect relationships	Empirical inquiry
Material progress	Mathematical models

In the mechanical paradigm, everything in nature was subjected to mathematical laws. The environment was seen as stable; there were definite truths in the world—absolutes. The underlying structure, as discussed by Kuhn (1970), was as follows:

The mechanical-scientific paradigm is in transformation. Much controversy

---

Values:
Developmental
Consciousness
Intrinsic capability
Exploration and discovery

Symbolic Generalizations:
Field/resonance
Complexity/ecological systems

Beliefs:
Regeneration
Emergence
Whole system education

Puzzle Solutions:
Holographic inquiry
Open systems
Qualitative models

---

exists as to what the new paradigm will look like or even what it will be called. We have selected to call it the *Paradigm of Process*. This decision was based on generally agreed-on insights concerning the underlying structure of the emerging paradigm. Sanford (1992) suggests, and we concur, that Kuhn's model will shift to this:

Although many of these values and beliefs are not new, they are resurfacing with new depth as the result of recent scientific underpinnings. Humanity is evolving, and we must honor the Mechanical Paradigm as a necessary prerequisite for the Paradigm of Process—because now we understand many ancient ideas with greater depth than we previously could.

Old Paradigm #7: *Only knowledge that is discovered through the use of sensing and thinking is worthy of acceptance and recognition.*

New Paradigm: *The processes of knowing through the use of feeling and intuition are valid and result in greater depth of understanding.*

As the United States begins to emerge from an overemphasis on individualism and materialism, we are witnessing a recognition that other ways of knowing have been suppressed. Carl Jung identified four psychological functions of knowing—sensation, feeling, thinking, and intuition. He attributed sensing and thinking with the masculine, whereas feeling and intuition were considered feminine. From this perspective, we shall use the concepts of masculine and feminine thought processes.

A shifting view of human beings is evident in many bookstores that are replete with literature on psychic abilities, self-healing, the mind-body connection, angels, visualization, meditation, and spirituality. There is a growing interest in knowledge that comes through feelings and intuition.

One might wonder why? Have not the rational, linear thought processes connected with current organizations led to a society in which we enjoy a standard of living far beyond that of most nonindustrial countries? We believe that this is a difficult question to answer. The answer to the question is defined by what people value and requires more than a yes or no response. Many people in our society are searching for inner peace and harmony that may result not from material acquisitions but rather from something deep within the human spirit.

The answer to the question may rest in the continual evolution of humanity. Humans are beginning to intertwine the knowledge of the ancients with the knowledge from the reductionists and are understanding the universe more deeply than ever before. From these new insights, we have experienced radical shifts in the way we see our world. We are beginning to accept that information is constantly *in formation*, that truths are only true momentarily, and that the world is in constant flux. As a result, new ways of learning, seeing, and knowing are becoming acceptable.

Just as we advocate for the spiraling together of content and process, we advocate for the intertwining of masculine and feminine thought processes. Hidden behind the evolving acceptance of feeling and intuiting, however, is a new problem. In our hierarchical society, the feminine processes are slowly being co-opted by men. The recognition of the importance of intuitive thinking is still leaving women in an inferior position. As Shepherd (1993) writes,

> During the nineteenth century it was claimed that women could not do science because they were not analytical enough. Now that scientists have discovered the value of a more intuitive approach, it is said that women are too rational and cannot make creative intuitive leaps. (p. xiii)

It is time to accept that within each individual, man or woman, is the capacity for development of the masculine and feminine processes. As people journey toward becoming whole, we must develop holonomous processes.

Through the blending of masculine and feminine processes, we will be able to shift from knowledge for knowledge sake to research that is grounded in truth, motivated by love, receptive to nature, and centered on creating harmony. We need to begin using the "whole" of who we are—our intuition, feelings, sensations, and thinking to make informed, reflective decisions. In essence, we need to balance the feminine and masculine cognitive processes.

Summary

Paradigm shifts do not come easily. They require letting go of old habits, old beliefs, and old traditions. But in the words of Sylvia Robinson,

> Some people think you are strong when you hold on. Others think it is when you let go.

How strong are we?

References

Adler, M. J. (1982). *The paideia proposal: An educational manifesto.* New York: Macmillan.

Bloom, B. (1956). *Taxonomy of educational objectives: Book I. The cognitive domain.* New York: David McKay.

Costa, A., & Garmston, R. (1994). *Cognitive coaching: A foundation for Renaissance Schools.* Norwood, MA: Christopher-Gordon.

de Tocqueville, A. (1969). *Democracy in America* (G. Lawrence, Trans.). New York: Doubleday.

Kuhn, T. (1970). *The structure of scientific revolutions* (2nd ed.). Chicago: Chicago University Press.

Liebmann, R. (1993). *Perceptions of human resource developers as to the initial and desired states of holonomy of managerial and manual employees.* Unpublished doctoral dissertation, Seton Hall University, South Orange, NJ.

Papert, S. (1991). *Situating constructionism.* In I. Harel and S. Papert (Eds.), *Constructionism.* Norwood, NJ: Ablex.

Sanford, C. (1992). *A self-organizing leadership view of paradigms.* In J. Renesch (Ed.), *New traditions in business.* San Francisco: Berrett-Koehler.

Shepherd, L. (1993). *Lifting the veil: The feminine face of science.* Boston: Shambhala.

Vygotsky, L. (1978). *Society of mind.* Cambridge, MA: Harvard University Press.

4

Curriculum

A Decision-Making Process

Arthur L. Costa

When I worked as assistant superintendent in charge of curriculum and instruction, I presented a social studies curriculum guide to my board of education for adoption. One board member voted against adopting the guide because, he said, "We already have a social studies guide. Why do we need another one?" Wouldn't educators' lives be easy if that were true! Adopt it once, and then we don't have to worry about it. Actually, this static concept of curriculum is true in some school systems and some countries in which curriculum decision making is vested in a few at the top of the hierarchy, and they work to enforce adherence to the curriculum guide, course of study, or syllabus by others who are expected to implement it.

The ever present need for curriculum development is not easily understood by many who viewed curriculum as the transmission of information. If content is valued over process, the curriculum guides endure by merely adding and updating content from time to time. I define curriculum, however, as a continual decision-making process at all levels of the educational establishment.

This chapter presents the notion not only that the curriculum should focus on processes as outcomes but also that curriculum itself is a process. The process of balancing the philosophical, operational, and political decisions of the curriculum decision-making process is described. This process includes three basic groups of decisions, depending on one's philosophical orientation. They are

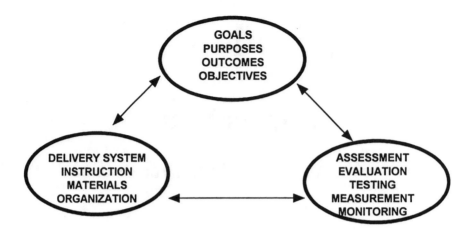

Sea Of Philosophical Beliefs And Values

Figure 4.1. Curriculum Alignment

deciding on outcomes, goals, intentions, purposes, and so forth; deciding on strategies, materials, and organizational patterns to achieve those outcomes; and deciding on how to assess whether those outcomes are achieved using the strategies that were adopted. A diagram of this dynamic process of balancing these ingredients of curriculum decision making is illustrated in Figure 4.1.

Philosophical Decisions

Education provides a public forum for the public's beliefs to be played out. Educators are constantly making decisions about curriculum on the basis of conflicting philosophies among board members, teachers, administrators, and the public. Examples of these public debates are related to misunderstandings of outcomes-based education, sex education, character education, values education, school prayer, and religion in the schools. Because of these differences, some parents have turned to alternative schools and home schooling.

Resolving, explaining, ameliorating, integrating, and responding to these often conflicting conceptions of the curriculum are continual challenges to the curriculum worker. Furthermore, as times change, as one political party gains philosophical dominance and then relinquishes that power to others, public opinion shifts. Liberalism and conservatism are in a constant ebb and flow. This sways public opinion, which in turn, influences educational decision making.

In their seminal work on educational beliefs, Eisner and Vallance (1974) describe five belief orientations that guide educators' curriculum decision making and fuel the debate among policymakers and the public. They are described as follows:

1. *Cognitive processors* are drawn to educational theorists and authors such as Jerome Bruner, Hilda Taba, Robert Sternberg, Jean Piaget, Reuven Feuerstein, Maria Montessori, and Edward de Bono. With their orientation to constructivist psychology, they may believe that the central role of schools is to develop rational thought processes, problem solving, and decision making. They believe that the information explosion is occurring at such a rapid rate that it is no longer possible for experts in any field to keep up with new knowledge. Thus, educators no longer know what to teach but instead must help students continue to learn how to learn.

Cognitive processors most likely select instructional strategies that involve problem solving and the inquiry method. When they talk about instruction, they use terms from Bloom's (1956) taxonomy: *intellectual development, cognitive processes, metacognition,* and *thinking skills.* They organize teaching around the resolution of problems and the Socratic method and bring in discrepant events for students to explore and analyze. They evaluate student learning by how well students perform in problem-solving situations that require developing meta-cognitive strategies to solve complex problems through time. Their metaphori-cal model of education is that of information processing: Human beings, there-fore, are meaning makers, and schools and teachers mediate those capacities.

2. *Self-actualizers* are oriented to Gestalt psychology and regard schools as child centered. They probably view the teacher as a facilitator for learning, and they believe the purpose of teaching is to bring out the unique qualities, potentials, and capacities in each child. They like multisensory instruction with many opportunities for auditory, visual, and kinesthetic learning. They value student choice, whether for classroom topics, the nature of assignments, learn-ing activities, or demonstration of achievement. They believe in self-directed learning, individualized instruction, and self-evaluation.

To provide for students' multiple needs, interests, and developmental tasks, self-actualizers may use learning centers focused around themes. They emphasize student autonomy and look for increases in autonomy as a central measure of their effectiveness as teachers. They are drawn to such humanists as Abraham Maslow, Sylvia Ashton Warner, Arthur Combs, Carl Rogers, Sidney Simon, and George Leonard. Their vocabulary includes words referring to the affective domain and terms such as *the whole child, nurturing, peak experiences, choice, democracy, holistic, self-esteem, continuous progress, dignity, creativity, climate for learning, individualize,* and *caring.* Because every child is different, self-actualizers are concerned with developmentally appropriate curriculum, whole language, and creativity. Their metaphoric model of education is that of a gardener—cultivating, nurturing, and providing the nutrients for maximizing each child's potential.

3. *Technologists* are influenced by the behavioral psychology of Skinner, Pavlov, and Thorndike and may be attracted to such education authors as Robert Mager, James Popham, and Madeline Hunter. They place strong empha-sis on accountability and measurable learning. Their metaphor for education is as an "input, throughput, output system" in which data and opportunities to learn skills are provided. They excel in handling details and have great ability

to analyze, project, and plan. They are skilled at task analysis and are interested in instructional computers and learning systems. They employ assessments for diagnosing entry levels and prescribe according to what is known and what is yet to be learned. They talk about *accountability, evaluation, task analysis, time on task, mastery, templates, diagnosis, prescriptions, desegregated analysis,* and *percentiles.*

4. *Academic rationalists* admire such authors as Diane Ravitch, E. D. Hirsch, Arthur Bestor, William Bennett, and Chester Finn. They are drawn to teacher-centered instruction, believing that knowledgeable adults have the wisdom and the experience to know what is best for students. Their metaphor for education is the transmission of the major concepts, values, and truths of society, and they consider students as clay to be molded or vessels to be filled. They value and are highly oriented toward increasing the amount and rigor of student learning. They are probably drawn to essential truths, classics, the great books, and traditional values. They appreciate basic texts and the teaching strategies of lecture, memorization, demonstration, and drill. They evaluate students through summative examinations, achievement testing, and content mastery. They speak about *discipline, authority, humanities, scholarship, standardized tests, basic skills,* and other aspects that value higher academic standards.

5. *Social reconstructionists* are concerned with the problems of society, the shrinking world, the future of the planet, protection of wildlife, and major crises such as destruction of the food chain, the hole in the ozone, deforestation of timberland, and overpopulation. Concerned with interconnectedness and systems thinking, they view the learner as a social being: a member of a group, a responsible citizen, one who identifies with and is proactive regarding the environmental ills and social injustices of the day. They agree with John Naisbitt, who reports that we have gone beyond the age of representative democracies. Because we no longer trust our elective officials to make important decisions, we have moved to a state of participative democracies.

Social reconstructionists believe that this is a world in which people must care for neighbors and take action at the grass-roots level. They engage students in recycling centers, social issues, cooperative learning, outdoor education, and global education. Their metaphor of education is as an instrument of change, and they believe that schools are the only institution in our society charged with the responsibility of bringing about a better future and a better world. They are drawn to such authors as Marilyn Ferguson, Willis Harmon, Alvin Toffler, Robert Samples, John Naisbitt, and Jean Houston. Their vocabulary includes terms such as *environment, consumer education, peace, student rights, 21st century, multicultural, futurist, global intellect, pluralistic, change, save the Earth, ecology,* and *love.*

The Pluralistic Curriculum Dilemma

Which of these sometimes competing philosophical orientations should drive the curriculum presents a dilemma for curriculum decision makers. Because belief systems don't change easily and because the older we become, the less likely we are to change, the forces needed to drive change are significant. For educators, these forces behind change have been found to occur in essentially two instances.

First, when the prevailing culture begins to persistently and pervasively shift its values, educators may begin to move our thinking in like directions. For example, the 1960s saw the spreading influence of individualized instruction, and many of us began to behave more like self-actualizers.

Second, teachers have a tendency to adapt their belief systems to accommodate new realities. For example, a 12th-grade history teacher may take a position as a kindergarten teacher, or an instructor may move from an affluent school to one lacking in financial resources. In cases such as this, teachers' paradigms change, and so do the beliefs they use to explain their role in their new environment.

There is also an eclectic view that all these belief systems are viewed as necessary and valued aims of education: We want students to become good problem solvers; we want them to be self-actualized and to be knowledgeable, efficient, and concerned. The task for curriculum decision makers is to become at ease with a variety of educational beliefs, to refine their ability to work with people whose beliefs may be different from their own, and to constantly ameliorate differences that arise from community groups, staff, and political philosophy about what knowledge is of most worth.

Curriculum Alignment

The task of aligning curriculum is usually composed of four major decisions: (a) establishing the purposes, outcomes, goals, or objectives of the educational enterprise, be it at the classroom, school, district, state, or national level; (b) designing the delivery system by which those goals will be achieved, including instructional design, materials selection, allocation of time, and placement of learnings; (c) developing feedback spirals for monitoring, collecting evidence of, and evaluating the achievement of goals as a result of employing that delivery system; and (d) designing response mechanisms to the information retrieved from the feedback spirals.

Decisions regarding the goals of education are made at each level:

At the national level: In the United States, education is basically the responsibility of each state. Nevertheless, in 1990, then President Bush, on the basis of a conference of state governors, produced a document establishing goals for schools for the year 2000. This document was later adopted by President Clinton (Secretary's Commission on Achieving Necessary Skills, 1992).

At the state level: State boards of education and legislators decide on goals, performances, and standards for students in 3rd, 6th, 8th, and 11th grades.

At the district level: School district trustees decide on mission statements and student outcomes. They must approve and adopt lists of performances and graduation requirements.

At the school level: Schools develop and adopt mission statements, purposes, outcomes, and goals for their students. They establish standards of performance and grade-level and graduation expectancies.

At the classroom level: Teachers decide what should be grade-level learning outcomes in reading and math for fifth-grade students. Teachers plan objectives for the science unit.

In a similar manner, the delivery system is designed to achieve those goals at various levels. For example,

At the national level: There is talk of a national curriculum. As of this writing, a debate continues about who is responsible for providing school lunches. Head Start, Chapter I, integration, and so forth are attempts to meet the needs of younger and needy children.

At the state level: Numerous states develop curriculum guides and adopt textbooks. States must decide on the number of required hours of instruction, days of attendance, graduation requirements, and so forth.

At the district level: Decisions are made about staff development, allocation of resources, school building design, evaluation of instruction, and so on.

At the classroom level: Teachers devise instructional strategies, time sequences, and classroom organizational structures intended to facilitate achievement of their goals.

Similarly, assessment procedures are selected to determine the achievement of the goals developed at multiple levels:

At the national level: The National Assessment of Educational Progress, for example, discloses how U.S. students score on a variety of topics. There is talk of a national report card. Scores on tests are compared with those of other countries.

At the state level: States decide on statewide testing procedures to assess student's achievement of the state curriculum.

At the district level: School boards adopt standardized tests and other forms of measurement to determine district standards and to compare their scores with those of other districts.

At the classroom level: Teachers devise tests and other forms of observation of student performance of desired behaviors.

In the curriculum alignment process, sound educational practice dictates that the first group of decisions (the goals) needs to drive the system. Like it or not, what is inspected is what is expected; what you test is what you get. The traditional use of norm-referenced, standardized tests has dictated what should be learned (the goals) and has influenced how it should be taught (the delivery).

Societal Implications

Because schools reflect society, curriculum is in a constant state of flux. Simply teaching students how to read the Bible was once a sufficient mission for schools. Modern educators are realizing, however, that new goals for the

next century are becoming increasingly necessary as survival skills for our
children's future, for the perpetuation of our democratic institutions, and even
for our planetary existence. Such goals include

- Capacity for continued learning
- Knowing how to behave when answers to problems are not immediately
  apparent
- Cooperativeness and team building
- Precise communication in a variety of modes
- Appreciation for disparate value systems
- Problem solving that requires creativity and ingenuity
- Enjoyment of resolving ambiguous, discrepant, and paradoxical situations
- Generation and organization of an overabundance of technologically
  produced information
- Pride and craftsmanship of product
- Knowledge and acceptance of self
- Personal commitment to larger organizational and global values

These new goals are driving the curriculum decision-making process. The
decisions about the delivery system—curriculum materials, instructional strategies, school organization, and the curriculum alignment—need to embody these
goals not only for students but for all the school's inhabitants.

Likewise, decisions about assessment are transformed to become more
consistent with the new goals. Educators cannot employ product-oriented
assessment techniques to assess the achievement of these new, process-oriented
educational outcomes. Norm-referenced standardized test scores provide static
numbers that reflect the achievement and performance of isolated skills at a
particular moment. Thinking, however, is dynamic: Humans learn from experience, react emotionally to situations, experience power in problem solving,
and are energized by the art of discovery. Thus, *testing thinking may indeed be an
oxymoron!*

We are witnessing a nationwide surge to "go beyond the bubble" of traditional standardized, norm-referenced computerized testing (e.g., as discussed
at the California State Department of Education Curriculum Assessment Alignment Conference in 1989). State departments of education (e.g., New Jersey,
Vermont, Colorado, Maryland, Michigan, and Illinois) are providing leadership
by experimenting with and advocating innovative assessment methods such as
writing samples, materials manipulation, open-ended multiple answer questions, portfolios, performances, and exhibitions.

Such innovative methods are more useful and "authentic" than traditional
testing procedures for several reasons. First, they resemble the situation in
which real problem solving and creativity are demanded; they are not contrived.
Second, they allow teachers to more accurately diagnose students' abilities.
Third, they take place during instruction, rather than after instruction is completed. Fourth, they provide more immediate results that assist teaching teams
in evaluating the effectiveness of their own curriculum decisions and instructional

efforts. Last, they provide "real-time" feedback to students themselves who are (or who must become) the ultimate evaluators of their own work and performance.

Students as Curriculum Decision Makers

Cellular telephones, fiber optics, Internet, e-mail, voice mail, Nintendo, pagers, interactive television, digital video cameras, voice recognition, ink-jet, laser, media integration, CD-ROM, information bases, laptop/personal computers, video telephones, modems, information superhighway—these terms are recent additions to our daily vocabulary. They are having a tremendous impact on curriculum decision making.

In *Supporting the Spirit of Learning: When Process Is Content* (see Costa & Liebmann, 1996), Melchior, Edwards, Gawith, and Keaney redefine curriculum through technology. With new technological resources, students will increasingly become their own curriculum decision makers. They will access, select, synthesize, and manage the information that is available through a multitude of avenues and present it in unique forms designed by them. Their understandings will be built from vast databases, more accessible than the reference books or encyclopedias of the past. They will have instantaneous, live communication with vast, worldwide resources previously unavailable to them.

Traditional texts, workbooks, and notebooks will go the way of the typewriter, slide rule, and adding machine. Although some of us may seem to be "techno-peasants," having been unable or unwilling to participate in the technological revolution, affluent students today are growing up with, living in, and expecting to participate in and learn through technological means.

As a result, the criteria for performance and learning will be self-developed. Ultimately, the students, in the final analysis, determine what should be learned, how it should be learned, and whether it has been mastered. Relevant goals and outcomes emerge from within the students. If they feel those goals imposed from the outside are irrelevant, uninteresting, too complex, or too distant, little commitment will be made to learning them. If the strategy of learning is not vibrant relative to students' readiness, learning style, culture, and duration for mastery, little engagement will be exacted. Finally, if the form of assessment is not relevant to learners' capacity for the expression of their knowledge, students will give little energy to the acquisition of proficiency.

Technology not only can become a significant tool to enhance learning efficiency but also can be a motivator for student engagement. It also can be a means of involving students in the construction of their own curricula—having to decide what learning is of most worth and when and how it should be learned. Of most significance, technology will provide opportunities for students to receive immediate feedback about their performance and, therefore, to be in a constant state of self-assessment about how well they are doing (see Kallick's chapter on feedback spirals in Costa & Liebmann, 1996, *Supporting the Spirit of Learning: When Process Is Content*).

In Summary

This chapter demonstrates that curriculum is not a fixed body of content to be transmitted to youths. Curriculum *is* a decision-making process—constantly balancing the emerging and ever changing needs of students, society, and the content to be taught. As research adds to the knowledge base, as political systems change, as trends in society change, as technology advances, as we learn more about learning, and as we gain greater insight into the functioning of the human brain, so too must the curriculum change.

As educators move from a content to a process orientation of curriculum, our view will shift from deciding *what* to teach. The emphasis will be on how we make decisions about what we value, what is teachable, how it should be organized, how much time should be devoted, who should be involved in the decision-making process, what materials best communicate our intentions, and what process outcomes or goals are served.

References

Bloom, B. (1956). *Taxonomy of educational objectives: Book I. The cognitive domain.* New York: David McKay.

Costa, A. L., & Liebmann, R. M. (1996). *Supporting the Spirit of Learning: When Process Is Content.* Thousand Oaks, CA: Corwin Press.

Eisner, E., & Vallance, E. (1974). *Conflicting conceptions of the curriculum.* Berkeley, CA: McCutchan.

Secretary's Commission on Achieving Necessary Skills (SCANS). (1992, April). *Learning a living: A blueprint for high performance* [Goals 2000]. Washington, DC: U.S. Department of Labor.

5

How Process Is Connected With the Human Spirit

Rosemarie M. Liebmann

One morning, we stop to notice the beauty of the dawn
One day, we cherish the laughter of the children
For each of us, our spirits rise to new joys and challenges.

Maggie Liebmann

As I began my research for my doctoral dissertation, I found myself intrigued by a new concept—that of a *holon* (Koestler, 1972). *Holonomy* is a person's cognitive capacity to accept the concept that he or she is a subwhole: whole in self and yet subordinate to a higher system. Recognition of this condition has led scientists and others to search for an underlying unity between differing things—between humans and the world around us. The questions that they probe are, "What is this force that unites vastly different entities in the universe?" "How might we come to know and understand it?" And for those of us who interact with groups of people, "How do we honor our differences so that we might better understand our similarities?"

As I pondered these questions, I found the answer seemed to rest in my learnings from the new sciences and emotional intelligence as well as from my intrigue with listening to and developing my own intuition. This has been a journey that started long before I embarked on writing a dissertation and that continues to this day. The journey takes me forward into contemporary research and backward into ancient teachings. There is a remarkable convergence of these two seemingly disparate worlds. In Figure 5.1, I have integrated the four

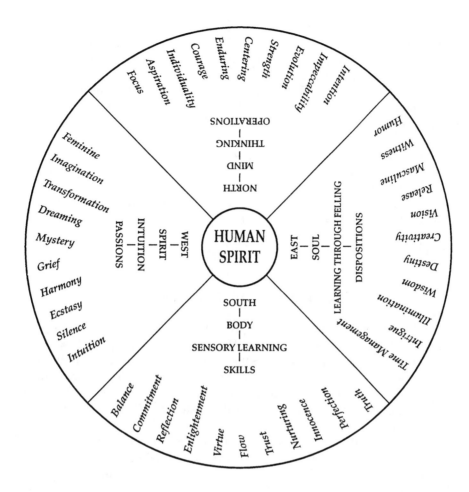

Figure 5.1. Integration of the Sacred Circle, How Humans Learn, and the Processes

levels of processes, the four directions of the Sacred Circle and their associated energy forces, and the four ways we as humans learn. Although these are not a perfect match, I found myself surprised by the large degree of congruence. The energy forces that appear on the circumference of the circle can be shifted into other quadrants. Their placement is not an absolute but rather one person's interpretation of the learnings associated with each direction in Native American teachings.

As I mentioned previously, this journey started while I was still in the classroom. It was one of those rare days when suddenly what always had made sense seemed no longer to fit. I found myself standing at the blackboard, actively engaged in my lesson. Half my brain seemed to be present in the classroom, and the other half was hovering above me looking down on the scene. I suddenly realized my increasing uneasiness with the curriculum as I knew it. My questions were similar to those of my students: "So? When will I ever use this? Why should I care?" Simultaneously, I was asking, "Why am I teaching this? How will this help them lead successful lives? Is this why I came into education—to stand here and teach facts?" There was an ever increasing disconnect for me, and I could not seem to resolve it.

A journey into process education started for me as I looked for ways to give my students skills they could carry with them beyond my classroom. As with most journeys, when the student is ready, the teacher appears. I was fortunate to have many wonderful teachers in the form of consultants, professors, supervisors, and authors. The following sections will illuminate some of that learning as it applies to the changes in views of science and the value of intuitive thinking.

Yes, both conservative and liberal members of our communities should be heard, but instead of being at opposite ends of the continuum, they need to work together collectively. They need to create unity from diversity. They need to let go of the win-lose model they've grown up with and adopt, from a genuine concern for students, a win-win model.

Research From the New Sciences

The impact of the "new sciences" (quantum physics, self-organizing systems, chaos theory, complexity, etc.) will be referenced throughout this trilogy. Western education has traditionally adhered to a reductionist mode of thinking in which the world is seen as a duality of subject-object, spirit-matter, female-male, black-white, right-wrong, content-process, inner-outer, good-evil, known-unknown, conservative-liberal, and so forth. Many times in these volumes, the authors discuss the need to eliminate this dichotomous thinking. Consistently, and in keeping with the break from the mechanistic Newtonian model of physics, the contributors advocate for a curriculum that is interdependent and interrelated. The emphasis on the basics as separate and unique—reading, writing, and arithmetic—ignores the reality of our universe—a universe that is in a continual state of change and transformation and that at first may seem chaotic but is, in fact, a blend of chaos and order (complexity).

Evidence of complexity has been found in many sciences from economics to mathematics, to physics, to psychology, and so forth. Wheatley (1992), for instance, points out, "[Mother Nature] has been stunningly successful with living systems by entrusting everything from energy fields to plants and animals to thrive on chaos" (p. 143). These living systems automatically adapt to ever changing circumstances, which has increased their capabilities, competence, and staying power.

Capra (cited in Vaughan, 1979) tells us that the universe of the modern physicist, like that of the Eastern mystic, is a system of dynamic, interacting, ever moving components of which the observer is an integral part. The task at hand for educators is not to reject but to expand experiences and understandings through integration. The new sciences have paved the way to rethink the curriculum to free up our ability to act, to be creative, to develop meaning in our work, and to unleash our intrinsic energy. These sciences do not propose formulas. Instead, they challenge us to leap beyond tradition, to consider the teachings from nature, and to translate these lessons into the everyday functioning of learning organizations.

One of these lessons is that time and space are concepts held within the rational mind. Scientists are beginning to see how their beliefs concerning time and space have placed limitations on their awareness and insights. The point is not to change how humans think about time and space but to accept that any type of thinking is only one of many possibilities and, as such, has limitations.

The scientific method has also been rethought. Although the power and value of this approach cannot be denied, it neglects the relatedness of the parts. Ian Mitroff (1983), who interviewed 40 eminent scientists, asserts that it also neglects the ability "to learn how to do science with feeling, how to develop a science that in its working methodology and spirit knows what feeling means" (p. 210). When we blend opposites, feeling with thinking, a magnificent diversity coexists within the oneness, like white light diffracted into the myriad colors of the spectrum. This process gives birth to new and superior theories. For example, our inability to explain blackbody radiation led to a toppling of the Newtonian world of classical mechanics. From this chaos grew the quantum universe. The new sciences are opening the way to even greater wisdom, to an understanding of the essence of nature.

By incorporating feelings into the scientific method, new research is being motivated by a love of nature, rather than a desire to control it. As Shepherd (1993) states,

> Wonder for the beauty of nature, a passion for the work, the excitement of learning new things, the joy of seeing a pattern emerge, the ecstasy of discovery, the zest of the quest for truth, the pleasure of relationships with colleagues—these feelings can inspire and augment the logical analysis of interesting problems. (p. 67)

Or in the words of Giambattista della Porta (1558/1957), "the whole world is knit and bound within itself; for the world is a living creature, everywhere both male and female, and the parts of it do couple together . . . by reason of their mutual love" (p. 14). This mutual love enables us to bring order and chaos into balance.

Founded in the mid-1980s, the Santa Fe Institute consists of an eclectic group of researchers who share the vision of an underlying unity, a common theoretical framework for complexity to illuminate nature and humanity alike. These researchers believe that the reductionist thinking that has dominated science for so long is inadequate in addressing the problems of the modern world. They believe that the crucial capacity for the 21st century will be the insight to see the web of connections. In addition, they believe that the universe is constantly unfolding. It is therefore fluid, ever changing, and alive. What is their point? Simply, "You have to look at the world as it is, not as some elegant theory says it ought to be" (Waldrop, 1992, p. 38). The new sciences have helped to see that reducing everything in the universe to a few simple laws has really led to an understanding of the enormously rich behavior in the world.

This rich behavior is exciting to those involved in continuous learning. It is similar to being in kindergarten, when we, as children, were exposed to all sorts of new things with a sense of wonder and intrigue. The whole universe was seen as an amazing place to explore in which new ideas emerged and took shape. The treasures that we discovered were guided by personal experiences, feelings, and the questions we raised. As we now consider a new way of looking at our universe, adults begin to experience anew the wonder and intrigue created by previously unknown possibilities.

Nature has also shown that large systems are able to maintain their overall identity and form only when the systems tolerate great degrees of individual freedom. The truth is that we inhabit a world that is always subjective and shaped by our interactions with it. The new sciences have brought to us an entirely new landscape in which the primary value is given to the relationships that exist between seemingly discrete parts—unity expressed as diversity. Perhaps that is the merit behind community, state, and national curricula. The primary value is in the relationship that exists between these discrete entities— the relationships embedded in the processes of learning. As Wheatley (1992) states, "To live in a quantum universe, to weave here and there with ease and grace, we will need to change what we do. We will need to stop describing tasks and instead facilitate process" (p. 38).

Why Value Intuition As a Process?

> Stop thinking and talking about it and there is nothing you will not be able to know. (Chinese patriarch of Zen)

There is much interest in today's society in achieving a sense of "balance." We are frequently led to believe that we are destroying the planet on which we live and that if we do not achieve balance between ourselves and Mother Earth, we will perish. Balance, however, is one face of the either-or coin. Heads we are in balance, tails we are out of balance. According to many mental health professionals, true happiness is achieved when the human spirit is in balance. And yet the maintenance of balance does not lead to growth. A sense of imbalance spurs intrigue, stress, and disequilibrium—all of which cause growth as a result of the desire to restore balance. This intertwining of chaos and order is essential if the human spirit is to be vibrant and healthy. This may also be true of the world around us. We need a sense of balance (order) as well as of imbalance (chaos) to foster continuous learning. Perhaps the current state of imbalance with nature will lead to greater understandings of our interconnections and dependence on Mother Earth.

When we, as adults, are granted the privilege of watching young children explore nature, we see the world through new eyes. Youngsters raise our consciousness to the beauty of a dandelion, the sweet smell of newly mown grass, the exquisite array of colors in a rainbow, the perfection of a snowflake, the music of the birds, the natural hum of nature, and the babbling of a brook. As children mature, they move away from this innocence into the world of experience. They learn that the dandelion is a weed to be disposed of, the grass is a chore that requires cutting, the rainbow is not magic but the refraction of light through water, the snowflake is merely frozen water that needs to be shoveled, the music of the birds is diminishing from ever louder sound systems, the hum of nature is lost to the noise of machines, and the babbling brook is polluted water. The more they learn, the more they begin to sense that something is not right. Just as they desire to experience because innocence feels uncomfortable, later in life adults search for innocence in response to too much experience, which has left us without joy and laughter. We long for the child who was playful, curious, and intuitive. If we are lucky, we can rediscover our intuition arising from our childlike qualities that were not lost to us but simply hidden from our senses.

These childlike qualities result in the dynamic inward freedom experienced when we can hear and trust our inner thoughts, ideas, curiosities, and wonderment. To recover this state of consciousness, we must awaken our intuition by developing the skills of self-trust and self-compassion. Intuition resides in the nonverbal, nonlinear side of the brain that looks for and is oriented toward pattern perception. We are all aware of our intuitive capabilities, but for many persons, they remain repressed or undeveloped. The misfortune is that intuition is a valid way of knowing, just as feeling, thinking, and sensing are. The interesting part about intuition is that it brings with it a sense of truth. As Vaughan (1979) states, "Learning to use your intuition is learning to be your own teacher" (p. 3). Intuition plays a primary role in creativity, problem solving, and interpersonal relationships.

The word *intuition* comes from the Latin *in-tuire*, meaning looking, regarding, or knowing from within. *Intuiting* is defined by Liebmann and Colella (see Costa & Liebmann, 1996) as the process of listening for and attending to quick and ready insights or convictions that lack rational thought or inference—contemplating perceptions based on feelings or other sensory stimuli, and knowing without knowing. It is the holonomous sense that the head and the heart are functioning as one, without any doubt. Intuition, when used correctly, is grounded in integrity, intellect, and inspiration.

Intuitive processing permits people to recognize possibilities inherent in any situation. When we become aware of these possibilities, we are free to make conscious choices. If we make choices without conscious awareness, as part of our automatic functioning in everyday life, freedom becomes elusive. Only when we awaken our intuition can we feel, sense, and reflect on the widest range of possibilities that are available to us. Only when we raise our intuition to a level of conscious awareness can we see clearly without limiting ourselves to the theories of others. Only then can decisions be made on the basis of "coulds" as opposed to "shoulds." Only then can we tap into the greatest knowledge bank—a knowledge bank that exists within and outside each of us.

At any given moment, conscious thoughts are a small portion of what a person truthfully knows. Unconscious thoughts, which are neither good nor bad, can benefit when they are brought into consciousness and analyzed. Learners who develop the skills, operations, dispositions, and passions for drawing on their vast storehouse of unconscious knowledge are able to transcend boundaries created by individual separateness as they access the infinite reservoir of the collective or universal unconscious.

Frequently, elders are surprised by the wisdom that comes from the mouths of babes. Children can see with a clarity that years of experience have distorted for adults. For example, a friend recently shared with me that she had to face a confrontation with family and greatly feared the aftermath. Her daughter, overhearing the conversation, responded, "Mom, you have to learn to do what is good for you, and everything else will fall into place." This 16-year-old young woman held a greater wisdom than her 49-year-old mother. The young woman was not hindered by years of abuse. Her experience was different from her mother's. She has learned to value her feelings and insights.

How might we tap into our unconscious reservoir of knowledge and bring it into consciousness? The answer is simple—reawaken our intuition. Wisdom comes when we can access both our experience and our intuitive nature. Both are teachers to us, and we must not resort to favoring one over the other. Let me provide an example for why I strongly argue for both.

Recently, as I was editing these books, I found myself lost in a struggle— triggered by a poem I had read—to understand the importance of recovering our innocence. Finally, in sheer frustration, I went upstairs, lay on my bed, and permitted my mind to grow still. As I did, connections were made with previous learning. It was as if puzzle pieces were falling into place. Not wanting to disturb this generative process, delighted by new insights, I stayed where I was. Suddenly, my little dog pounced on top of me, and I returned rather abruptly from never-never land. The following day, I shared many of my insights with colleagues. Speculating that innocence/intuition and experience are the combined cornerstones of wisdom, my colleagues and I are beginning to explore and collaborate on the implications for future research. Conscious thinking had been blocking my original progress. It was the ability to let messy impulses play around in my head through imagery that led to new insights and learning.

When I reflected on this process, I determined that it required the ability to (a) quiet the mind to expand awareness of possibilities (relaxation); (b) suspend disbelief and trust in myself to find answers (receptivity); (c) look honestly at the thoughts and ideas that seemed confusing (disidentifying); and (d) be willing to treat myself kindly and compassionately, permitting and acknowledging that insights might come at the most unexpected moments (self-awareness). Once the insights had presented themselves, the decision whether to act involved reason and choice that were based on experience. And the result? This chapter was conceived.

Why Value Intuition?

Knowledge has three degrees—opinion, science, and illumination. The means or instrument of the first is sense, of the second, dialectic; of the third, intuition. This last is absolute knowledge founded on the identity of the mind knowing with the object known. (Plotinus)

To choose a path in which life is lived wholeheartedly, people need to know how they feel. It is not possible for human beings to be passionate about their work or studies if they are out of touch with their feelings. Furthermore, because everyone thinks in pictures before learning to think in words, new insights and ideas frequently come in the form of mental pictures or images. These mental pictures color perception in ways that may not be immediately apparent. If we can raise conscious awareness of these images through which our perceptions are filtered, we can increase intuition and self-awareness.

Intuition is a basic prerequisite to empathy. It requires that we learn to hold our mental dialogue in abeyance, to have it stand aside to get in touch with a deeper level of experience. It is the process of learning to let things happen, rather than trying to make them happen. As Vaughan (1979) states,

> When you begin to observe your inner imagery and trust your subjectivity, you can easily feel the difference between the images which come to mind spontaneously and deliberate visualizations. People who have difficulty visualizing, imagining, or thinking in metaphors need to learn to let go of their tendency to control inner experience. Those who have no trouble in allowing the flow of imagery, on the other hand, need to learn to focus their attention in order to take responsibility for these experiences and not feel overwhelmed by them. The development of intuition depends on learning both control of the mind and the surrender of the egotistical will. (pp. 30-31)

In today's complex world, intuition is becoming increasingly important. Intuition comes from the development of a silenced mind in which clear vision can happen. For students, intuition is important because it leads to improved self-esteem and a sense of inner direction that arise from the development of nonjudgmental self-awareness. When individuals experience themselves as centers of pure consciousness, they have increased awareness of their original and timeless unity with *all* reality (Vaughan, 1979).

Western society has traditionally ignored the importance of intuition. Recent research in such fields as psychology, physiology, the new sciences, leadership, cognition, and philosophy is beginning to lend support to the importance of educating both sides of the brain, the intuitive and the rational. These two modes of knowing, when seen as complementary to each other, expand knowledge, perceptions, choices, insights, and understanding. In essence, when these two are integrated, viewpoints are heightened and sharpened by the knowledge of the other.

In addition, to be successful, we must begin to monitor our language. It is language use that leads to dichotomous thinking. The word *holonomy* is one attempt at trying to create a vocabulary that is inclusive rather than exclusive. Holonomy describes the state of being in which one is an autonomously interdependent individual. The paradigm shifts from *me-you* to *we*. Although only an attempt, holonomy is an effort to overcome the limitations that language places on the richness of the world.

Another such word is *autopoiesis*, the characteristic of living systems to continuously renew themselves and to regulate this process in such a way that the integrity of their structure is maintained—renewal and maintenance. Autopoiesis is an increasingly important concept. Citizens are being asked to renew their marketability skills almost daily while still retaining the integrity of who they are and what they believe. They are being asked to blend their intuition (inner knowing) with their experience (outer knowing).

The metaphorical language of intuition is embedded in nature. Rational language focuses on reason, structure, strength, skirmishes, control, authority, and hostility. The language of intuition speaks to magic, faith, visions, trust, flow, openness, order, renewal, and illumination. Such phrases as *weaving*, *rippling, seamlessness, swirling,* and *fluctuating* are used to describe the ballet of chaos and order, change and stability, and intuition and rationality—the complementary aspects of the process of growth. None of these are felt to be primary, yet all are seen as primary.

It is in the seeing with a sense of wonder and feeling with openness to new experiences that people begin to tap in to intuitive universal knowledge. It is in curiosity about phenomena and wondering about alternative perceptions and explanations, in the playful messing around with our thoughts, and in the answers to the following questions that our intuitive knowledge can grow:

- Why do we limit ourselves to one idea, to one structure, to one perception that all truth is quantifiable and knowable?
- Why do we stay locked in our belief that there is one right way of learning when we know there are multiple ways?
- Why do we assume that there is only one right answer to a problem or question when we know there are multiple answers, depending on one's perspective or mental models?
- Why do we ignore that the universe seems to thrive on multiplicity of meanings and welcome diversity?
- Why do we stop dreaming and believe we can have no impact on the future when we have witnessed the effects of small disturbances on large systems?
- Why do we fear openness when we know it avoids deterioration?

It is clear that in our constantly changing environment, people will need high levels of self-awareness, plentiful sensing devices, a strong capacity for reflection, and an intuitive as well as a rational mind. As Wheatley (1992) suggests,

> We are great weavers of tales, outdoing one another around the camp-fire to see which stories best capture our imaginations and the experiences of our lives. If we can look at our selves truthfully in the light of this fire and stop being so serious about getting things "right"—as if there were still an objective reality out there—we can engage in life with a different quality, a different level of playfulness. (p. 142)

The Processes of Emotional Intelligence

A different level of playfulness? Perhaps levels of playfulness could be explored in the lower grades, but certainly not in the upper grades in which content is already crushing the teacher? Or perhaps educators need to look through a different set of lenses. As we saw with the new sciences, feelings are becoming an integral part of successful survival in today's society. Wheatley is suggesting that the adventuresome mind be permitted to play with thoughts and ideas, to raise somewhat absurd but perhaps curious questions. Einstein admitted that he learned a great deal from playing with children. Just as there is a growing awareness concerning the ethical implications of certain research and scientists are beginning to listen to their feelings and their intuition as ardently as they do to their rational minds, students need to be permitted to playfully mess around with content and to weave their own tales.

Furthermore, concern is mounting over the increasing violence in schools, the workplace, airports, and so forth. Emotional abuse, drive-by shootings, and posttraumatic stress have all entered the daily vocabulary of millions of Americans. We have shifted in the last decade from simple statements such as "Have a nice day" to threatening statements such as "Make my day." Many people have suggested that the media are to blame. The media certainly have to accept an appropriate degree of responsibility. Frequently, people say they no longer watch the television or read the newspaper because there is never any good news. Unfortunately, Goleman (1995) indicates that "the present generation of children will be more emotionally disturbed than the last: more lonely and depressed, more angry and unruly, more nervous and prone to worry, more impulsive and aggressive" (p. xiii).

What might we offer the next generation as a solution? As their nurturers and caregivers, we need to become more responsible for the lessons we set before the younger generation. We need to examine our own lives to see if we can bring back into balance the freedom to live as we choose and the acceptance of the responsibilities that go with that freedom. Clearly, one of those responsibilities is the ability to be empathic with others. The roots of empathy in human development can be traced to 3-month-old babies. Studies have shown that infants do respond with empathy to one another (Goleman, 1995).

As adults, we tell our children to treat one another with respect and kindness, but too often we do not model this behavior. Children learn what they see, not what they are told. Altea (1995) writes,

> There are many who will refuse to accept responsibility for their own actions. . . . Blame . . . fault . . . these are words that you will use. A finger pointed at another in accusation. A finger, often harshly, pointed at your own self in accusation. Where is your *gentleness?* (p. 252)

Gentleness? In this competitive society, the older generation instructs the younger in winning at all cost. It is not how we play the game but whether we have won. Schools are structured around the concept of competition, winning or losing, passing or failing, accepting or rejecting. So why should we be concerned with a fluffy concept such as gentleness? Because in the end, social skills—not, as popularly believed, IQ—may be the final determinant of success.

Again, we are faced with a dichotomy—the emotional mind and the rational mind. These two minds normally operate in harmony with each other. They intertwine their different ways of knowing to assist each other and to serve us better. Feelings, we are finding, are essential to thought, and thought is essential to feelings. The thinking brain grew out of the emotional brain. This is why honoring our emotions is so crucial to making wise decisions and thinking clearly. There is a natural dance that occurs between the rational mind and the intuitive mind.

The Emotional Intelligences

Goleman (1995) indicates that emotional aptitude is a *meta-ability* that determines how well people can use other skills in conjunction with raw intellect. Some of the skills that Goleman refers to are self-motivation, persistence, controlling impulsivity, delayed gratification, regulation of moods, empathy, and maintenance of hope.

Although Costa (1991) speaks of the importance of metacognition—awareness of thought processes—Goleman (1995) addresses *metamood* or self-awareness—attention to one's internal states. Self-observation and self-awareness are important because they permit us to hover above or beside the main flow of emotions, aware of what is happening, rather than being lost or immersed in the feelings. When we can take this reflective stance, we are taking the first step in gaining some control over the appropriate feeling given the circumstance.

Studies have shown that young learners who have high hopes and are optimistic perform better in the academic arena than their peers of equivalent IQs who do not hold these self-efficacious beliefs. Bandura (cited in Goleman, 1995) states, "People's beliefs about their abilities have a profound effect on those abilities" (p. 90). Self-efficacious people bounce back from failure, learn from experience, and approach new experiences using the wisdom of the past.

Another emotional state that is seen as one of the healthiest ways to teach children is through flow. Flow is a state of self-forgetfulness during which one is so absorbed in the task at hand that one loses all self-consciousness. In this state, the emotions are directed toward positive, energetic alignment with the activity. Flow occurs in a delicate zone that exists just between boredom and anxiety (Csikszentmihalyi, 1990). Why is this seen as positive for young learners? Flow creates internal motivation rather than motivation by threat of punishment or promise of reward. As a result, students find learning to be pleasurable, which is a more humane, natural, and effective way to create positive models of education.

In addition, if schools can become positive models for emotional intelligence, treating all members of the community with empathic understanding and warmth, children become better at handling their own emotions and are more effective at soothing themselves when upset. They are also more relaxed, which opens the avenues for increased learning. They develop a sense of well-being, and through the adult models, which they astutely observe and imitate within the community, develop appropriate social skills. These benefits have been found to lead to higher academic achievement. Therefore, administrators and teachers need to monitor their actions so that they work to generate confidence, curiosity, pleasure in learning, and an understanding of the limits that help children succeed in life.

One compelling example is found in the work of Goleman (1995), in which he studied the ability of 4-year-olds to control their impulsivity and to delay gratification and then reviewed their SAT scores 14 years later. In this study, he compared 4-years-olds of equivalent IQs. The children were brought into a room and were told that they could eat the marshmallow that was on the table, or, if they could wait until the adult returned, they would be given two marshmallows to eat. Goleman found that the 4-year-olds who were able to leave the marshmallow until the researcher returned had a 210-point advantage in their SAT scores over their peers who immediately grabbed the marshmallow and ate it. The ability to control their impulsivity and delay gratification produced significant gains for the learners in test-taking ability, thoughtful problem solving, and measurable academic achievement.

Some additional ingredients to success in schools that are related to emotional intelligence are these:

- *Confidence:* Confidence arises from a sense of trust in oneself as well as in others. Children need to learn and experience that the adults around them will help them be successful. All too often, the lessons of the past centered on trying to catch learners off guard—surprise quizzes, pop tests, trick questions, and so forth. These activities inadvertently negate the building of self-confidence.
- *Curiosity:* Students feel free to explore new things, knowing that this is a valuable activity through which new learning and positive rewards occur.
- *Intentionality:* Students believe that what they are saying and/or doing will be heard, honored, and valued by the learning community.
- *Self-control:* Students have the ability to monitor their emotions and resultant reactions in an age-appropriate manner.
- *Relatedness:* Students are aware that it is important to be understood by others as well as to understand others. In this mutual give-and-take dialogue, much growth and learning takes place.
- *Capacity to communicate:* Students have the ability to exchange ideas, feelings, and thoughts with members of the learning community, trusting that they will be treated with gentleness.
- *Cooperativeness:* Students develop the capacity to blend individual needs with group needs.

This requires a movement away from the traditional competitive environment of schools to a sharing of experiences. As stated previously, the paradigm shifts from *me-you* to *we.*

Goleman (1995) and others indicate that many of these capacities are well in place before the child reaches school. In fact, Goleman cites one study that summed up the lasting consequences of the emotional lessons of a child's first 4 years.

> A child who cannot focus his attention, who is suspicious rather than trusting, sad or angry rather than optimistic, destructive rather than respectful and one who is overcome with anxiety, preoccupied with frightening fantasy and feels generally unhappy about himself—such a child has little opportunity at all, let alone equal opportunity, to claim the possibilities of the world as his own. (p. 196)

If educators continue to impose lessons of threat, fear, and compliance without regard to the individuals, if we continue to value clones who all act the same and have assimilated the exact same content, we will continue to create an environment in which some students experience a sense of worthlessness, helplessness, and mistrust. All these emotions hinder learning and create negative responses to education.

The role of discipline in schools is a wonderful opportunity to teach appropriate social skills. In our "quick-fix" society, however, the most efficient route is always sought. Yet disciplinarians and guidance counselors know well the repeated offender. Little if anything is learned from the current management system because it does not address the underlying emotions that caused the outer manifestations. Educators need to invest time in talking with youngsters about their feelings and in how to understand them—not being critical or judgmental but rather coaching the students into seeing alternatives to inappropriate expressions.

Parents, the media, and others speak of their concern regarding test scores and academic achievement. Yet as a society at large, we continually bemoan the increase in violence. As a secondary principal once stated, "Without a feeling of safety, there will be no learning." Curriculum design requires using opportunities in and out of class to help students turn moments of personal crisis into lessons of emotional competence. As such, schools need to become more than just academic learning communities. They need to become caring communities—places in which students feel respected, cared about, and bonded to classmates, teachers, and the school itself.

I believe that we need more "playfulness" in education. Schools need to be caring communities in which new discoveries are made through laughter and surprise, places in which the underlying unity of all things is examined, places in which thoughts are supported by intuition and emotional intelligence is nurtured—caring communities in which chaos and order meet to push the learning curve forward.

References

Altea, R. (1995). *The eagle and the rose.* New York: Warner Books.
Costa, A. L. (1991). Mediating the metacognitive. In A. L. Costa (Ed.), *Developing minds: A resource book for teaching thinking.* Alexandria, VA: Association for Supervision and Curriculum Development.
Costa, A. L., & Liebmann, R. M. (1996). *Supporting the Spirit of Learning: When Process Is Content.* Thousand Oaks, CA: Corwin Press.
Csikszentmihalyi, M. (1990). *Flow: The psychology of optimal experience.* New York: Harper & Row.
della Porta, G. (1957). *Magia naturalis* [Natural magic] (Facsimile ed., D. J. Price, Ed.). New York: Basic Books. (Original work published 1558, Naples, Italy)
Goleman, D. (1995). *Emotional intelligence: Why it can matter more than IQ.* New York: Bantam.
Koestler, A. (1972). *The roots of coincidence.* New York: Vintage.
Mitroff, I. (1983). *The subjective side of science: A philosophical inquiry into the psychology of the Apollo moon scientists.* Seaside, CA: Intersystems Publications.
Shepherd, L. (1993). *Lifting the veil: The feminine face of science.* Boston: Shambhala.
Vaughan, F. E. (1979). *Awakening intuition.* New York: Doubleday-Anchor.
Waldrop, M. M. (1992). *Complexity: The emerging science at the edge of order and chaos.* New York: Touchstone.
Wheatley, M. J. (1992). *Leadership and the new science: Learning about organization from an orderly universe.* San Francisco: Berrett-Koehler.

6

Process as Content

Nancy Skerritt

In order to transform schools successfully, educators need to navigate
the difficult space between letting go of old patterns and grabbing on
to new ones.

Deal, 1990, p. 11

The Tahoma School District in Maple Valley, Washington, like many school
districts around the United States, is in the midst of change. Six years ago, a
collaborative committee of school and community members studied reports
such as *Work Place Basics* (Carnevale, Gainer, & Meltzer, 1990) and the *SCANS
Report* (Secretary's Commission on Achieving Necessary Skills, 1991) so common to the educational reform movement and determined a core of knowledge,
skills, and attitudes believed to be essential for life today and in the future. These
student goals are reflective of a reform language and set of aspirations that echo
through many school systems as educators all strive to restructure learning:
complex thinker, collaborative worker, community contributor, self-directed
learner, effective communicator, and quality producer (Table 6.1).

As our committee task analyzed these goals, we soon discovered that the
curriculum needs to accomplish the goals were far different from the traditional
textbook-driven, content-bound curriculum that had characterized our district
and many other school districts. We acknowledged that to become the type of
educated individuals that we believed were necessary for our information
society, students must acquire a body of thinking skills and behaviors that
formed the basis of the learner goals. These thinking skills and behaviors would
become the foundation for each content area, the primary goal of instruction,
the target of measurement, and the driver for change.

Table 6.1 Outcomes and Indicators

Self-Directed Learners	Community Contributors
Set goals	Provide service
Have persistence	Are harmonious
Are decision makers	Are future oriented
Are reflective and evaluative	Improve welfare of others
Are inquisitive	Enhance the environment
Collaborative Workers	**Quality Producers**
Share	Have high standards
Empathize and respect	Reflect originality
Listen actively	Use a variety of resources
Are flexible	Are aesthetically pleasing
Encourage others	Are criteria-based
Effective Communicators	**Complex Thinkers**
Have clarity of expression	Are creative
Use range of methods: multiple intelligences	Are problem solvers
Are technologically literate	Are risk-takers
Are responsive to diverse audiences	Are analytical
Interpret and evaluate	Are metacognitive

Process as content would mean tremendous shifts: shifts in curriculum design, in resource materials, in instructional strategies, and in assessments. As the curriculum director for the Tahoma School District, I want to share our story of what process as content means to the system in which I work, the successes we are experiencing, and the challenge of our journey.

What are the old patterns that have driven our system and other systems in which content acquisition is viewed as the major goal of education? Let's visit a classroom that depicts a content-driven curriculum, then a transitional classroom that reforms instruction but not content, and finally a classroom in which process becomes the content and traditional content becomes the vehicle for acquiring processes. Imagine the three classrooms as numbers on a continuum from 1 to 10. The first visit takes us to Classroom 1.

As we walk into our first classroom (Figure 6.1), we notice that the physical arrangement of the room is the traditional configuration of desks in neat rows, with students intentionally separated from each other to help maintain control and order. The teacher stands at the front of the classroom, lecturing about the subject at hand and then assigning work from the textbooks for the students to do at their desks. The teacher monitors by walking around the room, checking that the children are on the correct page and filling in the asked-for content knowledge. On the bulletin board is a schedule that divides the day into discrete sections for each subject area—45 minutes for reading, 20 minutes for spelling, followed by 45 minutes for math. Writing, science, health, social studies, and handwriting are all assigned a particular time, and the teacher ardently uses the adopted district texts as tools for covering the curriculum.

At the secondary level, the day itself is divided in a similar fashion as students move from one classroom subject to the next, each taught by a different

Figure 6.1. Classroom 1: Traditional Content-Based Curriculum

teacher and each based on an adopted text. The teacher organizes the year to dutifully pace through each book. After all, the students will not be ready for the next grade if the teacher does not complete each assigned curriculum. The secondary teachers are concerned that the chapter goals be met so that they too can cover the content in the text. If Chapter 8 is not reached by holiday break, then how will the teacher possibly finish the book on schedule?

Tests and other assignments in Classroom 1 are also driven by the content and content skills within each book. Students are asked to record and recall information, to feed back information on the objective exams, and to reflect their knowledge through the daily assignments. Like Mr. Gradgrind in Charles Dickens's book *Hard Times* (1961), the primary interest is in knowing the facts:

> Now what I want is Facts. Teach these boys and girls nothing but Facts. Facts alone are wanted in life. Plant nothing else, and root out everything else. . . .
> In this life, we want nothing but Facts, sir; nothing but Facts! (p. 11)

As we leave this classroom and visit a classroom at the number 5 on our continuum (Figure 6.2), we may think that patterns have radically changed, but

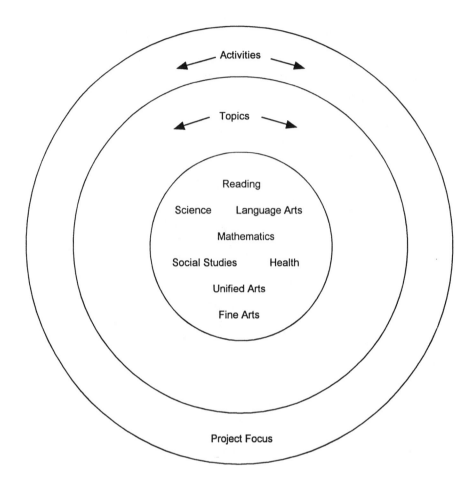

Figure 6.2. Classroom 5: Content-Based Integrated Curriculum

let's take a close look. On entering Classroom 5, we see significant physical changes. The students are working together in small groups, and the teacher is walking around the room assisting with the project work that is occurring. The first-grade class is studying whales. The teacher has been reading stories about whales, and the children have engaged in whale art, whale math, whale music, and writing whale stories. The children's project work fills the class, and we feel enthusiasm and excitement for learning.

The corresponding high school English class has just begun a unit on Chaucer and the Middle Ages. Students are presenting their reports on the art and architecture of the time period, the teacher opened class with Gregorian chant playing, and tomorrow's discussion will focus on the history and philosophy of the Middle Ages. Students are selecting culminating projects from a menu of options as well as writing a more traditional critical analysis of one of the *Cantebury Tales*.

Are these not transformed classrooms? The teacher has integrated the content areas around a topic, is using multiple resources, promotes collaborative learning, and facilitates rather than directs—but process is not content in

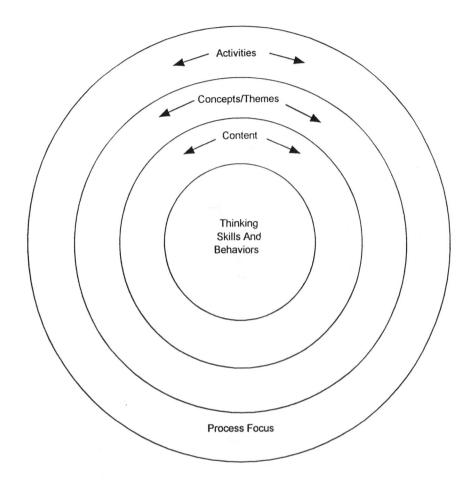

Figure 6.3. Classroom 10: Process-Based Curriculum

Classroom 5. We must visit one more room to observe the transformation from a content-centered curriculum to a processed-centered curriculum.

Classroom 10 on the continuum (Figure 6.3) looks much like Classroom 5 on the surface. The children are engaged in a variety of rich activities using multiple resources, and the teacher has integrated the curriculum around a particular topic. This time, however, the topic is broad—sea life rather than whales—and the teacher has focused the study to enhance three distinct district goals—community contributor, complex thinker, and collaborative worker. The unit outcome is this: Through a study of sea life, the students will discover the connections between people, the sea, and its life to make current and future choices that preserve and protect the environment.

The teacher has identified a core of thinking skills and behaviors as the principal content. The traditional content of sea life becomes a means to develop the cognitive processes of observing, classifying, and determining cause and effect and the thinking behaviors of inquisitiveness, empathy, and precision. The unit begins with the students' knowledge base by asking the question, "What do we know about sea life?" and then proceeds to direct the students through the acquisition of information necessary to answer the questions of "How are we affecting life in the sea?" and "What can we do to preserve and protect the sea life environments?" Collaborative service projects will culminate the unit so that students can practice the skills of becoming community contributors and collaborative workers in intentional ways.

On the day of our visit, the children have just completed a thinking skills lesson on a strategy for observing, using a variety of sea life artifacts—shells, sea creatures, and plants. The teacher has taught the class a song to the tune of "Have You Ever Seen a Laddie Go This Way or That?" to help them remember this strategy:

Now we go observing, observing, observing,
Now we go observing to learn what we can learn.
We look and we listen, we touch, taste, and smell,
Now we go observing to learn what we can.
First we have to focus, to focus, to focus,
First we have to focus to learn what we can.
We look and we listen, we touch, taste, and smell,
Now we go observing to learn what we can.
Then we have to write down, to write down, to write down,
Then we have to write down all that we learn.
We look and we listen, we touch, taste, and smell.
Now we go observing to learn what we can."

The children are recording their observations on a graphic organizer to reinforce the cognitive process, and the teacher mediates the learning by asking clarifying and probing questions.

The class segues into a lesson using the story *The Rainbow Fish* (Pfister, 1992) as a vehicle for introducing the thinking behavior of empathy. Community contributors demonstrate empathy in developing sensitivity toward the perspectives and needs of others. The children will identify a project that contributes to the quality of the sea life environment and will be asked to demonstrate inquisitiveness and precision in their work—thinking behaviors important to quality producers.

In classroom 10 at the high school level, the English teacher has identified a broad outcome for the entire year: "Students will apply thinking skills and behaviors to the study of traditional British literature in order to demonstrate the characteristics of complex thinkers, quality producers, community contributors, self-directed learners, collaborative workers, and effective communicators."

The teacher has organized the semester around the theme of perspectives, and the students have relfected on perspective in the 1990's as it relates to what we value in society today. Then responses are compared, using Venn diagrams, to perspective in the Middle Ages where spiritual belief focused and organized daily life. Students are systematically learning the thinking skill of analysis in order to determine the value systems that are represented by each perspective.

As the class transitions into a study of the *Cantebury Tales*, students review strategies for finding patterns in literature. In cooperative groups, students are assigned sections of the general prologue. Their task is to scan for patterns in language, imagery, syntax, tone, or any other literary convention. As they discover these patterns, they record them and reflect on the metacognitive strategy they used to discover the pattern. Strategies are shared as part of the

Table 6.2 Thinking Skills and Behaviors

Thinking Skills:

Goal setting	Finding evidence
Problem solving	Main idea
Decision making	Summarizing
Observing	Cause and effect
Comparing/Contrasting	Fact and opinion
Sequencing	Bias detection
Classifying	Point of view
Finding patterns	Analysis
Predicting	Evaluation
Inferring	Synthesis

Thinking Behaviors

Metacognition	Precision
Attending	Inquisitiveness
Persistence	Fluency
Empathy	Originality
Deliberativeness	Elaboration
Flexibility	Risking

class's discussion. Students are also asked to individually think about the characteristics of intelligent behavior they each employed that helped them to accomplish the complex thinking tasks in their collaborative groups and to give evidence for the beahaviors they identify.

Classroom 10's teaching and learning agenda is quite different from those of Classrooms 1 and 5. Although Classroom 5 may reflect improved instructional practices, the end goal is still the same as in Classroom 1—students learn content. In Classroom 10, the teacher focuses on the development of thinking and learning skills that enable students to process and create with information as well as to demonstrate the district's learner goals.

To assist our teachers in the district's shift from Classroom 1 and 5 to Classroom 10, we have identified a core of thinking skills and behaviors that provide definition for our system's process curriculum (Table 6.2). These skills and behaviors form the basis of each content area framework. Content goals reflect the focus of acquiring the thinking skills and behaviors through a study of the content area. For example, two of the five science goals read as follows: "Students will apply thinking and reasoning skills to enhance scientific literacy" and "Students will develop thinking behaviors that promote inquiry, problem solving, and the ability to recognize and manage change." The parallel goals in the language arts are "Students will apply thinking and reasoning skills to enhance language development and lifelong learning," "Students will apply thinking and reasoning skills to enhance language development and lifelong learning," and "Students will develop thinking behaviors that promote using the language arts as an integral part of their lives in an independent, self-motivated fashion." The analogous mathematics goals are "Students will apply thinking and reasoning skills to enhance mathematical reasoning and problem solving" and "Students will develop thinking behaviors that promote problem-solving abilities, self-reflection, and communication."

The content areas are integrated as much as possible into broad units of study organized by unifying themes. Sometimes these thematic units focus on a traditional topic such as the study of Africa or the human body; sometimes the units of study are open-ended questions such as "How do systems interact?" The question then is explored through the lenses of the different content areas in a team-taught situation, more typical at the secondary level. These units of study are designed around the thinking skill and the thinking behaviors and ultimately connect the learning to the district's learner goals. The primary content becomes acquiring the thinking skills and behaviors while using a traditional knowledge base in the core subjects as a vehicle. Learning is integrated and applied to life experience. The units of study are not ends in themselves but rather opportunities to progress toward the six learner goals of complex thinker, collaborative worker, community contributor, self-directed learner, effective communicator, and quality producer.

To aid the district's teachers in thinking skills instruction, the committee has task analyzed the 16 information-processing, critical-thinking, and life skills that made up the thinking skills core curriculum and has arranged them in a developmental sequence for the purpose of instructional emphasis. K-2 teachers are responsible for the skills of observing, comparing, classifying, sequencing, finding patterns, predicting, and setting goals. Third- and fourth-grade teachers introduce metacognitive strategies for inferring, finding evidence, finding the main idea, summarizing, determining cause and effect, and problem solving. Fifth- and sixth-grade teachers have responsibility for fact and opinion, point of view, bias detection, analysis, evaluation, decision making, and synthesis.

Strategy charts and graphic organizers as shown in the problem-solving example in Figure 6.4 replace the traditional textbooks as the basic tools for teaching the thinking skills. Teachers design formal lessons to introduce the thinking skills and then transfer the skills to an exploration of content within the integrated units. Multiple resources are used, and teachers brainstorm ways to interpret information through the application of the thinking skills. Some teachers have traded traditional worksheets for graphic organizers that represent the various thinking processes. Students access, interpret, and create with information through an application of the thinking processes that they are learning in their classes.

One fourth-grade teacher explained her next unit in the class newsletter by writing,

> In the Early American History unit, we will be focusing on the thinking skills of inferring and finding evidence. To infer, a person examines some information, selects clues or evidence within the content, and draws conclusions based on those clues. To find evidence, a person finds proof to support a given statement.

The next week's newsletter contained a short article written by one of the students. The article was titled "Inference." The child wrote,

> Mrs. Hard read us a story called *Seven Blind Mice.* It was about inferring. It gave clues about what was at their pond. During the story, each mouse would go and feel a part of something. When the last mouse went he felt the whole thing. We made an inference from the clues. The thing was an elephant.

Problem Solving

A Situation That Needs Resolution

1. **Define the problem**

2. **Invent alternatives**

3. **Critique alternatives** $+$

4. **Execute a plan**

Graphic Organizer:

Problem Solving Matrix

Situation:			
Define the Problem:	Problem:		
Invent Alternatives:	Alternative 1	Alternative 2	Alternative 3
Critique Alternatives: Pros			
Cons			
Execute the Plan:	Proposed Solution and Plan:		
	Reasons:		

Throw the DICE and solve the problem!

Figure 6.4. Thinking Skills Strategies Chart and Graphic Organizer
SOURCE: Tahoma School District, 1993. Used with permission.

The children were recognizing that the content of their instruction was the thinking skill. Inference became a familiar tool for reasoning about new information, and the instructional goal of teaching process was clearly communicated and understood.

The thinking skills curriculum is complemented by the thinking behavior curriculum, a set of attitudes and dispositions that are characteristic of good thinkers. Largely on the basis of Costa's (1991) work, the district has defined 12 thinking behaviors for the core curriculum. These include metacognition, attending, persistence, empathy, deliberativeness, flexibility, precision, inquisitiveness, fluency, originality, elaboration, and risk taking. Like the thinking skills, these behaviors are integrated into the units of study. For example, in a unit on America, students explore their relationship to the American community past or present to set goals and solve problems as contributing citizens. The unit's guiding questions included (a) What is the American community? (b) What are the characteristics of an American citizen? (c) How can we become better American citizens? In response to the second question, the students explored the thinking behaviors of persistence, risk taking, attending, and deliberativeness—qualities important to problem solving and goal setting as community contributors.

To reinforce the thinking behaviors, the district has defined each by its observable characteristics. For example, persistence means "keeps trying; does not give up easily." It looks like "stays on task, continued attempts, finds alternatives, uses multiple strategies, takes time to think." It sounds like "asks for help, self-corrects, makes affirmations such as 'I can do this,' 'I'll try this,' 'Let's try this another way.' " These tools help the teachers to make explicit the characteristics of the behaviors much like the Johnson model of cooperative learning makes explicit the social skills (Johnson, Johnson, & Holubek-Johnson, 1988).

Teachers are connecting the thinking behaviors to literature, are reinforcing the behaviors when they are demonstrated by children in the classroom, and are designing specific instructional activities to practice the behaviors. For example, one teacher asked children to randomly select a child to observe for his or her attending behaviors at an assembly program. The children used the observable characteristics that had been formatted into a checklist (Figure 6.5), obtained their data, and then drew a conclusion regarding the selected child's attending skills. The teacher also asked children to take the role of process observers in class while other children shared projects. The process observer gave feedback on their attending behaviors.

In the high school integrated block, the teachers use the thinking behaviors and skills as a basis for framing questions related to the topic under study. For example, students frequently analyze newspaper articles related to identified issues in the curriculum. For a weekly science column, the teachers have framed the following questions which reflect thinking skills and behaviors of self directed learners:

What was the scientist's purpose in conducting this inquiry?	Goal Setting
What obstacles or technical problems did the researcher overcome?	Persistence
What decisions were made to overcome these problems?	Decision Making
Give evidence of the scientist's reflective and evaluative attitude toward his work.	Finding Evidence and Metacognition
What has the scientist sought to discover?	Inquisitiveness

Students discover real world applications of the thinking skills and behaviors through their relevance to working professionals who are exploring real world issues and challenges.

Name_____   Date_____

Performance Checklist

Attribute: *Attending*		Often	Sometimes	Not Yet
	Observable Indicators			
What it looks like:	Eyes focused on stimulus			
	Body turned to stimulus			
	Appropriate facial response			
	Follows directions			
What it sounds like:	Takes turns in speaking			
	Talks about subject at hand			
	Asks relevant questions			
	Joins in when appropriate			

Notes:

Figure 6.5. Performance Checklist

SOURCE: Tahoma School District. Adapted from a checklist by Costa (Costa & Kallick, 1990). Used with permission.

Process as content demands a different set of assessment tools. The district teachers are becoming skilled in the use of developmental scales such as the Learner Outcome Scale (Figure 6.6), rubrics for assessing the language of thinking (Table 6.3), inventories designed to assess thinking behaviors, and performance checklists that are used to assess progress in mastering the thinking strategies. Portfolios enable students to self-select work representative of their progress toward the six learner goals, demonstrate growth through time, and help teach metacognition. Even at the primary grades, children begin to use

Developmental Level	Complex Thinker	Collaborative Worker	Self-Directed Learner	Community Contributor	Quality Producer	Effective Communicator
		Tahoma School District, Maple Valley, Washington — Student Assessment Profile — Student Outcomes		Name ___ Grade ___ Teacher ___		
V	Goes back to previous work and makes improvements based on new information and personal reflection. Takes risks. Demonstrates metacognition. Plans, monitors, reviews and revises.	Participates and contributes freely. Accepts group criticism and makes improvements. Encourages others to do likewise.	Works alone and is able to self-critique. Expresses a degree of self-satisfaction and can give reason for that self-satisfaction. Is able to determine what could be done to improve the product.	Seeks out opportunities for personal service. Contributes independently to the community as well as in class service activities.	Self critiques projects and uses this information to improve overall quality. Expresses pride in performance and can verbalize characteristics of quality - i.e. precision, creativity, use of resources.	Demonstrates sensitivity to diverse audiences and modifies methods of communication to the needs. Readily incorporates use of technology. Accesses and organizes complex information. Is interpretive and evaluative.
IV	Improves previous work based on new information. Uses both group and personal effort. Solves problems without teacher direction.	Contributes freely to the group. Encourages and helps others in the group to participate.	Works well alone. Is able to self-critique. Recognizes that there is a need for improvement.	Expresses concern for the welfare of others. Initiates ideas for class community service. Takes a leadership role.	Exceeds project expectations. Attends to details in project development.	Uses a range of methods to communicate including verbal, visual, body-kinesthetic, logical, and/or musical. Understands role of technology in accessing and organizing information.
III	Improves work using group-derived information or teacher direction.	Contributes freely to the group.	Works independently. Sets goals.	Takes an active role in classroom/community service activities.	Meets minimum standards for project completion.	Can communicate clearly through several different methods. Accesses and organizes simple information.
II	Can identify that he/she has used a thinking strategy.	Works in a group when assigned a role by the teacher.	Needs group direction or teacher interaction.	Participates in classroom service projects when directed by the teacher.	Completes projects. Meets some standards.	Limited ability to communicate. Lacks clarity and range of methods.
I	Unaware of personal thinking strategies.	Works individually in a group setting.	Non-directed work efforts.	Undeveloped interest in classroom service.	Begins projects without completing them.	Unclear communications.

Figure 6.6. Learner Outcome Scale

SOURCE: Portions adapted from "Breakthroughs Assessment Matrix," p. 23, in *Expanding Breakthroughs*, published by Zaner Bloser, Inc. Copyright © 1992. Used with permission.

Table 6.3 Developing the Language of Thinking

Sample Rubric

5   Qualifies thinking and feelings, gives evidence, uses precise language, asks questions, considers various possibilities or alternatives, makes inferences

3   Expresses thoughts and/or feelings in general terms, makes broad statements, suggests vague reasons, asks general questions

1   Relays information, provides no evidence of individual reflection or interpretation, uses little detail, gives summary only

the language of thinking. One second-grade teacher organizes the children's portfolios around the learner goals. Each week, a different goal is emphasized. Children select work that exhibits the week's goal and write a reflection that connects the selected work to the targeted goal. In one third-grade class, the teacher uses the Learner Outcome Scale as a self-assessment tool for student writing and other project work. She will teach to one area and ask the children to mark what they believe to be their developmental level as it relates to that goal.

Assessment practices are woven into the fabric of instruction. Teachers are continually refining tools, creating new tools, and expanding their techniques.

Process-based education cannot be effectively measured by content-generated tools such as recall examinations. Rather, students must be observed applying thinking skills and demonstrating thinking behaviors. They must ultimately develop the ability to self-assess and to grow from the insights acquired through reflection.

The school district faces the challenge of fostering and supporting broad-based, comprehensive change. Classrooms are at all numbers on the continuum from 1 to 10. The teachers hold diverse beliefs about the needs of today's children and model practices that reflect these beliefs. For some, old patterns are difficult to change despite support structures. A fundamental shift must occur for people in transition from a content-driven curriculum to a process-based curriculum. Teachers must first believe in the importance of thinking skills and intelligent behaviors for all children. They must themselves internalize an understanding of what this means for them and then for their students. The ability to articulate this understanding is critical for change to occur.

The district has designed one approach to defining process as content. The approach is motivated by a genuine commitment to the six learner goals. District values and beliefs about teaching and learning should influence school cultures, but district vision alone cannot transform the culture of the school. Change comes on a person-by-person basis. Educators first must recognize where we are on the continuum of classrooms and then develop a belief in the value of Classroom 10 for all children. Moving along the continuum requires new skills, new tools, and new definitions of curriculum, instruction, and assessment. Movement takes time, motivation, and continued support. For new patterns to replace the old, we must truly believe that process education is essential for acquiring the knowledge, skills, and attitudes needed for an information-based, global society. The children cannot learn that which we choose not to teach. Their needs, more than anything else, should motivate our desire to let go of the old patterns and grab on to the new.

References

Breakthroughs assessment matrix. (1992). In *Expanding breakthroughs*. Columbus, OH: Zaner Bloser.
Carnevale, A. P., Gainer, L. J., & Meltzer, A. S. (1990). *Work place basics*. San Francisco: Jossey-Bass.
Costa, A. L. (1991). *Developing minds: A resource book for teaching thinking* (2nd ed.). Alexandria, VA: Association for Supervision and Curriculum Development.
Costa, A. L., & Kallick, B. (1990). *Assessing student thinking*. Presentation at a Professional Development Institute of the Association for Supervision and Curriculum Development, San Francisco.
Deal, T. (1990, May). Reframing reform. *Educational Leadership, 47*(8), 6-12.
Dickens, C. (1961). *Hard times*. New York: New American Library of World Literature (Signet Classics).
Johnson, D., Johnson, R., & Holubek-Johnson, E. (1988). *Cooperation in the classroom*. Edina, MN: Interaction Books.
Pfister, M. (1992). *The rainbow fish* (English trans.). New York: North-South Books. (Original work published 1992 by Nord-Süd Verlag, Zurich, Switzerland)
Secretary's Commission on Achieving Necessary Skills. (1991). *SCANS report*. Washington, DC: U.S. Department of Labor, Employment and Training Administration.

7

Reading as a Thinking Process

Ruth M. Loring

Teaching reading as a thinking process is distinct from a more traditional way of teaching reading. In a nutshell: Teaching reading in a traditional way makes the act of learning to read, or reading to learn, the goal of the reading instruction. In contrast, teaching reading as a thinking process makes as its goal the types of thinking necessary to learn to read or read to learn (Herber, 1978).

Therefore, whether the central role of reading in school curricula is expressed as reading is the *object* of instruction or reading is the *means* of instruction (Perfetti & Curtis, 1986), the primary agenda should be to direct the attention of students to the thinking employed in the process. Now, this distinction is more than just semantics. Recent advances in the understanding of reading as a cognitive, rather than a behavioral, process clarify some of the differences (Harris & Hodges, 1995).

The information displayed in "Contrasting Views of Reading" (Table 7.1) shows the differences in our understanding of how we learn to read or read to learn. Even the use of this format for displaying the differences in our understanding of reading is itself an illustration of the type of approach toward reading as a thinking process rather than the more traditional format of simply interpreting connected text in a prose format. The graphic organizer in the first column makes explicit what the mind does naturally when we seek to find the way two concepts are different. The type of thinking employed when analyzing the differences in two concepts is a clarifying thinking skill of making comparisons and contrasts.

The aim of reading is to gain meaning from print for the purpose of being able to think with the author about ideas. Reading involves the translation and

Table 7.1 Contrasting Views of Reading

*with regard to...	Behavioral View: Reader...	Cognitive View: Reader...
meaning of connected text	reproduces	constructs
source of activation	receives from others	initiates from within
motivation to learn	depends on external factors	depends on internal factors
processing of print	starts with text	starts with self-knowledge
access to word meanings	stresses stimulus-response bonding	stresses metacognitive mediation
acquisition of reading ability	follows a linear and hierarchial development	follows a holistic and patterned development
method of reading acquisition	develops reading skills	develops problem solving strategies
achievement of comprehension	automaticity in basic skills	connects text to prior knowledge and experience

SOURCE: Adapted by Ruth M. Loring to make explicit the categories of differences from Harris and Hodges, 1995, p. 207 ("A Comparison of Behavioral and Cognitive Views of the Reading Process"). *"With regard to" is a format for clarifying and organizing thinking from Swartz and Parks (1994).

interpretation of graphophonic, syntactic, and semantic information. Therefore, "decoding and comprehending vie for the reader's attention. Readers must learn to process graphophonic information so rapidly that they are free to direct attention to comprehending the text material" (Vacca, Vacca, & Gove, 1987, p. 13). Models of reading that attempt to explain how this decoding and comprehension take place basically fall into three categories: top-down, bottom-up, and interactive.

In a top-down model, reading is activated by the reader's prior knowledge and experience to derive meaning from the print. In contrast, a bottom-up model proposes that reading is activated by graphophonic information such as letters, syllables, and words to derive meaning from print. Both models fail to take into account the role of the reader as the one who constructs meaning based on the interconnection of text and the reader's knowledge. The interactive model, however, does just that.

In the interactive model, reading is viewed as intentional thinking during which meaning is constructed through interactions between text and reader (Durkin, 1993). Kenneth Goodman makes reference to reading as being a thought-driven process in which the reader is "sampling, selecting, predicting, comparing and confirming . . . a sample of useful graphic cues based on what he sees and what he expects to see" (cited in Harris & Hodges, 1995, p. 207).

The degree of difficulty readers experience in constructing meaning from print is determined by the ease with which they are able to make connections between prior knowledge and graphophonic information. The more automatic the process of decoding, the greater the ease of interpreting (Samuels, 1979). The more self-knowledge readers have for accessing and monitoring their prior knowledge, the greater the facility of interpretation. The challenge of making this connection requires a view of reading as a thinking process. Such a perspective focuses instructional theory and practice on the type of thinking used in reading for understanding, the strategies used in the process of reading, the quality of thinking in constructing meaning, and the context in which this instruction takes place.

Types of Thinking in Reading

The thinking used in reading for understanding relies on the same skills and processes as thinking in general. Thinking can be understood as the "processes or products of cognition and a mediation or reflection on ideas or problems" (Harris & Hodges, 1995, p. 257). The very cognition people do in day-to-day living as we "recognize, interpret, judge, reason, and know" (p. 34) is employed when we read. Developing a useful framework for organizing the way we teach is a must if reading instruction is to explicitly identify, engage, and improve the type of thinking we do naturally.

The works of Robert Swartz, Sandra Parks, John Barell, and Arthur Costa that apply to all content areas have influenced my thinking about how to organize instruction in reading as a thinking process. Swartz and Parks (1994) have developed a comprehensive approach to infusing thinking across the curriculum. The map of thinking domain they propose can be applied to teaching reading as thinking as well. Thinking skills categorized as clarification and understanding, creative thinking, and critical thinking are embedded within skillful decision making and problem solving as thinking processes. Barell (1994) suggests that these categories of skills be encased in continuous reflection. So the categories of search for meaning, be adventurous, and be reasonable are understood to function best when there is a continuous attention to the metacognitive aspects of thinking. Finally, Costa's (1991b) conceptualization of thinking for, of, and about thinking has served as a superordinate structure under which the context for instruction, the content for instruction, and the evaluation of instruction in reading as a thinking process can be organized.

As a reader constructs meaning, clusters of thinking skills are activated as the printed message interacts with the reader's scheme to obtain an accurate understanding of the author's message. I propose a model, "Reading as a Thinking Process: A Framework of Cognition Categories" (Table 7.2), in which four clusters of thinking skills are employed in the reading process: connective, clarifying, creative, and critical. These clusters of skills are interdependent, function interactively, and are undergirded by metacognition.

Metacognition

Metacognition is the foundation for all four clusters of cognition. It is not a different set of thinking skills. Instead, it incorporates the same set of thinking skills but is applied to readers' thinking rather than the content being processed. Metacognition is expressed as the inner dialogue readers use to plan, monitor, and

Table 7.2 Reading as a Thinking Process: A Framework of Cognition Categories

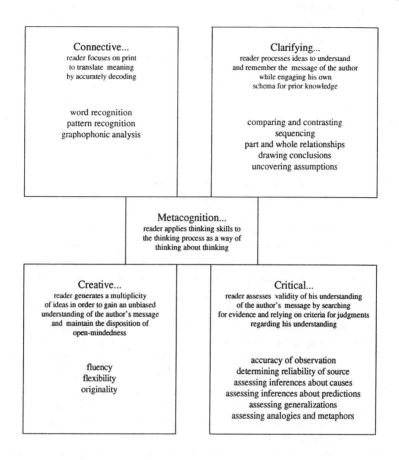

Connective...
reader focuses on print
to translate meaning
by accurately decoding

word recognition
pattern recognition
graphophonic analysis

Clarifying...
reader processes ideas to understand
and remember the message of the author
while engaging his own
schema for prior knowledge

comparing and contrasting
sequencing
part and whole relationships
drawing conclusions
uncovering assumptions

Metacognition...
reader applies thinking skills to
the thinking process as a way of
thinking about thinking

Creative...
reader generates a multiplicity
of ideas in order to gain an unbiased
understanding of the author's message
and maintain the disposition of
open-mindedness

fluency
flexibility
originality

Critical...
reader assesses validity of his understanding
of the author's message by searching
for evidence and relying on criteria for judgments
regarding his understanding

accuracy of observation
determining reliability of source
assessing inferences about causes
assessing inferences about predictions
assessing generalizations
assessing analogies and metaphors

SOURCE: Developed by Ruth M. Loring from *Frameworks for thinking about how thinking skills can be organized* by Swartz and Parks (1994), Barell (1994), and Costa (1991a).

evaluate their own thinking. It is tridirectional—introspective, retrospective, and "futurespective" (Flavell, 1976)—as readers take charge of their thinking.

Metacognition is an awareness and knowledge of mental processes such that readers can monitor, regulate, and direct them to a desired end: self-mediation (Harris & Hodges, 1995). In reading, metacognitive awareness is knowing when what one is reading makes sense by monitoring and controlling. For the teacher who is teaching reading as a thinking process, a focus on metacognition is essential. By looking back on thinking used to obtain understanding, the readers are taught to verbalize heuristic strategies that are naturally embedded in their own thinking. Making this type of thinking visible both to the readers themselves and to fellow students increases the repertoire of problem posing and encourages more careful thought about reading strategies.

Self-awareness and self-control over thoughts in problem solving (Flavell, 1976) in reading is referred to as *metacomprehension*. When readers adjust their thinking for more effective understanding, metacomprehension has occurred. The need for metacomprehension is aroused when expectations about the text are not confirmed or when unfamiliar concepts occur too frequently to be ignored (Robeck & Wallace, 1990). For this purpose, metacognition can be thought of as superordinate thinking (Swartz & Perkins, 1990) that functions at increasingly complex levels. A *tacit* use of metacognition means that readers employ a particular thinking skill without realizing it. At the *aware* level, readers are at least conscious that they are using the particular thinking skill as they are doing so. When readers organize their thinking in a conscious manner, the level of metacognition is considered *strategic.* Finally, if readers retrospectively consider the value of their thinking or efficiency of the thinking process, it can be said that their metacognition is *reflective.*

These increasingly involved, complex, and analytical stages of metacognition are continuous and reciprocal in their use. Reading taught as a thinking process means that metacognition is taught explicitly, recognized when it occurs, and modeled by the teacher as well as the students. For example, a social studies high school student who is asked to read what appears to be a short selection about the World War II treaty becomes confused about not understanding what he or she has read. The student is mildly mindful of the tendency to go back and reread it but is not fully conscious of doing so—a tacit use of metacognition.

An awareness level of metacognition, however, occurs if the student stops, puzzles over lack of comprehension, and thinks, "This is not making sense." Making a plan to reread, to create a cognitive map of what he or she does not understand, to ask some questions for clarification, and so forth, represent metacognition that is considered strategic. Finally, if the student's thoughts about the thinking processes used leads to a judgment about the effectiveness of the strategies, the thoroughness of processing, or the quality of understanding after use of the strategies, the student's metacognition has moved to a deeper level of reflection.

Metacognition is modeled when students and teachers take the time to verbalize their own thinking about their thinking at these levels. By allowing time for comments about metacognition to be recognized, the culture of the classroom begins to be transformed from one of merely teaching reading or reading to learn content to one that is focusing on reading as a thinking process.

Metacognition can be taught explicitly by the teacher in a direct manner. For example, scenarios can be devised by the teacher or collected from other classrooms in which metacognition at various levels is evident. Students can learn to identify the levels and make recommendations to move to deeper levels of metacognition. Practicing metacognition can be implemented in cooperative learning groups. Questions that prompt metacognition can be employed by students and teachers. Some questions that have been found useful for prompting metacognition have come out of the work of Perkins (1989) and Swartz and Parks (1994).

Connective Thinking

The connective cluster of thinking skills refers to the cognition that results in seeing the relationships between letters and sounds and between printed and spoken words. Making these connections is the primary task of those students just learning to recognize words and decode phonetically—Stage I according to Chall's *Stages of Reading Development* (1983). Even mature readers, however, function within this cluster of cognition when confronted with an unknown word, especially when the context cues are minimal.

Clarifying Thinking

Skills of clarifying are activated as readers seek an understanding of the author's message while engaging schemas. Skills frequently taught in reading classes include the ones listed under this category of cognition: comparison and contrast, sequencing, part-whole relationships, drawing conclusions, and uncovering assumptions. A commonly used approach in skill instruction involves identifying the skill, offering an example of its use in a text passage, and then providing similar passages for practice of the skill.

In contrast, teaching reading as a thinking process approaches the use of this skill as it reflects the thinking process. For example, using a graphic organizer, such as the one shown in Table 7.1, to "download" information in an organized manner is more reflective of what the mind actually does to sort out how ideas are different. By making the thinking explicit, the path is open for clearly designating the category of difference. The explicitness makes visible to all what the categories are and how they are derived. In this way, students learn how to think through comparisons and contrasts, to notice patterns of significance, and to formulate conclusions that are the result of their own thinking. A more traditional approach to reading tends to merely focus on "reading signals" to recognize when the author is making comparisons or describing a part-whole relationship. Teaching reading as a thinking process, however, encourages students to learn to unpack their own thinking by being guided to think clearly through the process and then take time to pay attention to their own thinking.

Creative Thinking

Creative thinking is that category whereby readers generate a multiplicity of ideas about messages being obtained from print. Mature readers, like good thinkers, cultivate the disposition of open-mindedness. Creative thinking can help foster that disposition. For instance, being able and willing to recognize different points of view is a characteristic of mature readers (Chall, 1983). Teachers can devise lessons that allow students to experience the benefits of questioning an initial response to an author's message or of participating in class conversations in which various perspectives are presented. In addition, generating multiple options when thinking about possible causes for an event encourages more skillful thinking in the critical thinking cluster described in Table 7.2. Creatively approaching a decision making or problem-solving challenge in a reading lesson engages skills of clarifying and of critical thinking as well as of creative thinking. Engaging students in meaningful reading assignments such as these is quite different from the "one right answer" approach to reading instruction.

Critical Thinking

Finally, critical thinking occurs as readers seek to substantiate their under-standing of the author's message by searching for evidence as support. Readers can also apply the same skills of evaluation to their own thinking in the constructive process. A term commonly used in reading for this type of thinking is *critical reading*. It involves "reading in which a questioning attitude, logical analysis, and inference are used to judge the worth of the text according to an established standard" (Harris & Hodges, 1995, p. 49). Teaching reading as thinking includes direct instruction in the development of those critical thinking skills of accuracy of observation, determining the reliability of source, evaluat-ing inferences with regard to causes and predictions, and assessing the precision of generalizations. A review of the research in reading comprehension led Fielding and Pearson (1994) to conclude that teacher-directed comprehension strategy instruction is one of four key components in effectively teaching students how to understand what they are reading. Along with this direct instruction, teachers must make ample time for reading, provide opportunities for peer and collaborative learning, and allow time to talk about what has been read. The teacher who teaches reading as thinking implements all these compo-nents with the goal of helping students become proficient readers who con-sciously employ metacognition and thinking skills in all four categories of cognition (see Table 7.2).

Reading Process Strategies

The strategies used in the process of reading are to help students make the connection between what they are reading and how they are thinking about it. Effective strategies will assist students in coping with three major pitfalls in reading that tend to inhibit a deep understanding of an author's message: complexity of the text, confusion about the task or text, and carelessness in the process.

Complexity is a continuing issue in constructing meaning from print because the density of ideas varies between types of texts. Teachers of reading have long recognized the need for the power to find and understand various thought relationships that exist (Niles, 1964) in different types of texts, for example, expository versus narrative. Vacca and Vacca (1986) describe numerous strate-gies that address text organization. Teachers can make use of these strategies while referring to the type of thinking used in clarifying text structure. For example, at times a text selection is difficult to understand because of an assumption that enough relevant information to explain the concept is pro-vided. Sometimes this assumption is not well-founded. Uncovering underlying assumptions is the type of thinking readers must do to identify inconsiderate text (Armbuster & Anderson, 1981) and to clarify its meaning. By making this thinking explicit through direct instruction, reading is taught as a thinking process.

It is possible that readers simply become *confused* while constructing mean-ing from print. Ruth Garner in *Metacognition and Reading Comprehension* (1987) describes effective strategies to reinspect and summarize text. She proposes that teachers can model and directly teach these learning strategies. Teachers can also encourage students to listen to themselves, to think aloud about their thought processes (Hayes & Flower, 1980), and to get in touch with what they know and what they don't know using K-W-L strategy (Ogle, 1986).[1] Furthermore, when deciding whether information is to be believed, rather than simply becoming confused, readers can apply critical thinking by investigating the reliability of the source to help sort out the information that may be confusing.

Carelessness in constructing meaning from print happens to the best of readers. A lack of attention to details, a loss of concentration, or a low level of interest can result in an incorrect or a shallow understanding of the author's message. Checking to make sure that a word is decoded correctly accesses the connective thinking that any close attention to details requires, such as matching parts in putting a machine together or following directions for making a dress. The more teachers can help bridge students' attention to thinking into day-to-day events, the greater the likelihood that carelessness will decrease. Also, carelessness can be addressed through self-monitoring. This metacognitive strategy makes use of the same categories of cognition that are applied in thinking about any concept. The difference is that the object of thinking is thinking itself (Swartz, 1989). For example, if a sentence or paragraph is not making sense, readers can be taught to think about the way they were processing the information. Asking questions such as "Do I need to reread this section?" "When I guessed at that unknown word, did I make a mistake?" "What plan can I follow to get a better understanding?" These questions reflect thinking that is connective, clarifying, and creative in the categories of cognition around which instruction can be organized.

Strategies that are embedded within the content being taught are retained by students at higher levels than those strategies taught in isolation (Fielding & Pearson, 1994; Garner, 1987; Jones, 1991). When teachers also use the language of thinking to draw attention to the type of thinking being used, students are helped to become aware of their own language and thought (Costa & Marzano, 1991), resulting in an even greater impact on learning. Therefore, in addition to recognizing the need to implement strategies to counteract complexity, confusion, and carelessness, the structure and content of instruction are important to consider as well. Strategies related to structure and content are organized around six areas of concern: (a) approach, (b) design, (c) language, (d) representation, (e) observation, and (f) communication.

Constructivist Approach

The constructivist approach to teaching reading as a thinking process is based on the idea that "an individual's prior experiences, mental structures, and beliefs bear on how experiences are interpreted. Constructivism focuses on the process of how knowledge is built rather than on its product or object" (Harris & Hodges, 1995, p. 43). Adopting an interactive model of reading is consistent with this approach to teaching and learning (Brooks & Brooks, 1993). PreP (Langer, 1981) is an example of a strategy that is rooted in a constructivist approach to teaching and learning and to an interactive model of reading. This prereading plan engages students in the discovery of what they already know or think they know about a topic before reading. The teacher begins by asking students what comes to mind when they think of a particular topic. Students brainstorm using creative thinking to generate many and varied responses to the idea in question. The teacher records these initial associations on the board around the concept in question. Next, the teacher asks for elaboration on the initial associations. At this stage, the connections among the ideas are made explicit by students exposing their thoughts about what and how they were thinking when their initial response came to mind. The teacher can also make those connections visible by drawing arrows between the ideas and adding students' comments on the group cognitive map. Finally, the teacher takes the students to the stage of reformulation of ideas by using the students' ideas already submitted and discussed. The constructivist view of teaching and learning, as well as the exposure of the content and process of students' thoughts, is evident in this strategy.

In a recent review of research on comprehension instruction, Fielding and Pearson (1994) concluded that *negotiating meaning socially* is among the most significant factors in successful comprehension development. Teachers who teach reading as thinking need to be sure that the constructivist mind-set is supported by organization that is compatible with optimal opportunity for peer interactions, such as cooperative learning (Johnson & Johnson, 1987), paired problem solving and think-pair-share (Whimbey & Lochhead, 1984), and opportunities for conversations as suggested by Harste, Short, and Burke (1988). The classroom should approximate the world outside the classroom where students can talk to each other in meaningful ways about meaningful ideas.

Design

The design of lessons that reflect the teaching of reading as thinking can be those that are highly structured three-level reading guides, which address levels of comprehension—literal, interpretation, or applied—(Vacca and Vacca, 1986), or those presented in a teacher-directed explicit instruction approach (Pearson & Dole, 1987), such as a directed reading thinking activity (Stauffer, 1969) or an anticipation guide (Vacca & Vacca, 1986). One of the most effective structured approaches to teaching not only reading but any subject area is the *infusion* method designed by Swartz and Parks (1994). Thinking skills and processes are taught directly as they are embedded within the content. The structure of lessons includes four components: introduction, thinking critically, thinking about thinking, and applying thinking. No matter what structured approach a teacher uses, however, it is essential that the type of thinking used during the reading process is understood and taught directly.

Language

By using the language of thinking, the critical transformation from traditional reading instruction to teaching reading as a thinking process can be achieved. For example, the powerful structure of before-during-after reading (Fountain & Fusco, 1991; Jones, 1991; McGee, 1995; Vacca & Vacca, 1986) offers a fertile opportunity for teachers to use the language of thinking to focus

Table 7.3 Strategy to Support Metacognitive Processing

QUESTION	PROCESS	➡	Embedded Cognition (*Categories of cognition)
		Before - reading/writing/speaking/listening	
1. What am I doing?	Create a focus (access short-term memory).	➡	"Ideas I already understand within this topic are..." (*Creative-fluency*) "The idea I need to identify as the point of this reading is ..."" (*Clarify - drawing a conclusion*) "The last time I did an assignment like this..." (*Clarify - compare*)
2. Why am I doing this?	Establish a purpose.	➡	"Some things I know that the teacher expects are..." (*Critical - Observe*) "What I know already fits with what is expected in this way..." (*Clarify - compare/contrast)*) "Some things I can do to help set a purpose are..." (*Creative - originality*)
3. Why is it important?	Create reason(s) for doing it.	➡	"Therefore, as I read this, I plan to focus on ____ because..." (*Clarify - drawing a conclusion*) "Other options I could consider for determining the focus could be..." (*Creative - flexibility*)
		During - reading/writing/speaking/listening	
4. How/Where does it fit in with what I already know?	Recognize context/ interrelationships/ analogous situations (long-term memory).	➡	"This is like what I already know in some ways but different in other ways..." (Clarify - compare/contrast) "The main ideas and supporting ideas are related in that..." (*Clarify - part/whole relationships*)
5. What questions do I have?	Discover a possible structure or method of approaching the topic.	➡	"Checking his position on that, I think..." (Clarify - assumptions) "Evidence I have to believe this is..." (*Critical-reliability of source*) "This word is unfamiliar to me, but I can say it..." (*Connective-graphophonic analysis*)
6. What plan would help me to understand or learn about this?	Design a possible structure or method of approaching the topic.	➡	"I can use ___ (cognitive map, graphic organizer, think aloud, etc.) to learn this information because I see how it organizes this information and I remember when I used it before." (Critical - generalization)
		After - reading/writing/speaking/listening	
7. How can I use this information in other areas of my life?	Consider application to other situations (connect long-term Memory).	➡	"I remember how this connected to my life before, so, I think it can be used in the future in the following way..." (*Critical-making predictions*) "The next time I have a problem like this I'll know how to..." (*Critical - causal explanation*)
8. How effective have I been in this process?	Evaluate progress.	➡	"On a scale of one to ten I would rate my use of strategies to learn this information ___ since I..." (*Critical - making inferences about causes*) "Analogies I can relate to my learning are..." (*Critical - analogical reason*)
9. What more do I need?	Monitor need for further action.	➡	"When I think about the way my thinking was activated and maintained in this assignment I realize I was thinking in the following ways..." (*Metacognitive levels within various categories of cognition*).

SOURCE: Developed by Ruth M. Loring, from Fountain & Fusco (1991).
* Refer to Table 7.2.

students' attention on the type of thinking they are using. The questions shown in Table 7.3 are typical of the type that can promote metacognition. Fountain and Fusco (1991) suggest that these questions be used before, during, and after reading. They also identify the processes implied in each question. These processes are covering the implied cognition. In the third column of Table 7.3, I suggest some of these cognitive categories and comments that could represent the embedded cognition that results in the behavior listed as process.

By being explicit about the language while using the before-during-after strategy, students become increasingly accustomed to the language of thinking as a common currency of exchange in the community of learners. Students who achieve greater control over their own learning process—self-efficacy—(Pintrich, 1995), tend to experience a greater motivation to read. Attention to affective factors in learning to read and reading to learn, as well as the thinking processes that make reading possible, must be addressed (Cramer & Castle, 1994).

All modalities of language, that is, reading, writing, speaking, and listening, should be incorporated into instructional strategies. Because only the results of thinking can be directly observed, students should be encouraged to speak and write every day. As students take the time to put themselves into words through writing or speaking, their thoughts are exposed. Opportunities for this exposure should occur in every class daily. To accomplish the goal of having each student speak does not necessarily mean that the entire class will hear from every student. Instead, small groups or partners in think-pair-share can provide the occasion for all students to speak or write. These encoding processes facilitate the formulation and clarification of thought. Teachers can also use check-up techniques to monitor students' understanding and clarity of their own communication. Effective techniques include one-minute papers, conferences, questionnaires, and sentence starters, such as "I am wondering about . . ." "One thing that really confuses me is . . ." and "The last time we did this activity, I thought it was . . . " Instructional decisions that keep the lines of communication open about how information is being received and incorporated makes visible the processing that mature readers do automatically. Peer interaction that allows students to teach and to learn from each other is at the heart of a constructivist approach.

Reciprocal teaching (Palinscar & Brown, 1984) is an excellent example of an organized peer interaction. Students learn to clarify, summarize, predict, and evaluate one another's understanding of a particular topic. This strategy puts an emphasis on using specific terminology to talk about what and how well fellow students are understanding topics. The concept of *scaffolding* is included as a temporary means of support for students as they move toward independence. Other ways in which teachers can focus on the language of thinking are to ask students to keep journals, take "notes to self," and devise matrices that keep track of questions missed on tests with plans to approach study differently as a result of really understanding how errors were made. The more students are involved in their own language generation about the type of thinking they are doing, the better they will become at both language and thinking.

Representation

The representation of text through mapping, webbing, graphic organizers, cognitive maps, pictures, and so forth helps students to see thinking involved in reading-connected text. Clarke (1990) offers a thorough explanation of the rationale behind communicating ideas through means other than connected text. The value of any type of representation of ideas in a nonconnected text format is twofold: (1) The creator, either student or teacher, is able to gain a deeper understanding of the topic being depicted, and (2) the recipient is provided with a window into the understanding of another person, giving insight into what that person is thinking. Because thinking cannot be directly observed, it is important to find varied ways both to share thoughts and to discover the thoughts of others.

Graphic organizers used in the infusion approach (Swartz & Parks, 1994) effectively organize information for processing ideas, guiding thought through specific processes, and serving as a place to "download" ideas during reading. Cognitive maps are self-generated renditions of what the creator of the map understands about a particular topic. Margulies (1991) offers creative suggestions for representing ideas to be used in the cognitive mapping process. Other excellent resources for the use of graphic organizers include *Organizing Thinking* (Parks & Black, 1992) and Karen Bromley's (1995) chapter, "Enriching Response to Literature With Webbing," in *Book Talk and Beyond* (Roser & Martinez, 1995).

Observation

One of the most important resources for teaching and planning instruction is the observation made regarding the reading behaviors of the students. Excellent observation forms seem to be readily available. Vacca and Vacca (1986) offer several in their text *Content Area Reading*. Reading journals and teacher magazines are also good sources. A questionnaire (Table 7.4) for students to use to reflect on their intelligent thinking behaviors (Costa, 1991a) can be used as a pre- and post-self-assessment.

Relevant behaviors from the "Recognizing My Intelligent Reading/Thinking Behaviors and Attitudes" self-reflection questionnaire shown in Table 7.4 can be used as a guide for observing students' progress in the development of these behaviors. For example, the third question relates to the ability to listen. Students' knowledge of how to be a good listener is one of the indicators of a classroom in which good thinking is occurring (Lipman, 1991). Observable indicators of good listening are that students display eye contact, nod at appropriate times, give responses that connect with what has been said, and so on. Teachers can take notes or develop charts to keep a record of students' progress. Observation notes used to determine patterns of intelligent behavior and attitudes provide valuable information to help create a classroom in which thinking is taught and being thoughtful (Barell, 1994) is valued.

Communication

The way students and teachers communicate not only sets the tone for a caring culture in which everyone is respected but also makes the difference in whether reading is taught as a thinking process. Communication about reading should be more conversational than the question-answer scenario so typical of classroom instruction (Alvermann, Dillon, & O'Brien, 1987). Simply asking fewer questions makes a great difference in the flow of conversation in the classroom. Teachers should use more statements than questions and give attention to the syntax of communication to avoid speaking in a questioning format.

Table 7.4 Recognizing My Intelligent Reading/Thinking Behaviors and Attitudes

---

Rank yourself on the following statements. Use the scale of 1 through 5 beside each item: 1 = *least true of me* and 5 = *most true of me*.

1 2 3 4 5   1. I am able to stick with something even when it is difficult to read or to find the information to reach answers to the questions.

1 2 3 4 5   2. I take the time needed to come to a conclusion in answering a question. I usually think about what I know as it fits with what I am reading.

1 2 3 4 5   3. I listen to others during discussions about what we read. I try to understand how my thoughts might relate to their comments.

1 2 3 4 5   4. I am flexible in the way I think about things. I can think of many possible solutions to problems I may read about instead of just one or two.

1 2 3 4 5   5. I am aware of my own thinking when I read and make adjustments in the way I read on the basis of how well I am understanding.

1 2 3 4 5   6. I am careful to check to see if I am correct when I come to new or especially difficult information I am reading because I want to be precise.

1 2 3 4 5   7. I ask questions of myself as I am reading. I also ask questions of others because I really want to understand the author's meaning.

1 2 3 4 5   8. I am likely to use what I already know when I try to understand something I read, and I try to use what I learn in new situations.

1 2 3 4 5   9. I use language that reflects my thinking as I read (comparing and contrasting, analyzing consequences, drawing conclusions, and making predictions).

1 2 3 4 5   10. I am alert to using all my senses (taste, touch, smell, sight, and hearing) as I construct meaning from what I read.

1 2 3 4 5   11. I recognize the characteristics of ingenuity, originality, and insight in me. My creativity helps me imagine as I read.

1 2 3 4 5   12. I think I am a good reader and a good thinker who is inquisitive and curious.

Developed by Ruth M. Loring, from Costa (1991a).

When questions are asked, open-ended questions, rather than closed questions that can be answered with one word or phrase, help to diminish the atmosphere of "one right answer." In a discussion, no one should have "the" answer, not even the teacher. So the communication pattern should reflect the tentative nature of a search for understanding rather than a simple parroting of answers for the sake of getting on to the next point.

Teachers can encourage the focus of attention toward the students by requesting more information be given "to *us*" rather than "to *me*." Allowing for waiting time before expecting a comment or response to a question is an often heard and difficult to hear admonition. Yet the result is usually a longer and more articulate response. There should also be enough time to formulate responses as a group. Teachers should use questions or comments to prompt responses from as many students as possible. Allowing time before and after responses often invites others to contribute without having to repeat or amend the question or statement (Loring, 1986).

The idea is to have a conversation about the topic being discussed (Eeds & Wells, 1989). A high level of integrity regarding communication patterns gives an authenticity to instruction that encourages genuine involvement in the discussion process. Students and teachers are more motivated to intellectually engage when the discussion is authentic rather than contrived. For example, in literature circles, there are two types of appropriate questions. One type is real questions about issues or events for which teachers do not have answers and truly want to know what students think. Another type of question asks students to expand on a particular opinion or interpretation. For instance, teachers might say, "That's interesting. Say more about what you were thinking when you said . . . ." Short and Kauffman (1995) suggest that "if we can encourage students to share more of their thinking instead of making telegraphic pronouncements, they will have a stronger base for group dialogue" (p. 146).

Listening to each other with an expectation to learn and with an attitude of appreciation for one another's contribution creates an atmosphere of trust and honesty.

> Insightful teachers invite all children to join in the conversations by creating a community of learners—a community in which members find meaningful ways to use language to learn about themselves and the world of literature. Their book discussions resemble natural conversations, with ebb and flow of shifting topics punctuated by students' thoughts and questions. (Wells, 1995, p. 132)

Quality of Thinking

The quality of thinking in constructing meaning ultimately can be known only by the readers themselves. Thinking is in essence a "construct" that is "a theoretical concept based on observable phenomena that aid researchers in analyzing and understanding some aspect of study" (Harris & Hodges, 1995, p. 43). Therefore, only the results of thinking can be actually observed. As teachers seek to assess the quality of students' thinking, whether it is about understanding an author's meaning in a literature piece, following directions to complete a project, or making decisions about how to go about solving a problem, teachers need objective ways to assess the quality of students' thinking. In addition, students need a means of assessing the quality of their own thinking.

The issue is how to objectively, thoroughly, and with integrity expose students' thinking for the purpose of assessing the quality of the thinking process as well as the products of thinking. In reading, traditional reading tests can reveal some products of thinking through questioning, usually at various levels of comprehension. Asking students to apply what they learned from the reading by creating a display of knowledge, developing an outcome of the information given, and devising a scenario of events on the basis of an accurate understanding of the text, however, offers more authentic ways of assessing reading and thinking than the traditional reading tests.

In addition to these products that can be collected and shared via portfolios (Stowell & Tierney, 1995), the thinking process itself should also be assessed. For example, scenarios can be devised by the teacher or collected from other classrooms in which metacognition at various levels is evident. Students can learn to identify the levels and make recommendations to move to deeper levels of metacognition. Some questions that have been found useful for prompting metacognition have come from the work of Perkins (1989) and Swartz and Parks (1994). By allowing time for comments about metacognition to be recognized, the culture of the classroom begins to be transformed from one of merely teaching reading or reading to learn content to one that focuses on reading as a thinking process.

Assessment becomes the tool in the middle: before instruction to shape the content, process, and methodology to be used, then after instruction to assess the extent to which content and process were learned and the methodology was effective. Assessment then takes on a vital role in making decisions about the next steps in instruction.

Portfolio assessment provides the richest opportunity to reflect, foster, and evaluate this cycle in teaching reading as thinking. Stowell and Tierney (1995) examined the "evidence on the effectiveness of portfolios . . . against tenets of constructivist view of teaching and learning" (p. 80). One of their conclusions was this:

> When teachers implemented portfolio assessment practices, the ease of the portfolio accommodation into the classroom was directly related to the level of the teachers' involvement with the whole language philosophy and adherence to the principles of authentic assessment, and to their roles on the school staff. (p. 82)

Context for Instruction

The context in which instruction takes place affects the type of thinking used to understand, the strategies used, and the quality of thinking. Giving attention to the context involves two key issues that influence the type of culture that encourages and supports teaching reading as a thinking process: environmental features and attitudes about self and others.

Environmental features influence the culture in which instruction takes place. Some examples include what can be done with furniture and walls. Students should be able to see each other during class so that conversations can be face-to-face, rather than students having to talk to back of heads. Arranging desks in groups facilitates cooperative learning activities and other interaction pairing strategies. Making the room a place for public display of students' thinking keeps the process visible for all to see. Students can use bulletin boards to display their thinking and their thinking in process. Cognitive maps are excellent for such a purpose. These maps can be put on large butcher paper to display group thinking throughout the process. Different colors of pen can code the progress in thought. Corrections, adjustments, new insights, and so on can be added not just by the teacher but by any student or group of students. This means of making thinking visible makes the connection between language and reading apparent to all.

Attitude has a great deal to do with creating an environment in which it is not only okay but also expected to take risks. This is probably the most important attitude to hold and foster. So much of reading includes making approximations in the construction of meaning. It is essential that teachers model and encourage the taking of risks to see if a word fits or an idea can be supported. As teachers, maintaining the positions of learners will foster an empathic perspective toward students. Respecting the diversity of ideas, abilities, attitudes, and interests will be apparent in the teachers' attitudes toward students.

Finally, teachers should continuously practice self-reflection, asking questions of themselves such as "Why am I doing this?" "What other ways can this be done?" "What have I learned from my students or another colleague today?" "Now that I have done this activity once, how can it be modified?" The checklist shown in Table 7.5 gives a point of reference for teachers to self-monitor their own behaviors and attitudes in the day-to-day experience of teaching.

Making decisions about reading instruction is like reading in that both are problem-solving situations. The core of teaching reading as thinking can be summarized around the following ideas:

- Clarify reading by taking it beyond decoding and skill building to a recognition that it is a thinking process.
- Organize reading instruction around a framework of cognition in which metacognition undergirds connective, clarifying, creative, and critical thinking.
- Reflect on thinking before, during, and after reading, using strategies based on the exposure of thought through metacognition.
- Evaluate reading as a construction of meaning from print using authentic tools of assessment.

In summary, reading as a thinking process is premised on a view that the reader constructs meaning that is initiated from within and is motivated by internal factors. The processing of print starts with self-knowledge. Access to word meaning is achieved through metacognitive mediation. Learning to read follows a holistic and patterned development through use of problem-solving strategies that connect text to prior knowledge and experience. In light of these insights, I propose that reading is best taught as a thinking process.

Note

1. The K-W-L strategy (Ogle, 1986) refers to: K = "What do I know?"; W = "What do I want to learn?"; L = "What have I learned?"

Table 7.5 Teaching Reading As Thinking: A Checklist for Self-Reflection

---

Using a scale of 1 to 5, rate teaching/learning in your classroom by 5 = *very often*,
4 = *often*, 3 = *sometimes*, 2 = *seldom*, 1 = *hardly ever*.

1. I expect students to rely on what the text states during text-dependent discussions.	5 4 3 2 1
2. I choose to cover the content even though only a few students are participating in the discussion.	5 4 3 2 1
3. I encourage students to find alternatives to problems and/or decisions to be made.	5 4 3 2 1
4. Students in my class usually include their reasoning and support with their answers.	5 4 3 2 1
5. Students generate their own questions from the subject matter being taught in my class.	5 4 3 2 2
6. Questions I pose in class usually need to be answered with more than one or two words or phrases.	5 4 3 2 1
7. Students spontaneously comment on and/or critique one another's thinking during class discussions.	5 4 3 2 1
8. Students relate topics of lessons to experiences in other subjects and in their personal lives.	5 4 3 2 1
9. Students work in cooperative learning groups to solve subject matter questions and/or discuss ideas.	
10. Discussions are characterized as students *and* teacher seeking answers rather than one person having "the answer."	5 4 3 2 1
11. Students listen to one another as evidenced by eye contact and comments that build on one another's ideas.	5 4 3 2 1
12. I devise lessons that focus on recognizing other points of view regarding the topic being studied.	5 4 3 2 1
13. Students seem to make connections between the subject matter taught in my class and what they learn in other classes.	5 4 3 2 1
14. I provide structured overviews of difficult subject matter to provide a frame of reference for my students.	5 4 3 2 1
15. I value students' ideas that laterally expand on ideas presented by myself or other students.	5 4 3 2 1
16. My instructional practice reflects a collaboration with other teachers in the department and/or school.	5 4 3 2 1
17. I monitor the type and quantity of questions I ask during reading instruction and discussions.	5 4 3 2 1
18. I use graphic organizers to depict the relationships among and between ideas.	5 4 3 2 1
19. I use the language of thinking as often as possible when teaching reading strategies.	5 4 3 2 1
20. Metacognition is a major focus of instruction in my classes.	5 4 3 2 1

SOURCE: Developed by Ruth M. Loring, from Barell (1991).

References

Alvermann, D. E., Dillon, D. R., & O'Brien, D. G. (1987). *Using discussion to promote reading comprehension.* Newark, DE: International Reading Association.

Armbuster, B. B., & Anderson, T. H. (1981). *Content area textbooks* (Reading Education Rep. No. 23). Urbana: University of Illinois Center for the Study of Reading.

Barell, J. (1991). Self-reflection on your teaching: A checklist. In A. L. Costa (Ed.), *Developing minds: A resource book for teaching thinking* (Vol. 1). Alexandria, VA: Association for Supervision and Curriculum Development.

Barell, J. (1994). *Teaching for thoughtfulness* (2nd ed.). New York: Longman.

Bromley, K. (1995). Enriching response to literature with webbing. In N. L. Roser & M. G. Martinez (Eds.), *Book talk and beyond: Children and teachers respond to literature.* Newark, DE: International Reading Association.

Brooks, J. G., & Brooks, M. G. (1993). *In search of understanding: The case for constructivist classrooms.* Alexandria, VA: Association for Supervision and Curriculum Development.

Chall, J. (1983). *Stages of reading development.* New York: McGraw-Hill.

Clarke, J. H. (1990). *Patterns of thinking: Integrating learning skills in content teaching.* Boston: Allyn & Bacon.

Costa, A. L. (1991a). The search for intelligent life. In A. L. Costa (Ed.), *Developing minds: A resource book for teaching thinking* (Vol. 1). Alexandria, VA: Association for Supervision and Curriculum Development.

Costa, A. L. (1991b). Teaching for, of and about thinking. In A. L. Costa (Ed.), *Developing minds: A resource book for teaching thinking* (Vol. 1). Alexandria, VA: Association for Supervision and Curriculum Development.

Costa, A. L., & Marzano, R. (1991). Teaching the language of thinking. In A. L. Costa (Ed.), *Developing minds: A resource book for teaching thinking* (Vol. 1). Alexandria, VA: Association for Supervision and Curriculum Development.

Cramer, E. H., & Castle, M. (Eds.). (1994). *Fostering the love of reading: The affective domain in reading education.* Newark, DE: International Reading Association.

Durkin, D. (1993). *Teaching them to read* (6th ed.). Boston: Allyn & Bacon.

Eeds, M., & Wells, D. (1989). Grand conversations: An exploration of meaning construction in literature study groups. *Research in the Teaching of English, 23,* 4-29.

Fielding, L. C., & Pearson, P. D. (1994). Reading comprehension: What works. *Educational Leadership, 52,* 62-68.

Flavell, J. H. (1976). Metacognitive aspects of problem solving. In L. B. Resnick (Ed.), *The nature of intelligence.* Hillsdale, NJ: Lawrence Erlbaum.

Fountain, G., & Fusco, E. (1991). A strategy to support metacognitive processing. In A. L. Costa (Ed.), *Developing minds: A resource book for teaching thinking* (Vol. 1). Alexandria, VA: Association for Supervision and Curriculum Development.

Garner, R. (1987). *Metacognition and reading comprehension.* Norwood, NJ: Ablex.

Harris, T. L., & Hodges, R. E. (Eds.). (1995). *The literacy dictionary: The vocabulary of reading and writing.* Newark, DE: International Reading Association.

Harste, J., Short, K., & Burke, C. (1988). *Creating classrooms for authors: The reading-writing connection.* Portsmouth, NH: Heinemann.

Hayes, J. R., & Flower, L. S. (1980). Identifying the organization of writing processes. In L. W. Greg & E. R. Steinberg (Eds.), *Cognitive processes in writing.* Hillsdale, NJ: Lawrence Erlbaum.

Herber, H. L. (1978). *Reading in the content areas.* Englewood Cliffs, NJ: Prentice Hall.

Johnson, D. W., & Johnson, R. T. (1987). *Learning together and alone* (2nd ed.). Englewood Cliffs, NJ: Prentice Hall.

Jones, B. F. (1991). Reading and thinking. In A. L. Costa (Ed.), *Developing minds: A resource book for teaching thinking* (Vol. 1). Alexandria, VA: Association for Supervision and Curriculum Development.

Langer, J. A. (1981, November). From theory to practice: A prereading plan. *Journal of Reading, 25,* 152-156.

Lipman, M. (1991). *Thinking in education.* New York: Cambridge University Press.

Loring, R. M. (1986). *Questions used by teachers during reading instruction with skilled and less skilled readers.* Unpublished doctoral dissertation, University of North Texas, Denton.

Margulies, N. (1991). *Mapping inner space: Learning and teaching mind mapping.* Tucson, AZ: Zephyr.

McGee, L. M. (1995). Talking about books with young children. In N. L. Roser & M. G. Martinez (Eds.), *Book talk and beyond: Children and teachers respond to literature.* Newark, DE: International Reading Association.

Niles, N. B. (1964). Patterns of writing in different subject areas. *Journal of Reading, 7,* 31-37.

Ogle, D. (1986). K-W-L: A teaching model that develops active reading of expository text. *The Reading Teacher, 39,* 564-570.

Palinscar, A. M., & Brown, A. L. (1984). Reciprocal teaching of comprehension-fostering and comprehension-monitoring activities. *Cognition and Instruction, 1,* 117-175.

Parks, S., & Black, H. (1992). *Organizing thinking.* Pacific Grove, CA: Critical Thinking Press and Software.

Pearson, P. D., & Dole, J. A. (1987). Explicit comprehension instruction: A review of research and a new conceptualization of instruction. *Elementary School Journal, 88*(2), 151-165.

Perfetti, C. A., & Curtis, M. E. (1986). Reading. In R. F. Dillon & R. J. Sternberg (Eds.), *Cognition and instruction.* New York: Academic Press.

Perkins, D. N. (1989, July). *Mindware: The new science of learnable intelligence.* Paper presented at the Fourth International Conference on Thinking in San Juan, Puerto Rico.

Pintrich, P. (Ed.). (1995). Understanding self-regulating learning. In R. J. Menges (Ed.), *New directions in teaching and learning.* San Francisco: Jossey-Bass.

Robeck, M. C., & Wallace, R. R. (1990). *The psychology of reading: An interdisciplinary approach.* Hillsdale, NJ: Lawrence Erlbaum.

Roser, N. L., & Martinez, M. G. (Eds.). (1995). *Book talk and beyond: Children and teachers respond to literature.* Newark, DE: International Reading Association.

Samuels, S. J. (1979). How the mind works when reading: Describing elephants no one has ever seen. In L. B. Resnick & P. A. Weaver (Ed.), *Theory and practice of early reading* (Vol. 1). Hillsdale, NJ: Lawrence Erlbaum.

Short, K. G., & Kauffman, G. (1995). "So what do I do?" The role of the teacher in literature circles. In N. L. Roser & M. G. Martinez (Eds.), *Book talk and beyond: Children and teachers respond to literature.* Newark, DE: International Reading Association.

Stauffer, R. G. (1969). *Directing reading maturity as a cognitive process.* New York: Harper & Row.

Stowell, L. P., & Tierney, R. J. (1995). Portfolios in the classroom: What happens when teachers and students negotiate assessment. In R. L. Allington & S. A. Walmsley (Eds.), *No quick fix: Rethinking literacy programs in America's elementary schools.* Newark, DE: International Reading Association.

Swartz, R. J. (1989). Making good thinking stick: The role of metacognition, extended practice, and teacher modelling in the teaching of thinking. In D. M. Topping, D. C. Crowell, & V. N. Kobayashi (Eds.), *Thinking across cultures: The third international conference on thinking.* Hillsdale, NJ: Lawrence Erlbaum.

Swartz, R. J., & Parks, S. (1994). *Infusing the teaching of critical and creative thinking into elementary instruction: A lesson design handbook.* Pacific Grove, CA: Critical Thinking Press and Software.

Swartz, R. J., & Perkins, D. N. (1990). *Teaching thinking: Issues and approaches.* Pacific Grove, CA: Midwest.

Vacca, J. L., Vacca, R. T., & Gove, M. K. (1987). *Reading and learning to read.* Boston: Little, Brown.

Vacca, R. T., & Vacca, J. L. (1986). *Content area reading* (2nd ed.). Boston: Little, Brown.

Wells, D. (1995). Leading grand conversations. In N. L. Roser & M. G. Martinez (Eds.), *Book talk and beyond: Children and teachers respond to literature.* Newark, DE: International Reading Associates.

Whimbey, A., & Lochhead, J. (1984). *Beyond problem solving and comprehension: An exploration of quantitative reasoning.* Hillsdale, NJ: Lawrence Erlbaum.

8

Mathematics *Is* Process Education

Carol T. Lloyd

Star Gazing

One night in early May 1976, as I looked into the sky and wondered at the stars, I experienced one of my first moments of intellectual crisis. It was 3 days before my college graduation. I realized that I had spent 4 years of blood, sweat, tears, and money to learn that I knew nothing and that no matter how hard I worked for the rest of my life, I would never "know" but a tiny, insignificant part of the vast amounts of potential knowledge. I reached the conclusion that being "educated" meant knowing how little I really knew.

Looking back on that experience now, I understand that what I thought of as a crisis was really the beginning of my journey, one that still occupies me today and has brought me to this moment. After teaching for 18 years, I feel I finally understand what teaching really means. In this chapter, I share what my fellow colleagues and I have learned from classroom experiences.

A Shoreline of Wonder

I have watched my own children go off to school filled with wonder and a joy of learning that I have rarely witnessed in my secondary math students. My vision, and the vision of many others, is to develop schools that nourish and support rather than stifle that wonder and joy. This will not happen overnight, but we must not give up hope. I often remind my Algebra II students about the limitations of their knowledge of mathematics. Just as a first grader may say you can't subtract 3 from 1, or a third grader may say you can't divide 2 by 5, my students will tell me you can't divide by zero. My response is that's true in the real numbers, you can't divide by zero, but you'll come close in calculus. Or when they say there is no square root of -4, I agree that there is no real answer to the square root of a negative number; they will have to wait until second semester when we expand the world of real numbers to the world of complex numbers, which includes imaginary numbers. I want them to continually wonder about what still lies ahead on their journey. This idea was expressed in a statement made by my minister, "As your island of knowledge grows, so grows your shoreline of wonder." If we are to develop the lifelong learners that students must become to be successful in the uncertainty of the 21st century, then they must accept this philosophy as well. This is my role as a teacher; I happen to use mathematics as the vehicle to reach my goal for my students.

My philosophy of teaching is stated in a three-part contract called "Excellence by Design" (see Table 8.1). Each student receives and completes a contract, which remains in the student's notebook for reference throughout the year.

The Ultimate Process

My friend Cathy is a secondary English teacher. As we were brainstorming ideas for this chapter, she made the statement that some people would wonder how a math classroom could support a process-centered curriculum. I have heard teachers from all disciplines, even mathematics, ask that very question. My answer is, of course, that mathematics is the supreme example of the inability to separate content and process. Life is a series of problems to be solved. My job is to increase the number of tools my students have for solving those problems they encounter, some of which can be solved by mathematics. So when my students lament, as they often do first semester, "Can't we just skip the word problems?" I answer emphatically, "But my darlings, they are the whole point!" If they do not understand how to use the knowledge they have, then, mathematics becomes nothing but mental exercise. It is exactly that feeling among students that leads to the question, "When am I ever going to use this?"

Yet it is the process of problem solving that they will use every day of their lives if they are to survive. The concept of problem solving as a survival skill is also what has redefined the meaning of the term in math classrooms. It no longer means just translating a "word problem" into a math equation that can then be solved to find the "right" answer. The use of equations is now only one of many strategies for solving problems that students learn. Other strategies included are guess and test, breaking a problem into smaller parts, drawing a graph or diagram, working backwards, and looking for patterns. The lists vary slightly from one curriculum document or textbook to another, but the idea is the same. Mathematics is no longer a set of isolated skills to be accumulated until someday when you know enough to use them but rather a tool for describing and making meaning from the world around us everyday. Until the day when we no longer teach students through a curriculum that is artificially divided into disciplines, students will never truly understand mathematics as a tool.

There are great changes currently taking place in mathematics curricula across the country. Most of these changes are based on the *Curriculum and*

Table 8.1 Excellence by Design

The Teacher's Goal:

My students will take responsibility for their own learning and feel confident about their ability to solve life's problems.

To fulfill this goal, I am committed to the following:

1. I will challenge your mind by providing activities at the highest levels of thinking.
2. I will provide an environment that encourages intelligent behaviors.
3. I will support your learning by helping you answer your questions.
4. I will never criticize you for what you do not know.
5. I will not allow you to say "I can't."

              Carol T. Lloyd

The Student's Goal:

_____

_____

To fulfill this goal, I am committed to the following:

_____
_____
_____
_____
_____

              (student's signature)

The Parent's Goal:

_____

_____

To fulfill this goal, I am committed to the following:

_____
_____
_____
_____
_____

              (parent's signature)

Evaluation Standards for School Mathematics (National Council of Teachers of Mathematics, 1989). In North Carolina, there is a state-mandated curriculum for every subject, for every grade, which teachers are required by law to follow. There is also a state end-of-grade testing program for grades 3 through 8 and end-of-course testing for grades 9 through 12. These tests are, of course, based on the prescribed curriculum. School systems, individual schools, and to some extent, even individual teachers are then evaluated on the scores of their students on these state tests. This structure provides little freedom for the individual school or teacher to spend much time outside the mandated curriculum. I have been torn the last few years because some of what I felt I should be doing with my students was outside the realm of the mandated curriculum.

The good news, however, is that this very lack of freedom is pushing the changes needed in the curriculum. During the last 3 years, the state has been implementing a new math curriculum for all grades K-12. Changes in the corresponding testing program are in the process of being developed. At all grade levels, these changes include students being tested on their ability to use the appropriate calculator as a tool for solving problems, to communicate mathematical ideas with words and drawings, and to solve various types of problem situations. To have increased time for teaching the operations and processes needed, there has been a corresponding decrease in the time spent on mastery of basic mathematical skills that can be done by calculators. For example, instead of algebra students spending a great deal of time learning to graph various mathematical functions, they now learn to use a graphing calculator to graph the function. Considered important for the students is the ability to take a problem situation, organize it for input into the calculator, and use the resulting answers or graphs for data analysis and prediction. The problems students are solving come from areas such as business, science, social studies, and even the sports world. This emphasis on integration and application is a definite move in the right direction. Students working within this type of curriculum will have the answer to the question, "When am I ever going to use this?" before them most of the time.

Supporting the Dispositions

For students to become the mathematically literate population needed for the 21st century, mathematics classrooms must nourish the development of the five dispositions (Costa & Garmston, 1994). For the last 4 years, I have been working with my students on the development of Costa's (1991) 14 intelligent behaviors. The teacher must constantly model these behaviors and support their growth in students by pointing out examples and counterexamples of their use and by providing opportunities for students to display them. Students who understand and can exhibit behaviors such as persistence, creativity, decreasing impulsivity, and metacognition will have a much greater chance of developing the dispositions of efficacy, flexibility, craftsmanship, consciousness, and interdependence.

Students who do not feel efficacious about their ability to succeed are not willing to tackle the type of problem situations previously discussed. Students should see their teacher experience failure and model persistence, metacognition, a sense of humor, and then flexibility by applying a number of problem-solving strategies until finding the one that works. Students must accept responsibility for their own learning. They should have opportunities to figure things out on their own or with the help of other students. The teacher must not be too quick to jump in and answer their questions or solve their problems. Assignments should be done not for the teacher but rather for the contribution they make to the learning process of the students. Students' sense of efficacy will grow through time as they experience success in an environment that scaffolds their learning, encourages failing forward, and makes the risk takers safe from humiliation.

One student, Sarah, came to me as a sophomore, quite sure that math was not her subject. She was generally an excellent student in all classes but felt math was her weakness and something to be tolerated because she had no choice. Because of the experiences she had in my class, her attitude changed a great deal through time. In fact, by the time she reached advanced math her junior year, she had become the one the other students turned to for help, and she knew she could help them.

Students will become interdependent by working in an environment that requires them to be interdependent and rewards them for being so. The environment of the classroom should support the idea of a journey that teachers and students are taking together, not teachers versus students or student versus student. The teachers should not be viewed as the persons with all the answers. Each group of students, in conjunction with the teachers, should be viewed as a learning community. Once again, the modeling by the teachers is extremely important. Students should see teachers working together with other teachers and with students in planning activities and solving problems of all types. Students should be asked for their input by providing feedback for the teachers about classroom procedures and activities. The implementation of cooperative learning techniques and the belief that we are all smarter together than we are alone will provide students with practice in the classroom of the interdependent behaviors they will be required to use outside the classroom.

Activities that develop students' problem-solving abilities will support the dispositions of consciousness, flexibility, and craftsmanship. Constant attention to metacognition in both teachers and students will increase their consciousness level. The two questions I ask students most often are "How did you get that?" and "Why did you do it that way?" Just getting the answer is not what is most important. The next time, the answer will be different. What matters is the students' understanding of the process they used to arrive at their answers so that the process can be refined, altered, or repeated for later problems. "I got that answer, but I'm not sure how," is not acceptable. By establishing an atmosphere of constant questioning, students are forced to clarify their thought processes, analyze their errors, and refine their own questions.

By supporting and appreciating diversity of methods, teachers teach flexibility. Students who are required to do things in exactly one way will have difficulty dealing with ambiguity, finding alternative ways to solve any type of problem, and trying something when they are not sure what to do. Math teachers, because of our own learning styles and belief that mathematics is an "exact" science, have been notorious for inflexibility. We must be willing to model flexibility for our students in many ways. My flexibility and my expectation of flexibility from my students have been some of the hardest things for some students to adjust to in my classroom. For so long, students have been told to follow these directions, do it just this way, that they are often at a loss when I refuse to provide those specific parameters in every case. Certainly, some things are mathematically incorrect, but there is also much more flexibility and ambiguity than most of my students have been led to believe. If they are to survive in a constantly changing society, then they must appreciate and practice flexibility.

Appreciation for flexibility does not preclude striving for excellence and producing quality work. In our fast-food, throw-away society, the under-standing of what constitutes quality is often missing in students. In whatever teachers ask our students to produce—a homework assignment, an essay ques-tion, or a project—we must continually work to develop their appreciation and understanding of what is a quality product. When through time, we see positive changes in the quality of their work, their writing, their questioning, and their responses, then we know they are striving for new levels of craftsmanship.

Experiences for Processing

The concept of journals is often discussed as a way of supporting growth in students' thinking skills. It was when I read John Barell's (1991) *Teaching for Thoughtfulness* that I first became excited about using "thinking journals" in my classroom. Barell gave examples from the work of several teachers with their students and journals, including those from a math teacher, Rosemarie Liebmann. Of course, my students have often been surprised by this "writing" they had to do for math class, which we begin on the first day! Yet as time goes on, it is the opportunity to be creative, thoughtful, and reflective that some students find most rewarding about my class. That they are given grades based on their thoughtful completion of assignments each quarter reinforces for them the importance I place on their thinking and writing. At first, they don't believe that I will actually read their journals, but when they receive them back with appropriate supportive comments and specific feedback, they realize I am serious about journals. When I make comments in class about the feedback and suggestions they give me and then act accordingly, their ownership of the class increases; so does their belief that they can make a difference.

It is important that early in the year I am open and willing to accept whatever responses I get. This often requires flexibility on my part. I remember one student in Algebra II, Eric, who started the year scared to death and quite sure that he would never pass my class. He had barely passed Algebra I. When I asked my students the second week in school to explain why a negative number times a negative number is a positive, he had not a clue. He did, however, respond quite creatively with a poem that ended, "Why ask why, ask why?" When he volunteered to read his response the next day, I applauded his sense of humor and his display of creativity. Eric soon began to display other intelligent behaviors, such as persistence and questioning. I am happy to report he passed my class and went on to a 4-year college intent on a degree in nursing. Table 8.2 shows some examples of the questions I have given for journal assignments that are not specifically math questions but that support the processing of students' learning and/or provide me feedback about our class.

Table 8.2 Questions for Journals

---

1. Ask students to complete the following: "When I hear the word *math*, I think _____, and I feel _____."
   "Problem solving means _____."
   "The hardest thing about problem solving is _____."
   "I took this course because _____."
2. Have students analyze a class activity. Ask students: "What did you like, and what did you not like, about the activity? What did it help clarify for you? What is still not clear?"
3. After the first few cooperative learning activities, ask students: "What did you like and not like about them? How did your group do at following directions, working together, and communicating?"
4. Metacognition practice: Ask students to explain some task or problem: "How did you think it through?"
5. Ask students to think of a nonmath problem they have had in the last few months: "Describe how you solved the problem and at least two other ways you could have solved the problem."
6. Have students compare and contrast concepts learned. For example, after learning four methods for solving a system of linear equations, ask students to compare and contrast using the four methods: "Which one seems the easiest or most efficient for you more often? Why do you seem to prefer one over the others?"
7. Ask students to propose criteria and their rationale for evaluation of a project. Follow this with a class discussion in which students must reach a decision on the criteria for grading.
8. Ask students to describe their intelligent behaviors: "Which two intelligent behaviors do you display most often? Which two have you improved most? How and when do you display them? With which two do you have the most trouble? How can you improve in these areas? Which two intelligent behaviors do I [the teacher] most need to improve? How can I work on those areas?"
9. As a review assignment, ask students: "Explain what concepts you should understand as a result of this unit. What should you be expected to know for a test? Suggest possible questions for a test."
10. After the completion of a project, ask students to evaluate the project: "What math skills or concepts did you have to use? What did you learn from completing it? What intelligent behaviors did you have to use? How did you use them?"
11. When trying new things in the classroom, have students give feedback: "Was the new strategy helpful to you? Why or why not? What suggestions do you have for making it better the next time?"
12. Have students use a three-circle Venn diagram for comparing and contrasting characteristics of themselves with two other family members.
13. Before or after a holiday or a *big* event (such as the prom!), ask students to describe using intelligent behaviors in that situation.
14. Have students analyze a test situation: "Was the test what you expected? What had you done to prepare for the test? How good a job did you do? What should you do again or do differently next time?"
15. Ask students to create new intelligent behaviors they feel should be practiced and explain them.

My students' journals have provided me with some of the most accurate assessment of my teaching and their learning that I have ever obtained. Sometimes they are painfully honest, especially after they know I will not hold their comments against them. Sometimes I agree with their assessment; other times I do not. For example, my honors students this year, who are mostly sophomores, were having a difficult time accepting some of my teaching practices first quarter. Because I did not check their homework every day, they did not always do their assignments. Because I did not tell them they had to do certain problems a certain way, they were confused by the ambiguity. They did not want to have to figure out that the way I did the problem or their partner did the problem produced an equivalent answer to theirs. As a result, many of them were not pleased by the grades they received first quarter. I even had a guidance counselor work with them one day so they could air their complaints. But I did not give up. When they realized I was not going to give in and accept responsibility for their lack of responsibility, they began to work harder. At the end of first semester, I asked them to rewrite their goal from the beginning of the year to consider what they needed to do differently second semester. I also asked them what the teacher and their parents could do to support them. Almost without exception, they said that we needed to encourage them but that the responsibility for the learning was theirs.

Another way I have provided process experiences for my students is through projects. One I have used was adapted from the *Curriculum and Evaluations Standards for School Mathematics* mentioned earlier (National Council of Teachers of Mathematics, 1989). I pose for the students the following problem: "For your birthday, I am going to give you a present, a big dog. For you to be ready, I am going to give you the material for a doghouse ahead of time, one piece of plywood, 4 feet by 8 feet, and some nails. You have a saw, a ruler, and a hammer. Your goal is to design and build (on paper) the *biggest* dog house you can." We talk about how they will need to define for themselves what constitutes a doghouse and how they will determine the biggest. On the day they bring in their projects, we have a class discussion to establish a definition for *doghouse* and how we will determine the *biggest*. These discussions can become very heated! By the time we have finished our discussions and tried to determine the biggest, they are truly amazed by how much math and how many intelligent behaviors they have used. Often, students comment in their reflective journal assignment after this project that next time they would think much longer when confronted by what they consider to be an easy little assignment!

One process that I have been constantly appalled to find lacking in my students is the knowledge of how to make a thoughtful decision. The problem, I suppose, is that the responsibility to teach decision-making skills does not fall under any specific curriculum. Many of my students are not taught by their families those skills that I was lucky enough to have learned around the dinner table. Several years ago, I decided I would not let my juniors and seniors graduate from high school without at least one formal experience in decision making. What decision they choose to use for their project varies. Most either work on choices for college or careers, but students also decide when would be the best time to get married or what to buy someone for a present. Table 8.3 provides a copy of the project as I present it to my students. My idea for the project was based on a presentation I attended in 1991 on a program titled CATS (Critical Analysis and Thinking Skills) (Applegate & Evans, 1977). The way in

Table 8.3 Decision-Making Project

The steps in the process:

1. Define the problem. What decision do I have to make?
2. Identify areas of concern. What are my options? (This step often requires research.)
3. Predict consequences. List for each option the positive and negative possible outcomes. (This step usually requires research.)
4. Prioritize. What is the likelihood of that consequence occurring, and how important is it to my decision?
5. Assess sources. How reliable is each source from which I received information? Is the information objective?
6. Make a decision. On the basis of information gathered, what is the best choice for you?

We will discuss each of the steps in the process during class. You will individually keep a record of the process for your own decision. At the end of the project, you will be expected to turn in a clear, well-organized presentation of the process you have completed. You will be graded on the evidence of the thoroughness of your process and the clarity of your presentation. Each step not completed and checked on time will result in a loss of 3 points per day late. The project will count as one test grade.

Step:	*Due Date:*
1. Decision to be made	November 17
2. List of options	November 21 and 29
3. Possible outcomes	December 1
4. Prioritize outcomes	December 6
5. Assessment of sources	December 6
6. Make a decision	December 9

Name: _____

Step 1. What decision do I have to make?

_____
_____
_____

which students are to document later steps is discussed with them in class as we go through the project. Many of my students have told me through the years that this was the most important thing they learned in my class.

During the last 5 years, my school system has been implementing many changes and has provided extensive staff development in a variety of areas. Although my major concern has been thinking skills, I have made many changes of various types in my teaching. As I have mentioned with the journals and projects, assessment was one of the areas in which I have experimented with different ideas. I also have attempted to use a variety of formal test questions, including open-ended questions that are now beginning to show up in testing programs. As has been discussed in many places, the world outside school does not function through multiple-choice or fill-in-the-blank tasks or evaluations. Students must have experienced in the relative safety of the classroom the same types of unstructured, ill-defined problems that they will encounter in life.

As I began to make so many changes in my teaching practices, I felt the need for some "hard" data that I could use for various reasons—but mostly for myself. My end-of-course test scores have remained fairly stable, usually with a slight increase from year to year. But this was not the data for which I was looking; much of what I was doing was not tested by the state tests. So I developed a student survey that I administered 2 years in a row. Students answered anonymously on scanner forms. The survey, including the percentage of students from my three Algebra II classes who agreed, disagreed, or were uncertain about each statement in a particular year can be found in Table 8.4. Of 77 students, 69 completed the survey. The other students did not attend class the day the survey was administered.

The survey's "hard" data was encouraging, but it is "soft" data such as the following story that warms my heart. Several years ago, one of my students, Ana, was in a minor car accident as she reached school. As she sat in the office waiting for her parents to arrive, Mrs. Adams, the assistant principal, was trying to keep Ana's mind occupied by asking her about her classes and teachers. When Ana told her she was in my class, Mrs. Adams asked how she felt about that. Her response was, "Mrs. Adams, she makes you think so hard your head hurts!"

I also know that my own children's teachers would be encouraged by the ways in which I see the results of changes in their teaching. When my family was leaving for vacation, Hannah, my 8-year-old, asked what I had in my "teacher" bag. I told her it was the material for working on my chapter. "But we're not taking the computer," she responded. "How are you going to work on the chapter?" I replied that I was going to think through what I wanted to say and write down my ideas. "You ought to make a web!" she explained. I agreed, and that's exactly what I did. Through time, the process skills that our students develop will transfer. Hannah's web is one small example.

The Infinite Journey

The quest for knowledge is never over. Teachers must never be satisfied that we are finished. The futures of our students are at stake. I know that I am a better teacher today than I was 5 years ago. I pray that 5 years from now, I will be a better teacher than I am today. There are certainly times when we are tired or frustrated, but we must not give up the journey. As our shoreline of wonder increases, so does our dissatisfaction with where we are today and our thirst for what is beyond the horizon. The educational system itself and those who compose it must be the epitome of the lifelong learner. I look forward to the visions of tomorrow that we are creating together today.

References

Applegate, T., & Evans, K. (1977). *The critical analysis and thinking skills program (CATS)* [Brochure]. Salt Lake City, UT: Author. (Program presented at the National Defusion Network conference, February 1991, Winston-Salem, North Carolina)

Table 8.4 Student Survey

Respond to each of the following statements by indicating the degree to which you agree or disagree with the statement. Try to respond with the entire year's experience in mind. Your responses are yours alone. The accuracy of your responses will enable me to make appropriate adjustments in the future that will lead to a better learning environment for other students.

Strongly agree A	Agree B	Uncertain C	Disagree D	Strongly disagree E

(Percentage of responses)

A/B	C	D/E	
51	16	33	1. I have succeeded in reaching my goal for this class.
90	9	1	2. I have enjoyed this class.
72	25	4	3. I am a better math student because of this class.
86	10	1	4. This class had a pleasant atmosphere.
97	1	1	5. I was treated fairly by the teacher.
88	7	4	6. I was treated fairly by other students.
94	4	1	7. Other students were treated fairly by the teacher.
100	0	0	8. The teacher is competent in the subject.
67	22	12	9. My attitude about mathematics has improved.
96	4	0	10. I earned the grades I received.
87	9	4	11. Instructional presentations were clear and understandable.
67	28	6	12. Content was related to other subjects.
74	17	9	13. Content was related to REAL life.
88	9	3	14. Proper study skills were encouraged and discussed.
80	16	4	15. The class maintained a high level of time on task.
87	7	6	16. I enjoyed the cooperative learning activities.
82	13	4	17. The cooperative learning activities were helpful to my understanding of the content.
81	14	4	18. The cooperative learning activities were helpful in developing my ability to interact positively with other students.
72	16	12	19. The cooperative learning activities were helpful in developing my communication skills.
75	20	1	20. My attitude toward other students in the class improved after working with them.
90	6	4	21. Communication between students was encouraged.
80	13	4	22. The room arrangement encouraged communication.
83	7	1	23. I felt comfortable with the room arrangement.
96	3	1	24. The teacher encouraged students to express themselves openly.
90	9	1	25. Questions were encouraged and answered in an appropriate manner.
86	14	1	26. Questions were valued for the thinking behind them.
93	3	4	27. Understanding of the content was more important than just getting the right answer.
58	36	6	28. My problem-solving abilities improved.
51	23	23	29. My attitude toward problem solving improved.
93	6	1	30. Creative ways of solving problems were encouraged.
87	7	2	31. Individual uniquenesses were valued.

(continued)

Table 8.4 Continued

75	16	3	32. The time required for preparation was appropriate for the class.
97	3	0	33. The teacher was prepared for the class.
90	10	0	34. The teacher displayed high expectations for student success.
90	7	0	35. The teacher acknowledged student success.
84	13	0	36. The teacher encouraged parental involvement in school.
87	9	4	37. The teacher had contact with my parent through a letter.
23	3	72	38. The teacher had contact with my parent through a conference.
10	12	78	39. The teacher had contact with my parent by phone.
57	23	17	40. The teacher showed concern for my life outside this classroom.
43	17	39	41. I discussed this class with my parents at least once a week.
52	35	13	42. My parents reacted positively to contacts with the teacher.
75	14	10	43. My parents encouraged me to reach my goal.
55	29	16	44. My parents reacted positively to class activities I described.
90	6	3	45. Activities were provided to accommodate different learning styles.
75	20	4	46. My experiences in this class have positively influenced my decisions about future plans for school or career.
87	7	6	47. Tests given accurately assessed the objectives taught.
84	12	4	48. A variety of methods were used to determine mastery of content.
91	7	1	49. An appropriate learning environment was maintained.
75	10	14	50. The thinking journal assignments encouraged me to think about the algebra concepts in a new or deeper way.
89	5	7	51. The thinking journal assignments allowed me to express my thoughts about topics related to class.
94	3	3	52. The display of intelligent behaviors was constantly encouraged.
54	33	14	53. The emphasis on intelligent behaviors has changed the way I behave outside this classroom.
64	25	12	54. The thinking journal assignments helped me to relate my learning to life.
59	23	17	55. The emphasis on problem solving has made me better at solving math problems.
86	12	3	56. This class has encouraged me to engage in metacognition.
77	16	7	57. As a result of this class, I am more concerned with HOW and WHY.
74	19	7	58. As a result of this class, I am a better decision maker.
62	28	12	59. I have become more creative.
83	13	3	60. I have improved my thinking abilities.

NOTE: Percentages were rounded to the nearest whole percentage, which is why the sum is sometimes greater than 100%. The sum is sometimes less than 100% because not all students responded to every question.

Barell, J. (1991). *Teaching for thoughtfulness: Classroom strategies to enhance intellectual development.* White Plains, NY: Longman.

Costa, A. (1991). The search for intelligent life. In A. Costa (Ed.), *Developing minds: A resource book for teaching thinking.* Alexandria, VA: Association for Supervision and Curriculum Development.

Costa, A., & Garmston, R. (1994). *Cognitive coaching: A foundation for renaissance schools.* Norwood, MA: Christopher-Gordon.

National Council of Teachers of Mathematics. (1989). *Curriculum and evaluation standards for school mathematics.* Reston, VA: Author.

9

Teaching the Process of Aesthetic Knowing and Representation

James G. Henderson
David M. Dees

Wisdom tells us that life and life in abundance lies only in work, love, laughter—and work. And when I use the word work, I mean work with head, heart, and hand.

Hubbard,
from Memorial Art Gallery
exhibit guide, 1994

Introduction

The statement that opens this chapter was written by Elbert Hubbard at the beginning of the 20th century. Hubbard established the Roycroft, a community for artists and artisans in East Aurora, New York. This community was inspired by the arts and crafts movement in England, which was initiated in the late 19th century as a reaction to the stultifying work conditions and the standardized, unimaginative work products of the industrial revolution. The Roycroft community, which included a press and book bindery, a leather department, a furniture shop, a chapel, and an inn for visitors and educational events, was based on a philosophy that aesthetic knowing and representation (AK&R) was the cornerstone of a quality, community-based lifestyle.

The focus of this chapter is on the process of AK&R. We believe the AK&R process is a fundamental form of human awareness. By identifying, appreciating, and understanding this qualitative way of experiencing, educators working within the AK&R protocol can help others to "see" the limitations of the process-content distinctions that control current educational environments. We begin this chapter with a general description of the AK&R process and an analysis of its educational value. After this theoretical discussion, our attention turns to concrete curriculum and teaching recommendations. We will offer advice to teachers on how to incorporate the AK&R process into curriculum design, development, enactment (teaching), and evaluation deliberations. We will conclude with a brief discussion on how teachers and other educational stakeholders, who understand the value of the AK&R process, can draw from national, state, and local policies in an effort to enact the process. This last section is included because current curriculum environments generally work against aesthetic educational considerations. Too many schools still operate under the influence of industrial era assumptions.

The Aesthetic Knowing and Representation Process

Elliot Eisner, in an interview with Buescher (1986), provides the following overview of the AK&R process:

> The ability to experience, to imagine, to represent . . . is a fundamental process of human intelligence. The process as well as the product that grows from it can have a deep, moving, and aesthetic character to it. Being able to experience what is subtle, to imagine what is interesting or useful, and to be able to adequately represent what has been experienced are each influenced by the conditions in which one lives. . . . Why do we have music or dance or poetry or stories? Because it is only through these modes and others that particular kinds of human experience can be communicated. We have to do this as a people. Human beings invented the forms that can meet that need to imagine and communicate. (pp. 11-13)

The AK&R process possesses two central features: qualitative experience and imaginative representation of that experience.

Dewey's (1934/1958) discussion of "art as experience" provides the foundational context in which to understand how the AK&R process is initiated. He notes that qualitative experience is based on the human capacity for sensitive perception in contrast to shallow recognition:

> Recognition is perception arrested before it has a chance to develop freely. . . . In recognition we fall back, as upon a stereotype, upon some previously formed scheme. . . . Perception . . . is an act of reconstructive doing, and consciousness becomes fresh and alive. . . . An act of perception proceeds by waves that extend serially throughout the entire organism. . . . The perceived object or scene is emotionally pervaded throughout. (pp. 52-53)

The AK&R process is fostered by teaching that encourages sensitive perception. Teaching that is based on shallow recognition would, by definition, not encourage this process. Whatever other value this type of instructional activity might have, it would not deliberately invite students' deep-seated perceptions or the aesthetic elaboration of these perceptions.

Dewey (1934/1958) further remarks that sensing, feeling, and thinking are all involved in discerning perception: "There is, therefore, no such thing in perception as seeing or hearing plus emotion. . . . When an aroused emotion does not permeate the material that is perceived or thought of, it is either preliminary or pathological" (p. 53). Because artful perception involves so much of the total being, so does its aesthetic elaboration. The AK&R process is one of the most intellectually engaging and challenging activities known to humanity. As Dewey further notes, "To think effectively in terms of relations of qualities is as severe a demand upon thought as to think in terms of symbols, verbal and mathematical" (p. 46).

The AK&R process cannot be properly comprehended and appreciated without understanding Dewey's point. Educators and others who make hard and fast distinctions between sensorimotor, affective, and cognitive development are trapped by the language they use. They are not predisposed to understand the integrated, holistic nature of the AK&R process. Abbs (1994) writes,

> Art embodies the invisible logic of the life of feeling and sentience and, in so doing, brings it to conception and consciousness. Once this is clearly recognized the common education distinctions between cognition and affect, between meaning and expression, between objective and subjective, between public and private break down and give way to what would seem a more valid differentiation between kinds of knowledge, between kinds of intelligence, between kinds of symbolic forms, between kinds of public language. (p. 224)

Eisner (1994) notes that "the tendency to regard cognition as something independent of both 'sense data' and feeling has a long history" (p. 23). This traditional interpretation of human cognition must be overcome to properly understand and appreciate the AK&R process.

Eisner (1994) provides a detailed description of the AK&R process. He points out that aesthetic experiences result from a sentient individual's transactions with an immediate environment. These transactions, which are partly dependent on a person's "internal conditions" (p. 46), such as prior experiences and current dispositions, result in qualitative experiences. Concepts, that is, meanings, are then constructed from these experiences. Some, but not all, of these concepts can be discursively rendered. Eisner argues that "much of our experience will not take the impress of a verbal label" (p. 47). His point is that humans know more than we can say. The individual then selects a form of representation to publicly render these concepts. This selection is made from a variety of expressive mediums, including words, photography, painting, music, movement, schematic diagrams, and so on. Eisner writes, "The choice of a form of representation is a choice in the way the world will be conceived, as well as choice in the way it will be publicly represented" (p. 42).

Eisner (1994) concludes his discussion of the AK&R process by noting that a public rendering of concepts becomes a potential part of the transactional environment of all people. The use of forms of representation result in the creation of new "environmental qualities . . . which, in turn, makes it possible to revise, correct, and strengthen the ideas expressed through the form chosen" (p. 47). In effect, the form of representation is a means of both personal and social expression and feedback. Finally, all forms of representation both enable and limit human meaning making. Any particular representative approach will highlight certain qualitative features of the environment and will use a limited range of human senses. As Eisner writes,

> When the skills necessary for using a form of representation are not available or the encouragement to use them is not provided, the kinds of meanings that an individual might secure from such forms are likely to be foregone. For example, children who are given no opportunity to compose music are unlikely to secure the meanings that the creation of music makes possible. Nor are they likely to regard the world in a relevant way to the creation of a musical equivalent. (p. 47)

Abbs's (1994) discussion of the AK&R process is remarkably similar to Eisner's. His description of this process, however, includes a discussion of "the aesthetic field" (p. 63), which serves as the basis for both aesthetic responses to, and evaluations of, aesthetic renderings. The aesthetic field "refers to that complex interactive system of allusion, reference and structure in which individual expressions of art are necessarily constituted" (p. 64). Different forms of representation rely on different aesthetic fields. For example, "Picasso's work can be viewed as a febrile ransacking of the entire visual history of western culture as well as primitive art" (p. 65). Abbs makes this point to highlight the distinctive cultural and historical foundations of all forms of representation.

A protocol can be gleaned from Eisner's and Abbs's discussion of the AK&R process. Although this protocol is an oversimplification of a highly complex and recursive type of learning, it provides a concrete referent for curriculum and teaching deliberations. The process of AK&R can be broken into the following overlapping and interactive phases:

- Teachers invite students' qualitative perceptions through some sort of aesthetically compelling activity.
- Students are asked to make sense of this activity through conceptually playful and imaginative exercises.
- Students are asked to publicly render their playful and imaginative explorations through the use of one or more forms of representation.
- At a critical point in this process, students are provided with foundational, cultural, and historical information appropriate to their use of one or more forms of representation.
- Students' expressive activities are submitted to both personal and public aesthetic critiques.

This protocol will help guide the curriculum and teaching advice that will shortly be offered. Before discussing this advice, however, we turn to an analysis of the educational value of the AK&R process.

A Discussion of Educational Value

The focus of all the processes in this book is on students' active meaning making during learning. When teachers work with the AK&R process, they help their students explore the many ways that humans can make sense of their lives. In effect, they help their students expand their constructivist repertoire and cultivate a broad humanistic, and perhaps spiritual, outlook on life. Eisner (1994) argues that education should be "concerned with fostering an individual's ability to construct, diversify, and deepen meaning [and, therefore, educators] should make it possible for students to become skilled in the construction of such meanings within a variety of the forms that are available" (p. 86).

Gardner's (1983) research has identified seven types of human intelligence: linguistic, mathematical/logical, spatial, musical, kinesthetic, interpersonal, and intrapersonal. Because the AK&R process can be designed to use all of these intelligences, it is a marvelous educational tool for ensuring students' balanced development. Furthermore, because students are not equally endowed with all seven intelligences, teachers can use the AK&R process to help all students develop their unique aptitudes and talents. Eisner (1994) writes: "Educational equity is not likely without a range of opportunities for conception and representation, opportunities that are wide enough to satisfy the diversity of talents of those who come to school and who share their future with us" (p. 89).

The educational use of the AK&R process is also important for the realization of cultural democracy. This normative concept refers to the synergy between democratic principles and pluralistic values in all aspects of life (McClelland & Bernier, 1993). Aesthetic projects can be organized so that students with diverse expressive talents work with one another. The math-able student is asked to work with the music-able, the dance-able student, and so on. This type of cooperative learning can enhance tolerance and respect for human diversity. Furthermore, the use of the AK&R process can help ensure the expressive vitality of society. This is an important consideration because a mature democratic civilization is a renaissance society—a place in which the arts and humanities flourish. Eisner (1994) writes, "As schools make it possible for students to optimize the realization of their potentialities . . . , the culture itself is enriched" (p. 89). Eisner notes that the human mind, as distinct from the human brain, is a cultural achievement. We construct our "minds" through the ways that we cultivate and refine our awareness.

Although the AK&R process has enormous educational value on its own terms, it can also be used to enhance the other learning processes described in this book. Research based on applications of Gardner's (1983) multiple intelligence theory has clearly demonstrated the value of using music, dance, poetry, and other forms of representation to enhance learning in the mainstream school subjects, such as mathematics, reading, and social studies. Teachers must be cautious, however, when they use the AK&R process as a means of enhancing other learning processes rather than as an end in itself. If they are not careful, they will reproduce the age-old Western prejudice that thinking, feeling, and sensing are compartmentalized in human intelligence. As mentioned above, this prejudice inhibits the use of the AK&R process. Furthermore, it can seriously limit advanced learning in the mainstream subjects. Mathematicians, physicists, and other sophisticated students of academic traditions regularly rely on the AK&R process. Eisner (1994) notes that qualitative thinking assists in mathematical inquiry and scientific research: "With qualities arrayed in space, certain relationships can be examined, the load on memory reduced, and forms of conceptual manipulation are made possible" (p. 37). In fact, experience with the AK&R process may be necessary for creative problem solving in all fields of inquiry. Ziman (1992), a research scientist, writes,

> On Mondays, Wednesdays and Fridays, I construct "normal" science, trying to solve the puzzles defined by the current paradigm: on Tuesdays, Thursdays and Saturdays, I take a "revolutionary" stance and poke subversively into the anomalous cracks. On Sundays, perhaps, I pray for guidance in what Kuhn called the "essential tension" between authority and rebellion, creativity and criticism.[1] (p. 15)

An understanding of the educational value of the AK&R process can help guide curriculum and teaching deliberations. We now turn to this practical topic.

Curriculum and Teaching Applications

To enact the AK&R process and to integrate it with other learning processes, traditional approaches to curriculum and teaching must be challenged and repositioned in an effort to reconnect the artificial distinction between process and content. The arts provide an important avenue for this repositioning of the process-content dichotomy. Artistic activities represent the tangible interconnection of process and content. Can the process of creating a painting be separated from the content of the work? Can the actor playing Hamlet be separated from the "Hamlet" on stage? By engaging in a particular artistic process, the artist creates an aesthetic content. We propose that teachers who are sensitive to the interplay between process and content in the arts can lead the way in creating a curriculum context that is supportive of the AK&R protocol outlined above. These teacher-leaders, however, should not just be art teachers. Educators representing all parts of the curriculum should be involved.

We are suggesting that curriculum be viewed as a collaborative work of art—a deliberative approach in which process and content are interrelated and interconnected. This type of curriculum context would bring the multiple visions of those involved into a decision-making process in which everyone benefits. For example, in a theater production, the visions of the designers (costume, set, lighting, etc.), directors (musical, artistic, production, etc.), actors, and stage crew, all meet, compromise, deliberate, and collaborate to work together to create a work of art that meets the demands for artistic integrity and expression.

This combined deliberative and collaborative curriculum approach is out-lined in Henderson and Hawthorne (1995). Drawing from van Manen's (1991) notion of pedagogical tact, Walker's (1971) views on deliberation, and the traditions of comprehensive curriculum work and critical curriculum studies, Henderson and Hawthorne (1995) propose a type of curriculum decision mak-ing that they call *transformative curriculum leadership* (TCL). As part of the TCL model, curriculum is viewed as four distinct, yet interrelated, spheres: design, development, enactment, and evaluation. Curriculum design is "the overall view of the educational journey" (p. 59). In architectural terms, it is the blueprint for the construction of the educational program. Curriculum development involves the day-to-day interactions of teachers in which their "beliefs, stimulated by curricu-lum design, and confronted by the climate and culture of the school" (p. 76) are thought through and developed as specific course, unit, and lesson plans. The curriculum enactment sphere represents the transactional moments of teaching—moments in which teachers think through the relationship between content and process in the context of their students' specific needs for active meaning making. Curriculum evaluation "is directed toward describing, understanding, and critically assessing the nature and qualities of all the curriculum spheres and their relationships with one another" (p. 80). All these spheres are distinct yet connected. As well, each of these spheres are created, shaped, re-formed, and enacted through continuous deliberation and collaboration.

In the TCL model, curriculum becomes an active process: the deliberations and collaborations of students, teachers, administrators, community members, educational professionals, and political leaders, all outlining, debating, and reaching a consensus on what should "happen" in the classroom. Process is, does, and creates content in this model. Curriculum is not a final "thing" delivered to students. It is alive, like a theatrical performance, shifting and changing with each event. The application of the TCL model to the AK&R process requires the active, community-based leadership of teachers repre-senting all parts of the curriculum.

To make the application of the TCL curriculum model to the AK&R process tangible, we will demonstrate how a particular thematic concern of an imagi-nary teacher could be developed through each curriculum sphere. Furthermore, because we believe that teachers sensitive to the AK&R process can be leaders in enacting the AK&R protocol throughout the entire curriculum, we will explore how this imaginary teacher can collaborate with other teaching profes-sionals in the implementation of this process. For purposes of this example, we will use a thematic concern drawn from the theater arts.

Our imaginary teacher will view theater as a powerful way to demonstrate, reflect, and challenge society's current and past perspectives on the human condition. To this teacher, theater can inform, validate, coalesce, or challenge different views of social reality. This is only one of many organizing themes that inform our imaginary teacher's theater arts work, but it will serve as the focus for an illustration of how the AK&R protocol affects curriculum design, devel-opment, enactment, and evaluation.

As our teacher enters the curriculum design sphere sensitive to the AK&R protocol, she considers how her theme can be enacted in playful, imaginative, and compelling ways to her students. How can she structure exercises that

demonstrate the frustration of Walter Lee's African-American experience represented in Hansberry's (1959) *A Raisin in the Sun?* How can students demonstrate Hamlet's confusion and anger toward his relatives in their own lives?
What about the hurt and pain of Biff Loman in Miller's (1949/1979) *Death of a
Salesman?* Our teacher can think of acting exercises, character analysis, historical
studies, and even public performances of these plays, all as legitimate ways to
demonstrate to the students how theater can help them to diversify their
perspectives on the human condition. This satisfies most of the pieces to the
AK&R protocol. Our teacher, however, must also provide access to historical
and cultural information that the students will need to make sense of these
exercises and analyses.

As part of her design deliberations, our imaginary teacher must also consider how these activities can be publicly critiqued using nonstandardized
forms of evaluation. She may try a holistic portfolio assessment approach,
allowing the students to demonstrate their knowledge of theater through a
variety of presentations. For example, a student could choose a theater piece
such as *A Raisin in the Sun* and then design set, lights, and costumes; provide
historical and cultural information about the work in the form of a paper; and
present scenes from the work—all of which would be submitted to personal,
peer, public, and professional critiques. This collaborative approach to assessment could provide important insights to student knowledge. This approach to
evaluation is quite sophisticated. As Eisner (1985) notes, artistic judgments,
because they depend "upon the ability to cope with ambiguity, to experience
nuance, and to weigh tradeoffs among alternative courses of action" are better
representations of "the skills that characterize our most complex adult life
tasks" (p. 67).

In the development sphere, our exemplary teacher meets the reality of the
day. She sees her students for 50 minutes a day. Therefore, her play selections,
exercises, studies, and so forth will have to be limited to the given time constraints. Her play selection will also have to be in tune with the political realities
of the school system. A play such as Sherman's (1979) *Bent*, outlining the
experiences of a homosexual in Nazi Germany, may not score many points for
theater instruction in some communities. She must also be prepared, given the
behavioristic climate of her school district, to justify her holistic and integrated
form of evaluation. How will she translate an honest assessment of student
performance into the given grade construction of her school? How will she
coordinate time schedules with those involved in the creation and evaluation
of the students' works? How can she provide all the information and materials
the students will need to accomplish their task? Cost, student interests, time,
energy, and a host of other considerations guide the teacher's deliberations.

The enactment sphere is the living curriculum. In this sphere, our hypothetical teacher examines the moments of teaching, trying to recognize student
dissonance, comprehension, limitations, and excitement, all in an effort to make
it significant to the students. In this sphere, she relies on her own knowledge of
the material and teaching; her students' needs, requests, and desires; and her
overall perspective of a solid educative experience. Put simply, she attempts to
practice pedagogical tact (van Manen, 1991). She notices that not all students
are comfortable on stage, in certain exercises, or publicly revealing personal

perspectives. In these moments, she must "know" her students, suggesting that particular students explore other aspects of theater, such as set, lighting, or sound design. She may have to adapt or delete certain exercises that may be uncomfortable for some. On the other hand, she may have to develop further exercises for those who are comfortable revealing and exploring personal issues. In this sphere, she explores her selected curricular themes in an interactive context. She cannot do this without knowing her students.

Within the evaluation sphere, she begins to assess how well the AK&R protocol has been addressed in the deliberations within the design, development, and enactment spheres. Are the exercises that are actually enacted aesthetically compelling, imaginative, and playful, or, because of time and money limitations, have they become meaningless? Are the students understanding the social, historical, and cultural significance of the works they study? Are the public renderings receiving honest and perceptive aesthetic critiques? Are the students internalizing the differences and similarities between their own reality and the reality portrayed in the world of theater? Are the portfolio presentations really providing an honest measure of student theatrical awareness? During this evaluation sphere, our exemplary teacher reflects on the appropriateness, accessibility, and depth of her own curriculum blueprint that she created in the curriculum design phase.

From this limited example, it is easy to see how design, development, enactment, and evaluation are distinct yet interconnected processes that create, form, shape, and re-create the curriculum context. We have demonstrated how an imaginary teacher could practice this type of comprehensive and integrated curriculum deliberation using the AK&R protocol as the guide to decision-making. We now turn to a brief exploration of how a group of teachers could deliberate over the enactment of the AK&R process.

As we stated earlier, we believe that the AK&R process is a fundamental form of human awareness. An important step in curriculum work is to connect this learning process with other forms of learning to explore the educational relationship between the AK&R process and subject matter learning in areas not normally associated with the arts. Again, in an effort to keep our example simple, imagine that teachers reach a consensus that their students should be exploring differing views of social reality. During the design phase, the teachers discover the areas of interdisciplinary connection. For instance, their deliberations might be guided by the following questions: How could a study of Magritte's painting *The Use of Language*[2] or Pirandello's play (1954/1973) *Six Characters in Search of an Author* inform a presentation of Heisenberg's uncertainty principle[3] that reframes our perspective of reality? How could a painting be used to give the students the "experience" of a mathematical limit, going on forever yet contained in a form of representation such as a canvas or a diagram? Do these artistic connections help to make the material more aesthetically compelling, challenging, and playful? Do they allow themselves to be presented in a public forum? How do these concepts relate to their social, cultural, and historical perspectives?

The deliberations within the development sphere of this integrated process revolve around important practical and political questions. Given the time constraints of the day, how can the different teachers collaborate together? How can the lead teachers convince others that the AK&R process informs their practice? How can science, math, history, and physics teachers work with teaching professionals from other areas without compromising the important aspects of their chosen field? The enactment and evaluative deliberations will then be guided by consensus responses to these questions.

As we move from the idiosyncrasies of these two imaginary illustrations to a more general curricular discussion, the following three principles of curriculum deliberation can be identified. First, curriculum creators must work at the level of content-process synthesis. In our examples, the individual teachers and the teams of teachers focused on common thematic concepts. This helped them avoid the trap of distinguishing content from process. Traditional philosophical and curricular perspectives invite curriculum deliberations to fall into this trap. Nevertheless, if those involved reflect on and remind themselves of the AK&R protocol, the process-content trap will be avoided. Continuous critical reflection on the AK&R protocol is vital.

The second principle that emerges from our illustration highlights the importance of the deliberative process. Curriculum deliberations must occur in the design, development, enactment, and evaluation phases, and each of these phases must be closely integrated with the others. Current curriculum creations occur in isolation, with curriculum directors, principals, or even book publishers deciding on what material is suitable for the classroom. This historic curricular approach has helped solidify the content-process distinction so well-known and understood. In this new model, teachers, students, community members, politicians, and others all come together to debate and collaborate, creating the best curriculum that they can envision for the children. As well, teachers in this model are viewed as professionals, individuals who understand and reflect on what material, information, and experience is best for their students. Deliberation, collaboration, creation, and re-creation all occur if the phases are followed and integrated. Given the current political climate and historical tradition, this deliberative-collaborative process may be met with resistance.

To counter the resistance that probably will occur, teachers, administrators, students, community members, and so forth should consider our third principle, which concerns the establishing of clear public rationales to justify all aspects of their deliberations. To keep this approach from appearing as just another educational fad, curriculum deliberations should be clear and specific in outlining the curriculum blueprints. Why are certain thematic concepts important for the students to understand? Why should a certain evaluation be used over another? Why does collaboration with other teachers and professionals help the learning process? The political and financial realities of classroom contexts create the need for public, community-focused justification. Teachers, sensitive to this reality, can provide leadership for implementing meaningful change.

Currently, principals are forced to worry about money and test scores. As collaborative leaders, they must redirect their priorities. They must consider how their schools can become a democratic learning community. Community members must also step forward, providing teachers with the support they need to implement change. As seen in our illustration, the AK&R process is the integration of many ideas and people, all in an effort to create an educative experience that is valuable to children. Teachers, artists, and community members sensitive to and able to work from the AK&R process need to become informed regarding local, state, and national policies and resources that can assist them in creating curriculum that follows the AK&R protocol.

Policy Support

One way to develop clear and valid rationales, given the political reality of schools, is to draw on the public policies that can support curriculum reform efforts. Currently, several national, state, and local policies exist that when viewed from a critical perspective, can provide spaces for the enactment of the AK&R protocol. For example, the National School Board Association (1992) and the National Art Association (1992) both have recently proposed that art education, given the visual reality of the current technological society, is vital for all students preparing for the 21st century (Votaw, 1995). These policies could be used by an astute educator as an impetus for creating a space for curriculum change sensitive to the AK&R protocol. Because of the scope and focus of this chapter, a comprehensive examination of national, state, and local policies is impossible. An in-depth exploration of one of these policies, however, provides a practical example of how policies can become political rationales for the enactment of the AK&R protocol.

One of the most visual and effective national policies for implementing curricular change in art education has been discipline-based art education (DBAE). The DBAE concept, a creation of the Getty Center for Education in the Arts (1985b), is a curricular approach to art education that integrates "the ideas, skills, knowledge, and creative activity drawn from the art disciplines . . . (studio art) . . . (art history) . . . (art criticism) . . . (aesthetics)." The successful implementation of this approach in many schools, given the political resistance to art education in the United States, demonstrates that with strong beliefs and political savvy, art educators can lead the way in implementing change. In *Beyond Creating: The Place for Arts in America's Schools,* the Getty Center for Education in the Arts (1985a) highlights some of the successful examples of DBAE implementation, such as in Virginia Beach (Virginia), Palo Alto (California), and Decatur and Champaign (Illinois). As a result of a comprehensive examination of these success stories, the Getty Center proposes five critical elements for creating advocacy and support for this program:

- The efforts of a politically skilled art advocate
- Strong district support
- Outside resources
- Support and involvement of teachers and principals
- Active involvement of an art specialist

The guidelines for successful implementation of DBAE outlined in this brochure demonstrate that with politically astute leadership, new curriculum creations are possible. The Getty Center also highlights the importance of understanding and promoting academic rigor in the arts, which they define as

- A clearly stated rationale and conceptual base
- A written, sequential curriculum
- Well-specified instructional goals
- Continuing in-service teacher training
- Strategies for program review and development

As seen in this model, the DBAE approach regards art education as an academic subject, with clear and definable evaluation measures that serve to "justify" the rationale for art education to the community at large. As noted earlier, we believe that this is a key principle for enacting the AK&R protocol as well.

When using a national policy much as DBAE as a guide for curriculum deliberations, educators need to proceed with caution, noting the aspects of the policy that inhibit their decision making. Because of its comprehensive approach to the qualitative appreciation and expression of human experience, the AK&R process differs somewhat from the DBAE approach: *The AK&R protocol is not limited to the visual arts; it is a holistic process based on a fundamental form of human awareness that crosses all disciplines.* The DBAE concept provides powerful insights for broadening the field of art and implementing curricular change. It fails, however, to view qualitative human experience from the comprehensive perspectives of the AK&R protocol. If our imaginary teacher were using DBAE policy to guide her design deliberations, she would need to recognize, realize, and be sensitive to the similarities and differences between this policy and the AK&R protocol. National policies can provide political clout, but without a critical eye, our teacher could unconsciously reproduce current invidious distinctions between aesthetic awareness/knowing and "nonart" subject matter learning.

Conclusion

In the most aesthetic moments of human lives, process and content are not separate. Educators who are sensitive to such moments can serve as curriculum leaders for the design, development, enactment, and evaluation of the AK&R process. Their efforts will result in the creation of educational communities that value the importance of aesthetics in the learning process. To educate in this way is to promote the wisdom celebrated by Elbert Hubbard in the opening statement of this chapter. To teach the AK&R process is to celebrate the joy of integrating the head, heart, and hand.

Notes

1. Ziman (1992) is referring to Thomas S. Kuhn's (1962) *The structure of scientific revolutions.*
2. This is the famous painting (1928-1929) of a pipe with the puzzling phrase "Ceci n'est pas une pipe" ("This is not a pipe") written underneath. For an in-depth discussion of Magritte and his work, see Schneede's (1982) *René Magritte: Life and Work.*

3. For a further discussion regarding Heisenberg's uncertainty principle, see Cassidy (1992).

References

Abbs, P. (1994). *The educational imperative: A defence of Socratic and aesthetic learning*. London: Falmer.

Buescher, T. M. (1986). Appreciating children's aesthetic ways of knowing: An interview with Elliot Eisner. *Journal for the Education of the Gifted, 10*(1), 7-15.

Cassidy, D. C. (1992). *The life and science of Werner Heisenberg*. New York: Freeman.

Dewey, J. (1958). *Art as experience*. New York: Capricorn. (Original work published 1934)

Eisner, E. W. (1985). Why art in education and why art education. In Getty Center for Education in the Arts, *Beyond creating: The place for art in America's schools* (pp. 64-69). Santa Monica, CA: J. Paul Getty Trust.

Eisner, E. W. (1994). *Cognition and curriculum reconsidered* (2nd ed.). New York: Teachers College Press.

Gardner, H. (1983). *Frames of mind*. New York: Basic Books.

Getty Center for Education in the Arts. (1985a). Critical elements in changing art education [Brochure]. In Getty Center for Education in the Arts, *Beyond creating: The place for art in America's schools* (pp. 54-63). Santa Monica, CA: J. Paul Getty Trust.

Getty Center for Education in the Arts. (1985b). *Discipline-based art education*. Santa Monica, CA: J. Paul Getty Trust.

Hansberry, L. (1959). *A raisin in the sun*. New York: Random House.

Henderson, J. G., & Hawthorne, R. D. (1995). *Transformative curriculum leadership*. Englewood Cliffs, NJ: Merrill/Prentice Hall.

Kuhn, T. S. (1962). *The structure of scientific revolutions*. Chicago: University of Chicago Press.

McClelland, A. E., & Bernier, N. R. (1993). A rejoinder to Steve Tozer's "Toward a new consensus among social foundations educators." *Educational Foundations, 7*(4), 57-63.

Memorial Art Gallery. (1994). *Head, heart, and hand: Elbert Hubbard and Roycrofters* [Gallery guide for exhibit]. Rochester, NY: University of Rochester, Memorial Art Gallery.

Miller, A. (1979). Death of a salesman. In A. W. Allison, A. J. Carr, & A. M. Eastman (Eds.), *Masterpieces of the drama* (4th ed.). New York: Macmillan. (Original work published 1949)

National Art Education Association. (1992). *Briefing paper*. Reston, VA: Author.

National School Board Association. (1992). *More than pumpkins in October: Visual literacy in the 21st century*. Alexandria, VA: Author.

Pirandello, L. (1973). *Six characters in search of an author* (F. May, Trans.). London: Heinemann. (Original work published c. 1954).

Schneede, U. M. (1982). *René Magritte: Life and work* (W. W. Jaffe, Trans.). Woodbury, NY: Barron's. (Original work published 1973 by M. Du Mont Schauberg, Cologne, Germany)

Sherman, M. (1979). *Bent*. New York: Avon Books.

van Manen, M. (1991). *The tact of teaching: The meaning of pedagogical thoughtfulness*. Albany: State University of New York Press.

Votaw, F. (1995). *Collecting research data from community-arts education collaborations for use in action research*. Unpublished doctoral dissertation, Kent State University, Kent, Ohio.

Walker, D. F. (1971). A naturalistic model for curriculum development. *School Review, 80*(1), 51-65.

Ziman, J. (1992, November 27). Subversive scholar. *London Times Higher Education Supplement*, p. 15.

10

Science as Inquiry

Transforming Science Education

Donald B. Young

This is an exciting time in science education—in the United States and elsewhere. We are in the midst of a major reform movement, initiated in 1983 with the publication of *A Nation at Risk* and stimulated by a sense of impending danger of being eclipsed economically and technologically by other countries—particularly Japan and Germany. The movement continues with the enactment of Educate America 2000 Act passed by Congress in 1994 and the establishment of national standards for science literacy. The last time there was such a national concern was after the first Russian sputnik was launched in 1957. Then, we were shocked that Russia might be more technologically advanced than the United States. We initiated multimillion-dollar projects in science and mathematics education to produce more scientists and engineers. Now, as then, science literacy is seen as closely connected to economic and technological development and progress.

The Changing Nature of Science

But this reform effort is more than just an effort to catch up or maintain our lead. At its core are fundamental shifts in our understanding of science itself and in our approach to education. Schwab (1966) called attention to our dilemma in describing two different conceptions of science that are widely misunderstood by both scientists and the public. *Stable inquiry*, the conception of science held by the public in general, is captured in the following definitions of science:

> Science, above all, is a methodology for acquiring testable knowledge about the natural world. (Gould, 1986, p. 152)

> Science is a method, a tool, used to learn about reality, and only this. It is a way of finding out what "is," what exists, and how parts of reality interact. (Bergman, 1983, p. 41)

> Science is what scientists do. Science is knowledge, a body of information about the external world. Science is the ability to predict. Science is power, it is engineering. Science explains, or gives causes and reasons. (Bremer, 1962, pp. 37-38)

Stable inquiry is characterized by the steady accumulation of knowledge in a particular field guided by the current principles or perspectives of that field. These principles are taken as givens and are not questioned. They define the problems, methodology, and interpretation of results of experiments. Stable inquiry is generally successful in that it finds what it is looking for. Our entire educational system, including the training of scientists, has been based on such a conception of science.

However, there comes a time when a stable set of principles no longer defines meaningful problems, when research seems at a standstill and contradictory data are open and recognized. Here, stable inquiry gives way to *fluid inquiry* as described in these definitions of science:

> Science is an attempt to understand the universe and humanity's relationship to nature. The essential activity of science consists of thought, which arises in creative perception and is expressed through play. This gives rise to a process in which thought unfolds into provisional knowledge which then moves outward into action and returns as fresh perception and knowledge. This process leads to a continuous adaptation of knowledge which undergoes constant growth, transformation, and extension. Knowledge is therefore not something rigid and fixed that accumulates indefinitely in a steady way but is a continual process of change. Its growth is closer to that of an organism than a data bank. When serious contradictions in knowledge are encountered, it is necessary to return to creative perception and free play, which act to transform existing knowledge. Knowledge apart from this cycle of activity, has no meaning.
>
> Science is essentially a public and social activity. Science is, however, at least in principle, dedicated to seeing any fact as it is, and to being open to free communication with regard not only to the fact itself, but also to the point of view from which it is interpreted.
>
> Although science literally means knowledge, the scientific attitude is concerned much more with rational perception through the mind and with testing such perceptions against actual fact, in the form of experiments and observations. (Bohm & Peat, 1987, p. 16)

When stable inquiry exhausts its usefulness, when it has generated as much knowledge of a subject as possible, fluid inquiry proceeds with the invention of new principles and conceptions and tests them against data for adequacy and feasibility. In fluid inquiry, the principles and conceptions themselves are open to question and reinvention. Its goals are not to add knowledge in a narrow field but to develop new guiding conceptions and principles that will further redefine the subject and the course of future investigation. Failure is an expected part of the process of invention. This conception of science makes the knowledge that science renders fragile, questionable, and always subject to change.

These contrasting modes of inquiry are at the heart of the current shift in science education. In the last 150 years, the nature of science has changed dramatically. Where once a professional scientist could spend an entire career generating knowledge as a stable inquirer in a field of study, it is now expected that the guiding principles of inquiry will be revised several times in a lifetime. Fluid inquiry has emerged as the dominant mode of inquiry due chiefly to the demands of industrial democracy. Science has replaced exploration, empire, and colonial exploitation as driving forces of change in our society. It is the foundation of national power and productivity, and it is public. Its failures and rapidly changing conceptions are open to public view and scrutiny.

By contrast, the general public has been taught what Schwab (1966) calls a rhetoric of conclusions—the results of stable inquiry—which are taught as if they are fixed and certain. We are given conclusions of inquiry as if they were facts, and worse, we learn them only in isolation—and facts don't change. The fact is, that science teaching as currently practiced does not reflect science as science is practiced. Such a contrast has given rise to a public mistrust of science. What was thought to be certain is now shown to be only tentative or a best accounting at the time. We learned in school that science had the answers or would have—that its findings were absolute and certain (e.g., there are nine planets). Now we find that what we learned is questioned; it is given up for new conceptions (e.g., well, perhaps there are only eight planets; Pluto may not be a planet after all). So science is not absolute but changing and fickle. So how can these knowers be trusted?

Teaching science as science is practiced means involving students in learning science as a community process. Content is not an end in itself but a vehicle for constructing knowledge. By actively generating and interpreting data and testing guiding principles and conceptions, students begin to see that theory is not converted into fact but into another theory that is more robust and accounts for more connections. Teaching science as a community process recognizes the organismic nature of science in which all methods, as well as conceptual and physical products, are meaningless unless treated as an invitation to further process. The emphasis is on the interconnectiveness of science ideas, the fabric that holds our knowledge together, rather than on the isolated bits of information.

The Conflict of Educational Systems

While we are struggling with new conceptions of science as continuous inquiry, the reform effort is also about two incompatible systems of education. Our educational system has been one of selecting and screening students—identifying only the best for science education—a system that Ruth Mitchell, Associate Director of the Council for Basic Education in Washington, D.C., calls the factory model of education. It began early in our history. Thomas Jefferson, for example, suggested that education should inform the masses with what they need to know to make a living—to instruct them in their rights, interests, and duties as citizens. For elites, on the other hand, he proposed to develop the reasoning abilities and habits of mind that include reflection, invention, and what we call today higher-order thinking skills (Padover, 1943).

Under the factory model, value is placed on students' abilities to recognize discrete statements, right from wrong answers, and information that is easily recognized in texts and memorized. Its purpose is gatekeeping, selecting and sorting, and providing for access to higher education and opportunity or denial of it. This is how science has been taught.

The conventional way of teaching science does not work for most students. Scientists, researchers, educators, and businesspeople agree on this point. Somewhere in the middle grades, students lose interest in science, and by high school many find science difficult, boring, and irrelevant. Given the choice, few take advanced science courses. The result is that most adult citizens are not scientifically literate. For example, it is not uncommon to find adults who do not know that the Earth revolves around the sun once a year or others who believe that humans lived at the time of the dinosaurs. According to many, this result is due to an emphasis on covering too many topics superficially rather than in depth, seatwork over hands-on activities, memorizing rather than critical thinking, and recitation instead of well-reasoned argument.

We are beginning to realize that we can no longer afford such an approach. We need to create opportunities for everyone to be well educated, including the opportunity to enter into science and technology careers. More important, we must better educate the 90% who have been traditionally excluded from meaningful participation in learning science. We have recognized as a nation that we must include everyone in science education, especially women and minorities who are currently underrepresented in science and engineering, if we are to successfully compete in the scientific-technologic world of the 21st century.

The contrasting view might be called the "community of learners model." Its purpose is to develop each student's intellectual, social, and emotional abilities to function in the world, not to serve as gatekeeper for educational opportunity. Such a model is also consistent with the view of science as a community process and emphasizes the development of everyone's thinking skills. The next generation must see science as a continuous fluid process of generating knowledge.

Science education is most effective when it captures the beliefs and habits of mind or methods of thinking that guide scientists in their own explorations of the world. What are these beliefs and methods? Among them are the beliefs that (a) the world is understandable, (b) ideas are not fixed but grow and change over time, (c) scientific knowledge is durable, and (d) science cannot explain all things. Science also values certain rational methods of inquiry. These include careful observation, thoughtful analysis, healthy skepticism, the blending of logic and imagination, and the development of sound and coherent predictions and explanations.

In keeping with these beliefs and methods, good science teaching encourages students to be curious, creative, open-minded, skeptical, willing to suspend initial judgments, able to collaborate with others, and persistent in the face of failure. In the effective science classroom, the activity of finding out is as important as knowing the answer. By continually moving back and forth between questions, observations, and experiments, students refine and validate their hypotheses and at the same time develop good thinking skills.

New Visions for Science Education

The transformation that is occurring in science education is creating a new vision of what it means to be scientifically literate in our technological society. Propelled by the professional science associations and informed by the recent research about learning and teaching, the reform efforts are about teaching science as inquiry.

For the past 25 years at the Curriculum Research & Development Group (CRDG) of the University of Hawaii, the science section has been working on creating science programs and experimenting with new approaches to teaching science. In this effort, we have employed an engineering approach, taking the best available research on learning and teaching and crafting it into practical, workable applications in classrooms. The measures of success are whether the programs work in real classrooms and whether they are acceptable to practitioners.

The science programs share some common characteristics:

- They are all inquiry based, with teachers and students asking questions about nature and students doing investigations about 80% of the time.
- They are student centered, with students constructing their knowledge of the world from the investigations they do.
- They are based on a constructivist philosophy that asserts that knowledge construction is incremental. Instruction is designed in sequences that help students connect new knowledge to what they already know.
- In these programs, students interact with one another. We want them to talk to one another, share their ideas and their data, and discuss different points of view in an open manner.
- The teacher is a facilitator and learns along with students as they co-construct their knowledge.
- Students learn science by studying first their own local environment—whatever that may be—then comparing their understanding to other environments. There is a continual movement from local understanding to global applications to local implications.
- A variety of instructional strategies based on the best research on learning and teaching are incorporated into the design. Sometimes students work individually, sometimes in small groups, and at other times with the whole class. Throughout there is an emphasis on team work and collaboration.
- The programs emphasize integration—building connections between the disciplines of science, other subject areas, and out-of-school experience.

Students study a variety of sciences each year in an interconnected way rather than isolating chemistry, physics, or biology.

- Investigations also focus on interactions between science and society—particularly cultural perspectives—by dealing with both local and global issues. The attempt is to develop students who think globally and act locally.

Such an approach to teaching science also reflects how science operates. We attempt to replicate science in the classroom as it is practiced, including

- its questioning nature
- seeking evidence versus opinion
- collaboration—drawing on the best ideas of all
- replication—not focusing on single events but looking for patterns
- prediction and testing of ideas against evidence
- decision making based on the best available data

These approaches attempt to teach science as science is practiced and to capture a view of science as process in continual change and growth—that is, to reflect both stable and fluid inquiry. Shifting to teaching science as inquiry cannot be done in isolation. It has implications that affect multiple areas of the curriculum, teaching, and assessment. From these, I have selected 10 areas to briefly describe. I have also included selected glimpses of classrooms and schools we have been working with, and where the transformation has begun to occur.

1. Establishing National Standards

For the first time in the United States, there is an acknowledgment that we need rigorous standards in science education that set high expectations for curriculum, teaching, and assessment. Led by professional associations such as the National Science Teachers Association (NSTA), the American Association for the Advancement of Science (AAAS), and the National Research Council (NRC), the new standards identify what students should know and be able to do and emphasize learning that is hands-on, inquiry oriented, cooperative, and integrated.

We now know that learners need a large amount of experience and information to understand new concepts and apply them to new situations. Thus, if true learning is to occur, concepts must be pursued in depth. Lectures are often not the most effective way to teach and too often result in a student's ability to say the right words without any real understanding of what they mean or how to use and apply that knowledge. Teaching science as inquiry is a multifaceted activity that involves observing; posing questions; reading accounts of others to see what is already known; designing and conducting investigations; collecting and analyzing data; interpreting findings; posing solutions to problems; using critical, logical, and creative thinking; and so on. Engaging students in inquiry enhances learning. Join me for a visit to an elementary classroom where inquiry is a way of life.

The principal welcomed me with a rush of words, "I can't wait for you to visit Mrs. C, she's now soaring like an eagle instead of hopping around like a robin. (Inquiry science) has opened the door to lifelong learning for our staff and students! Honest to goodness, you can't separate language, math, art, or social studies from science. It has enabled this school district to integrate its curriculum!"

Moving down the hallway the overflow of student activity was overwhelming. An entire wall was covered by a graph of sunrise and sunset. The sine-curve produced by the seasonal daylight and darkness pattern was emerging beautifully.

Entering the room, students Lindsay and Mary Ann grabbed me by the arm and dragged me to the classroom chicken coop. Carefully cradling the full-grown chickens, they introduced me to Mellow-Yellow, Snowball, and Cuddles. "Would you like to hold Cuddles? He's the gentlest." Mike described the life history of their chickens recorded in the Class Chicken Book, a collection of shadow drawings, height and weight charts, photographs, and so on.

Later I was instructed by Kiley on the art of growing crystals. "You know," she giggled, "You have to use a super-duper-saturated solution or you'll dissolve the baby seed crystals like we did." Eventual success was obvious from the quarter-inch salt crystals displayed.

Kelly proudly displayed her desktop pencil and supply organizer made from a recycled plastic milk jug, and a glance out the window revealed garden spaces for each classroom, a birdfeeder, a giant thermometer, and several wind measuring inventions the class had made.

Where was the teacher during all this activity? She was quietly moving from group to group as they worked on their propeller-driven boats, facilitating the creative thinking of her students with a gentle, "What do you think? Perhaps a look in the Inventor's Box would help." (Young et al., 1993, p. 4)

The new standards provide a common focus on what can be achieved. There is a high degree of agreement on what students should know and be able to do and that science should be taught as inquiry. We must ensure that the standards-based movement deals with both what students should know and how they should be taught. In the community of learners model, the overarching goal for students is "to continue individual growth, pursue knowledge, develop aesthetic sensibilities . . . (through encounters with) intellectually challenging educational programs. (Children) are thinkers and doers before they come to school . . . (and) are eager to remain thinkers and doers" (Sarason, 1990, pp. 156, 162).

Eisner (1995) points out that one of the negative consequences of our preoccupation with standards is that

it detracts from paying attention to the importance of building a culture of schooling that is genuinely intellectual in character, that values questions and ideas at least as much as getting right answers. . . . One of the important aims of education is to free the mind from the confines of certainty. . . . Genuine education reform . . . is about vision, conversation, and action designed to create a genuine and evolving educational culture. (pp. 758-764)

Teaching science as inquiry contributes to the vision making, conversation, and actions of reform.

2. Science Is for All Students

"Science is key to the basics because it promotes the development of the thinking skills, learning processes, and positive attitudes required for lifelong learning" (Mechling & Oliver, 1983). This shift is at the heart of the debate between the factory model and the community of learners model of education. Should our educational system select the brightest and best for a high-level science education or more fully develop the potential of all learners?

All citizens need to be scientifically literate to function effectively in an increasingly technical age and to help create and sustain a decent, just, and vigorous society. A scientifically literate person is one who understands key concepts and principles of science and uses scientific knowledge and ways of thinking in everyday life. Citizens today face a range of difficult choices, from the personal (how to avoid AIDS) to the global (what to do about the greenhouse effect). People who understand science are better prepared to sort fact from myth, make sensible decisions, and urge their leaders toward enlightened public policy choices.

Science education is also economically important. We will need scientifically literate people in a range of fields that are science, health, and technology related. There will be an increasing demand for workers who have flexible skills, a basic grasp of science and technology, and the ability to solve problems and think creatively. These are the things that quality science education provides.

Science as inquiry enriches peoples' lives. It opens the human mind to new aesthetic and intellectual pleasures and to a new appreciation of the beauty that surrounds us. Inquiry-based science education empowers people to take greater control of their lives and to face problems with courage and understanding. It liberates them to imagine new questions and to set about finding new answers. Science taught as inquiry helps develop critical thinking skills and gives practice in use of evidence in decision making.

Yet the 1990 National Assessment of Educational Progress (NAEP) survey indicates that fewer than half of fourth-grade students attend schools where science is a priority. Science is not taught frequently in schools: 28% of fourth graders reported having science once a week or less; only about half reported having science every day.

A colleague puts it this way, "Would you steal from the students in your class? But that is precisely what you are doing when you do not teach science to all students as a significant part of the core curriculum; you are stealing their future." An elementary teacher shares these insights:

I didn't realize it, but science is in the middle of just about everything. The whole curriculum is easily integrated into science or the other way around. It's certainly more meaningful than it was before when we picked words out of a book and wrote sentences to match. I thought you had to be really smart to teach science. I thought, "I don't know anything." I took geology and biology because that's what you had to take. And then I saw this stuff was fun. My friends are really amazed that I love science.

I used to just give the answers, just blurt it out. Now I'm trying to train myself to say "What do you think?" . . . Students have become more resourceful. I really saw it yesterday. They were really trying to get the answers using library references. They know now not to come up and always ask. They try to find out on their own.

And retention is there. The other day one of my students from last year came in and he said, "Oh, you folks are doing decomposition." I mean, it clicked and it stuck with him and that was a big impact to hear that it was something that was so internal in him. (Young et al., 1993, p. 22)

3. *Shift From Reading to Doing Science*

Hands-on, activity-based science instruction is well established as an effective teaching strategy (Bredderman, 1983). The most serious thing wrong with science education today is the failure to teach science built on experience. Typically, terms come first, not the experience. Students read about science or are told the facts of science by their teachers. Then we try to explain relationships between things that students don't understood in the first place. We compound the problem by attempting to teach an enormous number of facts for students to memorize (Haury & Rillero, 1992).

Professional scientists develop hypotheses and then test these ideas through repeated experiments and observations. They cannot simply "know" that something is so; they must demonstrate it. The education of students must also provide for this kind of experience, not simply to confirm the "right" answer but to investigate the nature of things and arrive at explanations that are satisfying to students and that make sense to them.

In our middle school science program we begin by doing investigations in physics, biology, and ecology. Students learn science concepts from their investigations; there are no answers in the book. The answers come from the experiences that students engage in.

If you start introducing words such as *force, mass, velocity,* or *pressure* too soon, you will confuse students. The result is that no one learns anything meaningful, not even the brightest and the best. They can pass tests, but the tests we use don't measure real learning or understanding. Such an approach develops "counterfeit knowledge"—it sounds like the real thing, but it is not real; there is no depth of understanding and, therefore, no ability to apply. Teaching science as inquiry results in the following kinds of learning in classrooms:

I can see a difference in the children. When I first taught science, you were given topics and you were given x amount of time to cover certain pages. We didn't have a lot of materials. It was basically your science book and whatever else you could come up with. And looking at pictures of things isn't all that exciting. You can look at a picture of a tree and in the book it would say, "This is a tree. There are different kinds of trees." or "This is a rabbit. There are many different kinds of rabbits." Somehow it kind of lost its zest.

Now in science we do things. A traditional science program is like someone showing you a picture of a roller coaster and saying, "Boy this is a fun ride," but experiencing science is like getting on the roller coaster and going up and down and feeling nauseous and feeling the thrill when you go up and down. You are actually experiencing it, not looking at something someone else has written down or a picture someone has taken. I think that is the best type of learning that there is.

I loved science, but it was by the book. That's where I thought we got science. Once in a while we used to do a science report on the solar system or what not, but we went through the chapters and we read about it and did discussion. I'd try to do experiment kinds of things. It certainly wasn't integrated. It was more fact science and the tests were there. We'd go through the book and I'd make leave out blanks where key vocabulary words were. Now, it's very student-centered and the children do the thinking rather than a one-right-answer kind of approach where you read the book. (Young et al., 1993, p. 19)

4. *Students Learn by Constructing Knowledge*

"We cannot teach directly, in the sense of putting fully formed knowledge into people's heads. It is our charge as teachers to help people construct powerful and scientifically correct interpretations of the world" (Resnick & Chi, 1988, p. **000**). The view of students absorbing knowledge has shifted to one of students actively constructing knowledge, called the "constructivist approach," by being involved in interpreting and understanding new content and by linking new knowledge to existing knowledge in a meaningful way.

According to Howard Gardner (1991), in his book *The Unschooled Mind*, learners come to new situations with preconceived notions. As children develop, and long before they enter school, they begin to construct sets of ideas, expectations, and explanations about the world around them. Because their ideas are different from those of science, they are often called "naive conceptions."

Naive conceptions are strongly held and must be examined and challenged in the course of instruction over time for new understandings to develop. We must take into account learners' existing conceptions yet at the same time help them to alter fundamentally their scientific misconceptions (Resnick & Chi, 1988).

Teaching for understanding requires teachers to continually diagnose student ideas and consider where they are in the process of conceptual change. Naive conceptions must be explored through experience and discussion with opportunities to test ideas, even those that are false. Ideas change only when students face evidence from nature that their naive conceptions don't work.

For younger children (K-3) it is wise to stop at observation and description. By Grades 4 through 6, students have enough experience and are developmentally ready to move beyond observation and description to creating explanations. In Grades 7 through 12, students should be continually refining their explanations based on new evidence, new ideas, and greater experience with the world.

Constructivism is based on a set of assumptions about learning that have a long developmental history. Among these are the following:

- Humans construct a unique view of the world out of personal experience
- The process of construction is incremental, involving adding to, making connections with, and modifying previously established constructs
- Constructs are normalized through interactions with others
- The process of normalization where other humans are involved constitutes teaching

Some strategies that illustrate constructivist teaching include these:

- Accepting and encouraging student initiation of ideas and student questions
- Using open-ended questions and encouraging students to elaborate on their ideas
- Encouraging students to test their own ideas, answer their own questions, hypothesize causes, and predict consequences
- Encouraging self-analysis, collecting data to support ideas, and reforming ideas in light of new experiences and new evidence

In middle school, we spend a great deal of time doing experiments involving density. Most major textbooks give only two or three pages to this very difficult concept. Density is not directly experienced. It is an abstract relationship between two more concrete ideas of mass and volume that can be directly sensed and measured. Understanding density takes many experiences and applications and requires a fundamental knowledge of mass and volume as well as the relationship of these two concepts. Because they lack direct experience with mass and volume and practice in application, most students and adults do not understand density well and cannot apply the concept.

A constructivist approach to teaching also builds student confidence and efficacy as we see in this teacher's report:

Their whole feeling of their self-esteem was raised during the year. One girl sticks in mind. She was very unsure of herself. Besides having a lot of family problems she had a very low self -esteem and seemed to be the type of child that when you called on her for an answer, would give you an off-the-wall answer. And you would think, "Where did that come from?" But instead I would ask her to explain her answer. And sure enough, when she was explaining it, it did make sense in her own way. And the rest of the children would understand what she meant and they would applaud her or say, "Yes, that is right." I guess now whenever I compare back to three years ago when we used the science, and social studies, and health books, we didn't give them enough credit for what they were really able to learn. . . . I haven't felt this much gratification in teaching since my student teaching years and first year I taught. I've been rejuvenated. (Young et al., 1993, p. 19)

5. *Learning Is Social*

Learning is interactive and occurs in a social context. Misconceptions, biases, and wrong ideas that we all hold can be corrected only if we know about them. We seem to learn best by talking through things and by explaining and teaching what we know to others, giving examples and evidence and asking questions of one another about what we don't know. Therefore, students should be talking to one another and writing about science.

In our middle school science program, for example, discussion among small groups of students as well as between students and the teacher and the organization of ideas, data, and arguments to support a particular point of view are important strategies for developing understanding. We want students to share their data, their ideas, and their explanations, just as scientists do. Every effort is made to have students ask questions and then use their questions to initiate further investigations.

But that does not mean using collaborative or cooperative teaching strategies all the time. Effective science instruction incorporates a variety of teaching strategies. Competitive activities are good for practice, recall, and review. Individual activities are appropriate when a student must learn a specific skill or concept and attainment of the goal is important to the student. Cooperative learning is most appropriate for activities calling for problem solving, divergent thinking, and inquiry. There must be an opportunity for independent exploration, as well as guided group activity, for quiet reflection and for animated discussion. Small-group work enables every individual to participate fully in activities and discussion and allows students to develop leadership skills, learn from one another, and take risks in developing their thinking.

Our vision is "to transform the classroom into a learning community where ideas are shared, evidence is used to strengthen ideas, and there is a willingness to change ideas through exploration, dialogue, and discourse" (Sivertsen, 1993, p. 7). This vision also reflects the view of science as fluid inquiry.

> So many improvements that I saw through the year that I hadn't seen in 17 years of teaching. Students didn't have as many adjustment problems to first grade as students usually do. There was no crying or wanting to go home. The day didn't seem as long for them. Children became much more responsible than I have ever seen any first graders in all the years I've been teaching. They had specific jobs to do each week, including cleaning pet cages, taking weather data, and other activities that had to be done daily. I didn't have to remind them. They would just come in and get started on their jobs. They were able to work in groups and individually. They seemed to know which was appropriate to the activities. As an observer, I could see they were all attending to the problem at hand. By working together the whole group seemed to succeed. Students would volunteer to help each other, especially in other subject areas, once they learned that they could work in groups and be successful in groups. When one child was having problems in math, another child would ask if they could help them. And indeed, they did help them. They didn't tell the answer. I could see them up

there actually teaching them how they came up with the answer. (Young et al., 1993, p. 19)

6. *Focus on Key Concepts*

According to the AAAS (1989), the science curriculum is "overstuffed and undernourished." The typical life science course for middle school students introduces over 2,000 new concepts. High school biology classes introduce more new vocabulary than typical foreign language classes.

The transformation in science curricula is from coverage of a large number of facts and terminology to a more in-depth study of fewer, major concepts (Sivertsen, 1993). Science is more than a collection of facts. It is a fabric of interconnecting ideas that enable us to interpret the world around us and guide the generation of new knowledge. Emphasis should be on sequencing instruction to intentionally build on previous experiences and connect new ideas to existing knowledge.

Using common themes of science, such as systems, cycling, conservation, energy, and change—ideas that pervade science and technology—helps students make connections. In our middle school program, we organize instruction around themes, such as understanding the local environment, the flow of matter and energy through the biosphere, and change over time. In this way, we help students make connections between substantive science concepts and build a personal construct of the scientific view of the world.

Others suggest different organizations, but the common element is that the science curriculum highlights major ideas, concepts, themes, or "big ideas" so that detailed information about science becomes connected, becomes meaningful, and contributes to success in problem solving. It is in focusing on key concepts that there is hope in the standards-based reform movement. Both AAAS and NRC have identified major unifying ideas of science and made it clear that it is the responsibility of all teachers to teach toward understanding of these connecting ideas. Focusing on such connecting ideas helps students to see the relevance of science and its applications all around them, including out of school, as we can see in these parent comments:

> My child seems to like science. I can see a difference between my child that has been involved in this kind of science and my child who has not. I think it allowed students to stretch themselves with their new knowledge. It made them think. It made me think because my child taught me. I don't usually pick up the daily paper, but it's been a must so she can check up on the weather.

> I know my child benefited from the science activities. She experienced projects that normally wouldn't be offered in the old school curriculum and had a good taste of science. She never stopped babbling about all the projects.

> She continues to watch the moon and name the phases. She keeps track of the dates on her own calendar. Science has been really stimulating for her. She always told me about the science activities and she was very conscientious about doing the home activities. (Young et al., 1993, p. 17)

7. *The Teacher as Facilitator of Learning*

"The role of the teacher is changing from one of disseminator of information to facilitator of learning. This is a more demanding role in many ways. It takes deep understanding of basic science concepts and a willingness to not always be the 'authority' to be comfortable teaching science in an experimental mode" (Sivertsen, 1993, p. 8).

This change is accompanied by the movement from students as passive receivers of information to active learners using hands-on investigations to develop manipulative, thinking, and communication skills as well as knowledge of science concepts. Such shifts in teacher and student roles is altering our views of what constitutes a learning environment. For example, typically, we now assume that students who have no questions are not learning, whereas those who have pointed and specific questions are. Thus, teachers can evaluate their teaching by asking themselves, "Are my students asking better questions?"

Similarly, quiet classes with little student talk are typically classes where little learning is occurring. We know that students can often provide correct answers, repeat definitions, and apply formulas without understanding those questions, definitions, or formulas. Real understanding enables students to explain events in their own words, give evidence and examples of scientific principles, and teach others what they know.

Teachers promote student inquiry by engaging them in problem solving, asking probing questions, and guiding discussion with the use of hands-on investigations. They focus on the important questions of science:

- How do I know?
- Why do I know?
- What do you mean?
- How do you know that? (and perhaps most important)
- How can we find out?

In our middle school program, we ask such probing questions about the nature of light and heat and the relationships between these and other forms of energy. We conduct investigations to find indirect evidence for the existence of atoms, including experiments on the analysis and synthesis of compounds. The difference is that the experience comes before learning new concepts, not after. In elementary school classrooms, we see the following happening:

There is more hands-on now. . . . (I) improved my questioning technique and as I said, it's child centered. It is better to let them discover things—they learn more than just having to memorize things. It carries over into all of the other areas of teaching, too. I can see myself questioning them about everything now.

I think that probably the one thing it has done for me is change my whole philosophy of teaching. I've been doing things much differently in my classroom than I have done in the last seventeen years. I'm not telling the children the answers. When they want to find something out, we find it out together. . . . You'll probably be able to tell by just looking around . . . how the class is being run. That they are doing it in group— the atmosphere of the room. I know my atmosphere has changed greatly. I used to be more structured. I was strict. . . . Now, I think it's freer. If you walk around the room, the children are on task, you can hear them discussing what they're supposed to be doing, and they're really involved with the activity. But it probably is a little bit louder than before. (Young et al., 1993, p. 17)

8. *Continuous Professional Development for Lifelong Learning*

The teacher is the key to improved instruction. For teachers to be successful facilitators of science learning, a great deal of support must be made available to them both within the school and from the broader professional community. They must have opportunities to exchange ideas and experiences with other teachers, reflect on their teaching, and read and apply research (Loucks-Horsley et al., 1989; Loucks-Horsley et al., 1987).

Because teaching for understanding demands a role that few teachers' preservice training provided, opportunities for inservice professional development are essential. Professional development programs that result in meaningful changes allow for intense study of and engagement with the new knowledge over an extended time period and combine theory and application, time to reflect and practice, self-study and cooperative learning (Sashkin & Egermeier, 1993; Turnbull, 1991).

We know that the most effective staff development activities

- are continuous and ongoing
- model the constructivist approach to teaching that teachers will use with their students
- provide opportunities to examine and reflect on present practices and to work with other teachers to develop and practice new approaches
- and provide good support within the group, among the group and the instructors, and from the school (Fullan, 1990; National Center on Teacher Learning, 1991)

At the Curriculum Research & Development Group, we believe that teacher inservice is so important that science materials for classroom use are available only to teachers who have received intensive instruction in their use, in the philosophy and pedagogy of the program, and in the inquiry investigations that students will engage in. We engage teachers first as learners in the same kinds of inquiry they will carry on with their students and then focus on the instructional strategies that facilitated their learning. In addition, we provide an extensive array of support services for teachers once they begin using the new approaches in their classrooms. We believe that program developers and authors too are lifelong learners and can learn how to improve practice by working with teachers in their classrooms as they implement new approaches to teaching science. Such modeling of lifelong learning at all levels provides students with a view of schooling as only one approach to intellectual development. Veteran teachers as well as novices respond to continuous learning as we see in this teacher report:

> First grade, it's all reading. And the materials we had were very few for the content subjects and it was just open the book, look at a picture, and talk about it. We knew that what we were doing in our classroom we weren't happy with. We wanted to change in some way but we didn't know where to start. We were skeptical about inquiry science and taking the training, but then as we used the activities and in the classroom we were seeing some results that we hadn't seen before. Now after three years of teaching and using an inquiry approach, I see that the philosophy has really fit in for me and it's changed my other curriculum areas too. . . .
>
> To me science is being open, not always thinking there is a right answer. Or expecting one right answer. And not always giving what we know of as the right answer. And letting the students do more of the thinking than myself. Basically, I changed my teacher style and it's still changing. (Young et al., 1993, p. 17)

9. Shift From Testing to Multidimensional Assessment

Our view of assessment is shifting dramatically to its role as the servant, not the master, of curriculum. We know from the research on learning styles, multiple intelligences, and cognitive psychology that there are many ways of knowing. Conversely, there are many ways of teaching and of assessing. The prevalence of assessments that are focused on isolated facts and not on conceptual understanding has led to a curriculum that favors facts and vocabulary. By using more authentic assessments, such as performance-based or portfolio assessment or multiple-choice tests that require thought beyond recognition and recall, more higher-order thinking skills can be assessed and students can learn through the process of assessment itself. Children must be offered many different options for communicating what they know and understand and for raising new questions about a subject (Sivertsen, 1993).

Perhaps the most compelling reason for developing multidimensional assessments is that they can provide an opportunity to appraise what society currently values but is having difficulty measuring with multiple-choice tests. We want students who have both the mastery of subject matter knowledge and the more general abilities to think, solve problems, communicate, and collaborate. Opportunities to demonstrate ideas, quantify results, and make written, oral, or visual presentations of findings and hypotheses are essential in school, as they are in science. Our very emphasis on test scores has led to a narrow definition of human abilities. If students keep portfolios and engage in investigations about water quality in the community, what information can a multiple-choice test provide about students' abilities and experiences that we could not glean better from sampling their portfolios?

The real issue is the conflict between the factory model and the community of learners model of education. Science taught as inquiry clearly values the centrality of the community of learners. In the following, a classroom teacher tells how she is struggling with this conflict:

> They can do the research. I've got to find ways to get the information that they're looking for in a manner that they can understand it. It's not that I can say at the end of the month, "This is what they all know and they have all passed this test." It's developmental and they're on their way to coming to an understanding about a lot of things. They've got curiosity and desire and confidence in their own thinking skills.
>
> Before, I would demonstrate science. Now, I won't teach a lesson unless every child has materials, each child has their hands on. You can use everyday materials. You don't have to have a science kit.
>
> I'm carefully going through questioning strategies. They have the background and inquiry gives them the sense of wanting to know more. They have become better problem solvers. (Young et al., 1993)

10. Alternative Views on Teaching Science

Our views on teaching science (or anything else) are generally based on different underlying assumptions and acceptance about the nature of learning. Today, in science education, we have several alternative views about science teaching that are often in competition with one another. Gallagher (personal communication, 1993) has described five such views of science teaching, all of which are prevalent in schools today. The traditional view of science teaching is that of an expert telling students what they need to know. I often refer to this view as the "funnel model" of education. I have this image of a funnel at the top of the learner's head, and if we just had enough time and got it just right, we could pour all the knowledge one needs to know into the funnel and we would produce an educated person. It is, unfortunately, the view often held by the general public—that teaching is pretty simple work that anyone can do if you know the information.

In a slightly more sophisticated view, teaching is seen as "organizing the content." It recognizes that teaching is a complex activity in which the teacher's job is to break down complex content into small enough chunks for students to "get it." Furthermore, the teacher's job is to present the content in an interesting and motivating way. However, we now know that for many students focusing on the parts does not give them a sense of the whole. They need to see the whole picture before the parts make sense.

A third view sees teaching as "hands-on," engaging students in the activities of science. This was a common approach of some of the post-Sputnik programs of the 1960s. Students are presented with manipulatives and expected to discover science principles and meaning from their hands-on experiences. Unfortunately, many times, the activities become ends in themselves. Engaging in many isolated, hands-on activities may be fun, but if they are not sequenced and connected in a meaningful way, little learning of any value takes place. Students are often left with an unclear picture of what the purpose of the activity was and what was supposed to be learned. We know now that real learning from such activities takes place only with significant teacher assistance.

Still another view of science teaching prevalent in the United States today is called "the learning cycle." It follows a sequence of activities that engage students in exploration, explanation, and application of scientific ideas. Students explore using hands-on activities, followed by explanation of phenomena, usually by the teacher. Then students demonstrate their understanding by applying what they have learned in a new context (Lawson, Abraham, & Renner, 1989). This view has dominated hands-on elementary science education from the 1960s to the present.

However, the learning cycle model is increasingly being challenged by a new vision of science teaching called the "co-construction of knowledge" (Pottenger, Young, Brennan, & Pottenger, 1993). Based on constructivist philosophy and inquiry teaching, this new view places teachers in the role of facilitator helping students construct meaning from phenomena they experience. At the same time, teachers continually reconstruct their own knowledge of science concepts and of how students learn.

Teaching strategies are varied and include group work, student experimentation, individual and group writing, and concept mapping—strategies that help foster understanding and application of scientific knowledge. Initial exploration is followed by extensive opportunities for students to apply their developing ideas and test them out against natural phenomena. Only after multiple exploration and application activities are students able to develop explanations that take into account their beginning naive conceptions and the evidence they have collected from their own investigations.

How is the co-construction view different from the learning cycle? In both cases, learning begins with exploration through hands-on activities. The difference lies in the shift of responsibility to students for developing understanding, for making connections, and for applying their ideas in new ways. In the co-construction view, exploration, application, and explanation are not activities controlled by the teacher; they are all student responsibilities.

The difference also lies in the amount of emphasis that developing understanding must be given. It is a slow process. It requires that teachers find ways of engaging students in multiple activities to give them many opportunities to work through their ideas and build understanding of concepts over weeks, months, and years. It is not just keeping students on task so that they memorize. It is causing them to think deeply about ideas and their meaning and to constantly test those ideas. This means repeated use of the key concepts of science in a spiral curriculum. Significant ideas such as buoyancy, density, states of matter, pressure, force, work, and energy, once introduced, are revisited again and again during the course of the year and from one year to the next in different contexts and with different connections. In such a repeated exposure over time, students continually reconstruct and refine meaning. Ideas and explanations are fluid, in a constant state of change, just as they are in science.

Summary

The vision of science in a Renaissance school is about creating sequences of instruction in which students actively engage in science as a way of knowing about the world around them. It is an attempt to present science in the classroom as science is practiced—as one way of describing, explaining, and appreciating the natural world.

Science is experiential and it is social. Therefore, students should be engaged in hands-on activities, in communication with other students and the teacher, that build on their prior knowledge and skills to reach new levels of understanding and concept development. Investigations should include both stable and fluid inquiries so that students can appreciate the dynamic, evolving nature of science and develop their own skills for lifelong learning.

References

American Association for the Advancement of Science. (1989). *Science for all Americans.* Washington, DC: Author.

Bergman, J. (1983). What is science? *Creation Research Society Quarterly, 20,* 39-42.

Bohm, D., & Peat, D. (1987). *Science, order, and creativity.* New York: Bantam.

Bredderman, T. (1983). Effects of activity-based elementary science on student outcomes: A quantitative synthesis. *Review of Educational Research, 53,* 499-518.

Bremer, J. (1962). *What is science? Notes on the nature of science.* New York: Harcourt, Brace & World.

Eisner, E. W. (1995). Standards for American schools: Help or hindrance? *Phi Delta Kappan, 76*(10), 758-764.

Fullan, M. (1990). Staff development, innovation, and institutional development. In B. Joyce (Ed.), *Changing school culture through staff development.* Alexandria, VA: Association for Supervision and Curriculum Development.

Gardner, H. (1991). *The unschooled mind: How children think and how schools should teach.* New York: Basic Books.

Gould, S. J. (1986). "Creation science" is an oxymoron. *Skeptical Inquirer, 11,* 152-153.

Haury, D., & Rillero, P. (1992). *Hands-on approaches to science teaching.* Columbus, OH: ERIC Clearinghouse for Science, Mathematics, and Environmental Education.

Lawson, A. E., Abraham, M. R., & Renner, J. W. (1989). *A theory of instruction: Using the learning cycle to teach science concepts and thinking skills* (Monograph of the National Association for Research in Science Teaching, No. 1). Cincinnati, OH: National Association for Research in Science Teaching.

Loucks-Horsley, S., Carlson, M. O., Brink, L. H., Horowitz, P., Marsh, D. D., Pratt, H. J., Roy, K. R., & Worth, K. (1989). *Developing and supporting teachers for elementary school science education.* Andover, MA: National Center for Improving Science Education.

Loucks-Horsley, S., Harding, C., Arbuckle, M. A., Murray, L. B., Dubea, C., & Williams, M. K. (1987). *Continuing to learn: A guidebook for teacher development.* Andover, MA: Regional Laboratory for Educational Improvement of the Northeast and Islands and the National Staff Development Council.

Mechling, K., & Oliver, D. L. (1983). *Science teaches basic skills.* Washington, DC: National Science Teachers Association.

National Center for Research on Teacher Learning. (1992). *Findings on learning to teach.* East Lansing, MI: Author.

Padover, S. K. (1943). *The complete Jefferson.* New York: Duell, Sloan, and Pearce.

Pottenger, F. M., Young, D. B., Brennan, C. A., & Pottenger, L. M. (1993). *DASH instructional guide.* Honolulu: University of Hawaii, Curriculum Research & Development Group.

Resnick, L. B., & Chi, M. T. (1988). Cognitive psychology and science learning. In M. Druger (Ed.), *Science for the fun of it: A guide to informal science education.* Washington, DC: National Science Teachers Association.

Sarason, S. B. (1990). *The predictable failure of educational reform: Can we change course before it's too late?* San Francisco: Jossey-Bass.

Sashkin, M., & Egermeier, J. (1993). *School change models and processes: A review and synthesis of research and practice.* Washington, DC: U.S. Department of Education, Office of Educational Research and Improvement.

Schwab, J. J. (1966). The teaching of science as enquiry. In *The teaching of science.* Cambridge, MA: Harvard University Press.

Sivertsen, M. (1993). *Transforming ideas for teaching and learning science.* Washington, DC: U.S. Department of Education, Office of Educational Research and Improvement.

Turnbull, B. (1991). *Using research knowledge in school improvement.* Washington, DC: U.S. Department of Education, Office of Educational Research and Improvement.

Young, D. B., Lai, M. K., Brennan, C. A., Gallagher, J., Taylor, A. B., Hallinen, J., Ledford, C., Mattheis, F., Weaver, H. P., Hoover, K., Evans, A., & Kazemek, F. (1993). *Developmental approaches in science and health (DASH): A report on seven case studies assessing effects on students and teachers.* Honolulu, HI: Curriculum Research & Development Group, University of Hawaii.

11

Paper Thinking

The Process of Writing

Peggy M. Luidens

My fear about the process of writing started a long time ago. As a schoolgirl, I froze in the face of writing assignments. I didn't understand how to convert a blank sheet of paper into a page of meaningful prose. I just didn't get it! I didn't know where to begin, and I didn't understand how to go about writing.

My first formal writing class was as a senior in high school. By then, my fear of writing was well developed. My anxieties had been shaped by misperceptions about what writing actually entailed. I had been taught that it was mostly a mechanical process of following rules and guidelines down a well-worn path; it was producing a thesis that explained an esoteric topic that had been assigned by my teacher and was of no particular consequence to me. Just as its content was "teacher-driven," so too was the format. I had come to believe that writing involved the inevitable hemorrhaging red pen, bleeding over my lines with all sorts of correct "teacher language." I thought of writing as that time in the school schedule analogous to swallowing bitter-tasting medicine. I took it because it was supposed to be good for me. I thought this was writing.

I thought wrong!

I have since come to realize that instead of being a mechanical exercise in rule following, *writing is thinking*. It is about believing that you have something to say. It is about discovering, analyzing, synthesizing, and evaluating your ideas. It is about unfolding, in print, images that are swirling inside your mind.

It is about being vulnerable by revealing your thinking, at that moment and on that occasion, for others to read. In its fullest measure, all these make up the process of writing.

Donald Murray (1987) maintains that writing starts "with an individual human being's thoughts and feelings. Much of the most important writing takes place before words begin to appear on blank paper" (pp. 2-3). He continues,

> Writers write to learn, to explore, to discover, to hear themselves saying what they did not expect to say. Words are symbols for what we learn. They allow us to play with information, to make connections and patterns, to put together and take apart and put together again, to see what experience means. In other words, to think. (p. 3)

Thinking is an elusive concept. We can't hold it, touch it, or smell it. Yet it is the heartbeat of writing. What we can hold, however, is the manifestation of our thinking—the written piece—the artifact that reveals the thinking. Far from being a life-draining dose of medicine, writing is a life-giving experience.

Still Pictures

Written pieces are analogous to snapshots. They are the *still* shots that hold, for the moment, dynamic ideas stationary in a coherent order. They represent the best of one's thinking at that moment. As with snapshots, written pieces drive further thinking about dynamic events. Like snapshots, written pieces are stationary images while our minds are racing. That is their strength.

Consider the implications of this strength for a few moments.

While I sit at my desk and tap the keys of the word processor, I glance away at a special picture—taken at the recent wedding of a young friend. The bride and groom and my two daughters are smiling out at me from the photo, which is held grandly in a gold-gilded frame. Sometimes I just smile back, but often my mind jumps from their faces to the love I have for them. Depending on what's going on in my head, the picture interacts with my thinking in different ways. At one moment, my thinking drifts back in time from the 20-something bride to the young girl who was once our baby-sitter and the special love of my children's lives. She brought great delight to them.

Then my mind shifts again. Today, the bride is a beautiful young woman with her college degree in hand, and she is beginning the adventures of adult life with her husband-lover. There is so much promise in their squinting smiles and almost-grownup postures.

At other reflective moments, I focus only on my daughters, and I'm re-minded of the passage of time. At other times, my eyes are drawn to the details of the picture. The backdrop is an arched window of an 1888 church with its Gothic curves and balanced symmetry. I muse quietly; if only life could be so symmetrical and ordered.

Written artifacts—the still pictures of a writer's thinking—have much the same impact on both writers and readers. The still is a catalyst reminding us as readers of the crescendo of ideas that came together in coherent patterns to create the initial piece—and that point to new learning in our lives. The reading of a piece stirs our thinking. For writers, the still represents the best presentation of their ideas at that moment, whereas for the readers, the written piece presents the challenges of examination, analysis, and evaluation. For both parties, writing is about thinking.

In this chapter, I hope to accomplish two goals:

1. to invite the reader to explore with me the act of writing through two Writing Process lenses: (a) consideration of the *various stages of the Writing Process* that a writer encounters along the way from a blank page to a completed piece; and (b) examination of the *mental dispositions* that enable a writer to bring meaning to the paper
2. to examine a sample written exercise and reflect on the ways that the writing process in that assignment has or has not been effectively influenced by the teacher's awareness of the mental dispositions

Arthur Costa and Robert Garmston (1995) describe states of mind as the "the passions which drive, influence, motivate and inspire our intellectual capacities" (p. 2). As writers and teachers of writing, we must pay as much attention to the manifestations of thinking along the writing journey as we do to the finished, written piece. Our job when we write and when we engage students in writing is to be simultaneously conscious of what we learn about the ideas and concepts we (and our students) write about and about the mental dispositions we exercise as we go about the process of writing.

The theme of these volumes, Process as Content, challenges us to acknowledge and verify the types of thinking that authors—whether ourselves or our students—engage in as they write. In addition, we must consider the authors' capacity to transfer what they have learned about being writers to other writing tasks. Rather than placing all the emphasis on the written artifact, it is important that the *process of writing* becomes the *product to be examined and assessed*.

Let's examine how this might be done.

Writing as Process

Choose from a list of five topics and write a paper. It should be at least 15 pages long, and it will be due in 5 weeks.

For some of us, these words parrot interminable assignments from our school days. They exemplify the writing experience as a magical mystery gamble: by gosh or by golly, pulling the words out of a hat—somehow the message would magically appear, and a piece would be delivered up.

We've come a long way! During the last 25 years, the writing process has been defined, discussed, and dissected in myriad ways. The focus has shifted dramatically from an onerous and mysterious assignment to an invitation to writers to be conscious of the process that gets their thoughts on paper. Researchers are much more aware of the rehearsing, (multiple) drafting, and revising tasks involved in the writing process (Graves, 1978). Peter Elbow (1973) describes the process of writing as

> an organic, developmental process in which you start writing at the very beginning—before you know your meaning at all—and encourage your words gradually to change and evolve. Only at the end will you know what you want to say or the words you want to say it with. You should expect yourself to end up somewhere different from where you started. Meaning is not what you start out with, but what you end up with. Control, coherence, and knowing your mind are not what you start out with but what you end up with. Think of writing then not as a way to transmit a message but as a way to grow and cook a message. Writing is a way to end up thinking something you couldn't have started out thinking. (p. 15)

Others echo this interactive, dynamic message. Tom Romano, author of *Clearing the Way* (1987), borrows the language of Mayher, Lester, and Pradl, who describe the process of writing as *"percolating, drafting, revising, editing and publishing"* (italics in original; p. 55). In her classic discussion of writing, *In the Middle*, Nancie Atwell (1987) provides this cryptic message that she displays on a large poster in her classroom:

WHAT WRITERS DO

WRITERS:

- rehearse (find an idea)
- draft one
- confer
- draft two/revise
- confer . . .
- decide the content is set
- self-edit
- teacher-edit
- final copy/go public (p. 127)

For each of these authors, the emphasis is on the dynamic process involved in the exercise of writing. It is not sufficient to rush, unthinking, to an end product; rather, it is imperative that writers give careful consideration to the crafting stages along the way. We tip our hats to these scholars. Along with others, they helped to crack the code of the writing process. The structure these writers have framed comes from analyses of their own process of writing and a synthesis of the hundreds of observations they have made about the students they have taught.

Yet a cautionary note is important. Each of these authorities would agree that his or her description of the process is not to be taken as a step-by-step model or recipe. Each would reject such a static model as not reflecting the dynamism of writing. Instead, they have provided a platform for understanding the writing process on the basis of their experiences and research. In my own case, they enabled a fledgling English teacher to articulate the illusive process of writing and, more important, to acknowledge that my responsibility to my students was to unravel, with them, their own thinking processes as they write. Plumbing these thinking processes can be accomplished only when teachers and students are engaged frequently and intentionally with the writing craft.

What a gift to teachers—and what a burden! The teaching of writing takes on far-reaching implications. This is exemplified in Lucy Calkins's first book, *Lessons From a Child* (1983). She describes researchers from all over asking her questions about the research data she and her colleagues were collecting about writers and writing. One of her subjects was a schoolgirl named Susie, who Calkins followed for several elementary grades. Calkins describes one question that related to Susie's writing progress:

> It was Howard Gardner who asked the simplest, most difficult question of all: "What is Susie trying to do when she writes?" he asked. "What are her goals, her concepts of good writing?" . . . Gardner's question has been omnipresent, for Susie's intentions were at the root of her activities. Because her writing involved an interplay of creation and criticism, her writing was propelled by concern for making meaning, . . . and it was guided and shaped by concepts of good writing. Susie built and rebuilt her sense of good writing while she operated within it. (p. 142)

When considering the parts of the writing process, the reader might do well to visualize an artist painting a picture. Instead of working systematically from the top, left-hand corner of the canvas across to the top, right-hand corner, and then down the canvas, the artist engages in a series of activities: application and reflection, revision and reflection, close-in painting and long-range perspective, balance and color. Each step entails action and reaction without prescribed sequence.

Calkins's (1983) final words about Susie's conceptual development between grades 3 & 4 were these:

> Just as Susie's process became, in time, less systematic and packaged, so too her sense of the components of good writing became less absolute, less discrete. "This feels wrong," she'd say. She didn't elaborate with reasons, for her once clear distinctions between good and bad had become more tentative. Susie's sense of good writing was no longer a preset list of absolute values. "It's better now," she'd say. "I can tell because I listen to it, and I look it over. It just feels better." (p. 151)

During the last 15 years, it has become apparent that teachers of writing have a different homework required of them. No longer is teachers' primary work the marking of technical errors or the rewording of students' awkward prose or the inserting of paragraph marks. Rather, their tasks are much more complex and much more compelling. They are about having students unravel and verify the process of writing in which they are engaged. It's about collecting two artifacts, the written piece and the reflections on the personalized process, which the students are using to transform a blank page into a transcript.

As you can imagine, the latter can easily fall by the wayside. No matter how articulate the gurus are about this reflective piece, it is easy to grab on to the written text and to dismiss the process that has been experienced. For a variety of reasons, as I visit schools throughout North America, I see little evidence of the valuing of the process of writing as valuable product. What I see more often is a lock-step method of mechanically going through the steps of writing with little reflection on the process involved.

Certainly this lack of attention is not for lack of conviction on the part of the experts. Donald Murray (1989) underscores the importance of reflection on the process of writing:

> It is vital that the process is drawn out of the class experience so the class learns together that each writer is capable of identifying and solving writing problems. Learning will not stop with this class. This class will not be dependent on this teacher; this class will graduate individuals who know, through their own experience, that they can respond, rationally and skillfully, to the demands of the writing tasks they will face in the years ahead. (pp. 25-26)

Nancie Atwell (1987), who seemed to concretize the writing process through cryptic notes on poster paper, is cautious to say that she displays the poster for only 2 weeks at the beginning of her school year because she feels this is enough time for her students to have a general understanding of the procedures and some of the language of the writing workshop: "I want them to make their own decisions about what to do next as writers by looking at and thinking about pieces of their writing" (p. 127).

Our job as educators is about cultivating writers so that they will have understanding of the process in which they are engaged, along with the skill to pull it off. As an old adage of the classroom goes, "What gets checked, gets done." The challenge for teachers of writing is to treat the process as a product, just as they do for the final paper. Indeed, in the long run it will be this process-product that will carry a student through subsequent tasks.

Writing as Mental Dispositions

In Chapter 1 of this volume, Costa and Liebmann underscore the radical cognitive shift that accompanies the notion of "process as content":

> Understanding the process-content dynamic requires a fundamental shift in perceptions of what learning, teaching, and schooling are about. It is a shift from valuing right answers as the purpose for learning to knowing how to behave when we *don't* know answers.

In the writing process, this means that students need to know how to behave when the blank sheet is staring at them. They need to know how to respond when their ideas run dry or when the writing doesn't connect and how to go about designing and mending language. This requires a framework for teachers and students to hold on to and by which they can check their progress.

The framework that I have found to be particularly useful is Costa and Garmston's five dispositions of the mind: consciousness, efficacy, interdependence, flexibility, and craftspersonship. I believe these states of mind are useful catalyst/energy sources that fuel human thinking in different ways. Through the years, a group of us from the Institute for Intelligent Behavior have been refining our understanding of these catalysts.

Briefly, Costa and Garmston (1995) describe these dispositions as follows:

> **Consciousness:** Humans uniquely strive to monitor and reflect on our own thoughts and actions.
> **Efficacy:** Humans quest for continuous, life-long learning, self-empowerment, mastery, and control.
> **Flexibility:** Humans endeavor to change, adapt, and expand their repertoire of response patterns.
> **Interdependence:** Humans need reciprocity and are inclined to become one with the community.
> **Craftsmanship:** Humans yearn to become clearer, more elegant, precise, congruent, and integrated thinkers and actors. (p. 2)

Ponder with me these five mental dispositions as they fold into the writing process.

Consciousness

The mental disposition of consciousness is at the heart of the writing process. As we compose, we bring to our conscious minds the ideas, experiences, and feelings that we have collected about a topic or event. Through writing, these perceptions become tangible. Murray (1987) encourages writers to be conscious, not just of the material under consideration (represented in the "ideas, experiences, and feelings" mentioned above) but especially of their personal model of writing. He describes his own writing process as encompassing several steps: collecting, focusing, ordering, developing, and clarifying. This is not a linear process but rather a recursive one (p. 6ff.; see also 1989, p. 57).

One dimension of consciousness is being aware of the prior circumstances or actions that set the stage to write. As I compose this passage, I am conscious of the process I am using: (a) I had something I wanted to write about, something I felt passionate about: I wanted to fold the writing process into these mental dispositions and to expand on the notion of process as content; (b) I brainstormed all the words about these concepts that held significance for me so that I could see the full range of related concepts before I organized my thinking; (c) I reread some of my mentors' writings about writing. Calkins, Graves, Murray, and Atwell always inspire me and help me get focused. These readings seem to refresh my brain and give me confidence to begin.

Each of us has rehearsal behaviors and procrastination behaviors when we get ready to undertake a task. Being conscious about one's start-up rituals can make the difference between time well spent and time wasted. We all need approach ramps that get us over the starting hump. For some of us, each day can present a starting hump. I remember when my husband was writing his doctoral dissertation. Every day, before he began to write, he played solitaire for about 30 minutes. It was his opening ritual. Warm-up activities and readiness rituals are part of one's work. Students need to be invited to be conscious about how they approach their tasks. They need to look for and know what their readiness rituals are. "Just do it" doesn't always work.

An organizing technique in which I consciously engage is webbing. Once I have brainstormed a list of topics, concepts, authors, and so forth, I structure my thinking by sketching a web of these words and phrases, connecting related concepts and sources. I tend to think in visual terms, and this task of arranging related concepts on a page enables me "to see" the connections more clearly. This helps me concretize the initial flood of ideas that are swirling in my head. It also shows me I have something cooking. If the web looks slim, I do more of what Murray (1989) refers to as "collecting" (p. 57).

Next, I write some beginning lines as introductions. I usually write something personal that gets me connected with the piece. These introductory comments will look very, very different when I am done. Indeed, many of them wind up on the editorial floor. What is important now is to get me on the road. Starting to write, for me, often happens in fits and starts, much like the old Model T Ford that must be cranked up and typically has false starts before it actually gets rolling. For me, the writing process is initially a cranking process.

After my initial start, which may even turn out to be a false start, I outline what I'm about to say. Then I proceed to write as fast as I can to get the larger conceptual pieces jotted down. I make notes as I go along to check resources that need to be referenced and to designate key ideas that need elaboration. If I'm writing about something I've been thinking about for some time, this approach works well. If I'm writing about something for which I need more background, however, the marginal reading and research notes become imperative. As I write, I keep saying to myself, "get it down and don't stop to worry about the technical parts of the language. Maintain the energy and the flow of thinking. Don't interrupt that thinking process." This flies in the face of my training, which stressed the mechanics of the process to the extent that I would continually get bogged down in dictionaries and reference sources.

Consciousness about the process is imperative for teachers as well as for students. Teachers of writing need to practice and model the craft and design their own metaphors and personal understandings of the process to query students and lend insights into what they are doing.

Traditionally, teachers have been trained to be conscious only about perfecting the writing craft—paying particular attention to the stylistic and technical parts of the language. My plea is that teachers will become conscious of where the student-writers are throughout the journey of writing. Furthermore, I hope that teachers will be so aware of their own writing experience that they will develop vital metaphors that can enhance the students' self-awareness.

Questions, Questions, Questions

I thought it might be helpful for teachers if I developed sample questions to illustrate some of the issues considered in each of the mental disposition sections: consciousness, efficacy, flexibility of thinking, interdependence, and craftspersonship. The questions follow each section. It seemed appropriate to formulate these questions first to articulate what teachers want to understand about their students, and then to pose the questions in student-friendly terms. There are certainly no limits to the number of questions one could generate within this mental disposition.

These questions are merely to jump-start your thinking. Their intention is to elicit information about the mental dispositions students use in the writing process; about personal reactions and feelings they are having about their identity as writers; about the analytical thinking they do when they examine their work up close; and about predictions, goals, and future applications for their writing.

Consciousness Questions

Teachers might consider asking their students and themselves the following questions to evoke consciousness about the writer's self in relationship to the writing process. In addition to these set pieces, teachers should feel free to design other questions that would most probe students' consciousness about themselves as writers.

1. UNDERSTANDING THE WRITING PROCESS	Teacher Question (TQ): How do students describe their own processes of writing? Student Question (SQ): Tell me what processes you use to go from a blank page to a completed piece. Describe the steps you go through when you are writing.
2. RESEARCH QUESTIONS	TQ: How do students know when they have sufficient information for their text? What do they do if they don't have enough information? What are students' favorite strategies when they need more information? SQ: When do you know that you have sufficient information for your text writing to begin? What helps you determine that amount of information? What are your favorite ways of retrieving more information when you need it for a piece? Do you look for specific types of information, or do you

just expand your text to respond to the information that is most readily available?

**3.
ROADBLOCKS**

TQ: Students can experience roadblocks at a variety of intervals in the writing process. What do students do when they get stuck?

SQ: What do you do when you get stuck? How do you get back on track with your writing?

**4.
GETTING STARTED**

TQ: What approach ramps or rehearsal activities do students use when they start a piece? What setting, tools, and/or atmosphere is most conducive to a student's positive productivity?

SQ: When you get ready to write, what do you need to make it happen? What does your writing space look like? What "stuff" do you surround yourself with to get the job done? Do you have to have your pencils sharpened and your sheets of paper in front of you? Do you like music in the background? Is there a special place in which you like to work? What starter techniques get your ideas from your head to the paper?

**5.
SELF-ASSESSMENT**

TQ: What parts of the writing process are easy and what parts are hard for students? How can teachers support them in their struggles and encourage them to build on their strengths?

SQ: As you think back over your experiences as a writer, what parts of the writing process are your strengths and with what parts do you struggle? What is it that makes some parts easy, and what is it that makes other parts hard? What type of support, encouragement and celebration would you particularly appreciate from your teacher?

**6.
CONFERENCING
COMMENTS**

TQ: When students invite others to read or listen to a draft, what types of response are they inviting? What do they want to know from the reader? How can their teacher support their writing?

SQ: What types of feedback do you ask for from your readers when they read your early drafts? What are the most helpful types of advice you can receive from your readers to extend your thinking and not shut your thinking down?

**7.
FINISHED PIECE**

TQ: How do students know when a piece is done? What do they hope the piece will accomplish and how will they verify its success?

SQ: How do you decide that one of your pieces is done? What do you do to verify if the piece has achieved what you set out to communicate to your readers?

Efficacy

Efficacy, as related to the writing process, is the disposition of writers believing that they have something worthwhile to say. It is proactively implementing the strategies needed to commit these ideas to paper. Efficacious writers don't hesitate to seek out authorities, whether personal or informational, that may lend their expertise to overcome the challenges the writers encounter. This also involves seeking other resources when they are needed.

Efficacious writers have a sense of internal locus of control, taking responsibility for their own compositions. They cope with writing opportunities and with bringing these opportunities to fruition. They are not afraid to look at their task from multiple vantage points and to ascertain that they are accomplishing what they set out to do. The opposite of efficacy is powerlessness.

One of the most difficult aspects of writing for me as a young writer was my lack of ownership of the subject of my writings. I felt powerless to select the topic about which I was to write; there always seemed to be a precanned topic ("what I did last summer," "the most impressive person I have ever met," "a major U.S. battle," and so on). Central to efficacy is the sense of writers that they are the architects of the matter to be covered. This enhances the authors' commitment as well as awareness of the process being undertaken.

Efficacy Questions

Teachers might consider the following questions to learn about the degree of efficacy students have about themselves as writers.

1. TOPIC OWNERSHIP	TQ: What sense of ownership and interest does the student have in relationship to the topic?
	SQ: How do you feel about this topic? What is it about this topic that invites you to write about it? Have you thought about this topic before?
2. BELIEVING THEY HAVE SOMETHING TO SAY	TQ: What evidence do the writers show to verify they have something to say and are targeting appropriate audiences?
	SQ: For whom are you writing this piece? Why did you choose these ideas to communicate to this group of readers?
3. IDENTITY AS WRITERS	TQ: What competencies do the students exhibit that verify they are writers? Competencies might include knowing how to get started, knowing how to problem solve when ideas are not forthcoming,

exhibiting eagerness to invite others to read a draft and to participate in conferencing, and showing receptivity to the readers' questions and perceptions about a piece.

SQ: As a writer, what parts of the process are you able to do well? As you approach writing, what do you say or do for yourself to ensure that you can successfully complete the writing task? When you get bogged down with your research and/or writing, what do you say or do for yourself that gets you over the hump? What do you say to yourself when readers don't necessarily applaud your writing? To whom or to what resources do you go to fuel your thoughts?

4.
RESEARCHING
THE UNKNOWN

TQ: What are the students' willingness and capacity to research their subjects for information that is not known? What are the students' range of resources when digging into a topic and collecting information?

SQ: How do you decide if you need more information? How do you push yourself to find out what you don't know? How do you encourage yourself to dig into resources that may be unfamiliar or scary to you (personal interviews, World Wide Web, etc.)?

Flexibility

In writing, flexibility of thinking is a disposition of looking at writing from multiple points of view. One aspect of this flexibility is thinking about the audience and what the audience would find most useful. Writers soon learn that they are not writing only for themselves. Rather, there is a target readership "out there" whose interest must be engaged and whose understanding must be advanced.

One way the writers can learn to be aware of readers' concerns occurs when others read and respond to early drafts. Their insights and reactions may surprise the writers. Indeed, their comments may lead their work in entirely new and unexpected directions. Writers need to be flexible enough to evaluate and potentially follow those new insights and leads. Although, at first, other readers may be the best agents for initiating this flexibility, experienced writers learn to take the role of the reader and adjust the script accordingly.

Flexibility also involves what Kurt Vonnegut might describe as "having the guts to cut." Frequently, as one writes, ideas come tumbling out, often overlapping or with no clear connection to each other. It is always tempting to force everything into the written piece; after all, all the concepts and ideas were generated by the same processes of brainstorming and reflecting. Nevertheless, it is important to be able to separate the valuable contributions from the more tangential material. This calls on writers to exercise judicious cutting—always a painful experience.

On the other hand, flexibility in the matter of writing is often analogous to silly putty. Written material regularly needs to be stretched and shaped and remolded in a variety of ways. In particular, elaboration of initial ideas for greater clarity calls on writers to show dexterous flexibility.

In the end, being flexible in writing permits writers to move with the dynamics of the pieces being written. It lets the writers continue to be engaged in a thinking dialogue with the piece, shifting and bolstering where it becomes appropriate to do so.

Flexibility of Thinking Questions

Teachers might consider these questions to evoke students' flexibility of thinking about their writing endeavors.

1. MULTIPLE AUDIENCES	TQ: What audiences do your students consider when they write? SQ: What audiences are you targeting with this piece? What writing genres (play, poem, prose, etc.) could you use when you put your ideas together? What other audiences might be interested in this piece?
2. TOPICS AND GENRES	TQ: It seems important to have a sense about how students are perceiving themselves as flexible writers. In our growing-up years, we often stick to topics and writing genres we are most comfortable using. How do students gradually encourage themselves to become flexible with their styles, their genres, and their topics? SQ: What writing genres do you like best and in which ones haven't you given yourself much practice? What has discouraged you from choosing other genres? How do you go about challenging yourself to try something different with your writing? How do you like to be stretched and challenged with your writing? What is something you are experimenting with in writing? When you experiment with something new, how do you encourage yourself to keep going even when it's not easy? What genre would be a stretch for you as a writer?
3. REHEARSAL STRATEGIES	TQ: What rehearsal techniques (finding ideas) do students have as part of their repertoire? What opportunities do students have to experiment with different rehearsal techniques? Some

students primarily web their ideas, others have little notebooks to jot ideas down, some use note cards, some brainstorm and categorize ideas, some make outlines, some talk with others about the ideas swirling around in their head, some just talk to themselves, and some just start writing.

SQ: What variety of rehearsal techniques do you use to collect your ideas? With what other rehearsal techniques might you experiment?

4.
ANALYSIS FROM MULTIPLE PERSPECTIVES

TQ: It seems appropriate to have students analyze their writing from multiple vantage points. What are the multiple perspectives students use to analyze whether the writing is accomplishing what the authors intended?

SQ: When you read your piece, how do you think it sounds from your audience's perspective? What other audiences might be interested in this piece? How would you design your piece differently to suit other audiences? Are there other ways you would write your piece if it was designed for different audiences? How is this piece similar to or different from other pieces you have written?

5.
PERCEIVING THEMSELVES AS FLEXIBLE WRITERS

TQ: To gauge the connections students are making about themselves as writers and to have them want to extend themselves are two goals that often challenge teachers. What are students learning about themselves as writers? What is the next step to extend their capacity as flexible writers?

SQ: What are you learning about yourself as a writer? What are several different writing topics and genres you could design to extend your capacity as a writer? What reading genres have you never read, and what influence might they have on you as a writer? What consequences do you experience when you experiment with different audiences and different writing styles? How does your participation in different reading genres influence your writing style? What reading genres, authors, and classes have influenced your writing style? When you think about the styles you use as a writer, are there some types of writing you have never done, and which ones would you be willing to try? What are some goals you have for yourself as a writer?

Interdependence

A mental disposition suggested in the foregoing comments about flexibility is interdependence. Interdependence recognizes the importance of others in relation to oneself. In writing, this means that interdependent writers seek out others both as resources and as respondents to written pieces. Realizing that written pieces are dialogues between the writers and the readers, the former depends on the full engagement of the latter to be successful in their writing. These respondents, who have been chosen on a variety of bases, invite writers to reanalyze, reevaluate, and resynthesize their work. Readers bring unique perspectives and experiences with which they challenge the writers' own thinking. This forces writers to consider carefully the comments readers have made in light of their initial intentions. Was the intended message communicated effectively? Did the written pieces say to the readers what the writers wanted said? This part of the writing process is typically labeled *conferencing*. It is generally considered one of the most important steps in the writing process.

Interdependent Thinking Questions

Teachers might consider these questions that evoke interdependent thinking by their students.

1. INVITING FEEDBACK	TQ: At what points in the writing process do the students elicit responses from others about a piece?
	SQ: During the process of your writing, when do you request others to read and respond to your work? About what aspects of your writing do you ask people to give you feedback? In what format do you appreciate responses to your work? Whom do you ask to participate in conferencing with you? Who else might you ask to read your piece? When you ask people to give you feedback, what specific directions do you give so they know what to look for and what to comment on? How frequently do you seek out others while you are writing? What advantages do you see in conferencing with others?
2. RECEIVING FEEDBACK	TQ: Putting ideas together on paper makes many students feel vulnerable. What do your students need to support and enhance their growth as writers in a nonthreatening environment? How do your students interpret responses from you and their classmates as they test their writing with real audiences?
	SQ: What concerns do you have when receiving feedback from others? When another student or teacher gives you responses about your work,

what reactions do you have? What do you like about getting feedback from others? What do you find less desirable about other people's feedback? What are the benefits and what are the disadvantages to working with others when you write? What effects do conversations about writing have on you as a writer? What ways do you appreciate feedback from others about your written piece?

3.
GIVING FEEDBACK

TQ: We learn in reciprocity to others. Students invite each other to engage in conferencing about their writing. What protocols do they establish so the recipient of the feedback gets maximum mileage from the exchange?

SQ: How do you go about finding out what other authors want you to consider as you read their pieces? How do you inquire about the manner and format in which your writer would like to receive your feedback? How do you go about giving feedback to classmates?

4.
CODESIGNING

TQ: If students could design optimum ways they would grow as writers, what would they say?

SQ: If you want to take advantage of interacting with your teacher and classmates about your writing, what design would best fit your learning style? To maximize your growth as a writer, how would you design writing assignments to fit your learning style?

Craftsmanship

Craftsmanship is the disposition that involves refining the written piece in preparation for its dissemination. It includes both stylistic and technical editing. This is the point when fussiness comes into play.

When engaged in craftsmanship, writers are striving to attain written pieces that comply with the appropriate grammatical, structural, and linguistic requirements. There is no way to get around this crucial stage. What the writing process teaches, however, is that it should not be the sole criterion on which writing is assessed, nor should it be the only focus of writers. Indeed, if this disposition is the only one that engages the writers' minds, then the full richness of writing will be lost on those writers.

Craftsmanship Questions

Teachers might consider these questions to evoke the degree students perceive themselves as craftspersons of language.

1. THE WORK SPACE	TQ: All crafts use space and tools to get the job done. When your students "set up shop" for writing, what does it look like?
	SQ: Where is your favorite writing space? With what stuff do you surround yourself when you write? Some writers have prime writing times when they are most productive: When is your ideal time?
2. THE WRITING PROCESS	TQ: How do your students generate ideas, write, and then edit their work for stylistic and technical accuracy? In what ways do you ascertain the personal achievements students are making in this aspect of the writing process?
	SQ: How do you generate ideas for your writing? How do you choose what writing genre you will use for your piece? When you are researching a topic, what resources do you primarily use and how do you record the information that is pertinent? How do you get started writing your first draft? After you engage in conferencing with someone about your piece, how do you integrate the new ideas that may have been generated with the original text? What process do you use to edit your work for technical and stylistic accuracy?
3. PERSEVERANCE	TQ: Students' perceptions of the technical parts of the language are crucial. It is common for students to have rich ideas yet lack the labor and perseverance to perfect a piece. How do your students feel about how they are doing as writers who are not reluctant to go public with their work?
	SQ: How do you feel about your ability to take a piece to completion? How do you like editing your own work? What do you like and what do you dislike about the editing process? How might you take what's difficult in the writing process and turn it into an easy thing?
4. SELF-ASSESSMENT	TQ: It is important for students to self-assess their capacity to take a piece to completion. As you think about your students, what parts of the writing process have been achieved, and what parts need bolstering?
	SQ: As you look at your work for stylistic and technical accuracy, which aspects provide you the most difficulty, and to what do you attribute to that phenomenon? With what do you have the

most success, and to what do you attribute that? What methods work best for you when retrieving information and storing it in a usable fashion until you need it? How well do you integrate new insights, ideas, and audience feedback into your text?

5.
REFINEMENT

TQ: It is important for students to have a sense of their own progress with the writing process and to design learning plans to accelerate the parts of the craft on which they need to concentrate. What do your students say are their next steps as writers?

SQ: What type of writing do you want to practice that will encourage your self-expression? What topic would be interesting for you to investigate and communicate to an audience of your choice?

A Concrete Example

As we look at each of the five states of mind, consider the following writing experience. Notice how the apparently random process of creativity oscillates between points of clarity and those of uncertainty. Notice the dynamic process involved, as the author selects first one focus and then another, and then melds the information and perspectives into her final product.

A tenth grade English class, in which one student was my daughter Sara, recently was given an assignment to compose a research paper on the topic of each writer's own choosing.

Sara's teacher said,

> Make sure you pick a topic that interests you. This is an opportunity to take something you're curious about and write a research paper on it. This assignment will take us about 6 weeks. Our class time will be spent retrieving information in the school library, taking notes on note cards, learning about bibliographical notation, and then synthesizing notes into an interesting, well-written, technically accurate piece.

Sara decided to write about the Salem witch trials of 1692. Why did she select this topic? That's not immediately clear. She said the idea just popped into her head, and it sounded better than the topics her two friends chose—pencils and orchids. To Sara, the witch trials seemed like something worthwhile to think about; she also figured it was something that would hold her interest for the (ugh!) full 6 weeks of the assignment.

During the next 6 weeks, I observed Sara poking in and out of five books, reading about this 17th-century American phenomenon. One book seemed to suit her best. It was a small volume, succinctly written, with its principal thrust the people involved in the episode. Other books, which spent more energy on the legal debates or the religious doctrines of the people of the area, seemed to get only half-hearted attention from Sara. What grabbed her fascination was the humanity of the accused and the accusers. She wanted to figure out what made them tick. What were they thinking as they went to the gallows or as they escorted their former friends and neighbors up those steps? Transported by the humanity of the event, Sara found she was well motivated to undertake the research required. She had developed a "consciousness" of the participants, and it was their perspective that she wanted to research and portray.

The class sessions were congruent with what the teacher had told the class. After they went to the library and retrieved books, other rehearsal techniques—such as brainstorming ideas and developing thesis statements—were learned and practiced. Sara's initial interest was further stimulated by the growing amount of information with which she was contending.

The first draft of Sara's paper was written in and out of class with support from her teacher when Sara had questions. Her teacher diligently read her paper and made blue notes, blue arrows, and an occasional blue word use correction. The teacher was calling attention to the craft of writing but was not using that as the sole criterion of his comments. The first draft ended with a personal note: "Sara, an interesting paper—some problems with punctuation—but the content flows fairly well. I look forward to the final version of your paper."

Six weeks of hard work ended, and Sara's expressed hearty satisfaction that the piece was done to her expectation. Her teacher confirmed her positive perceptions with a grade of 98 points out of 100. Sara was pleased!

Reflection on the Assignment

As I observed and discreetly dissected this writing episode, I began to wonder what this experience would look like if the foreground of the writing process and the background of the five mental dispositions had been operating for the teacher. I started by asking myself: What would efficacy look like if it had been consciously built into this exercise in the teaching of writing? If I wanted Sara to have a sense of efficacy about this experience, to what efficacious outcomes would I point?

Two efficacious outcomes came immediately to mind: (a) She believed she had something significant to say, and she had confidence in her capacity to say it; (b) she had courage to access resources that might be unfamiliar or even scary. Certainly, one could list many other outcomes, but let's just think about these two. What strategies would a teacher design if these two outcomes were considered important?

For the first outcome, one approach may be to have students log their reactions and experiences as they carry out the writing assignment. Sara's experiences would have been instructive. Because she wrote her paper on our home computer, which is located in the kitchen area, I had a chance to observe many of her comments and behaviors. Among other things, I heard her say, "This is interesting. I like what I'm writing about. This is good stuff." Not once did I see her falter or rant and rave about how stupid the task was (as has been the case with some assignments!). Nor did she complain that she absolutely couldn't do it. She did, occasionally, admit that this type of writing was harder than the poetry or narrative pieces she had done before. She did acknowledge that this task required a different structure and a different discipline. All of these comments have been ideal indicators of the efficacy of the experience, and much of it might have been revealed in a carefully kept log.

The second outcome was about accessing unfamiliar resources to go deeper with the research. Although Sara had initial satisfaction in the extent of her research endeavors—and her satisfaction was echoed by her teacher—within a few days of the completion of the assignment, she realized that she had missed out on a special opportunity. It happened that Sara and I were being introduced to the World Wide Web on our new computer. Within 15 minutes of starting, we pulled up a message from a researcher living in Texas. We had retrieved a 1623 letter written by a high-ranking Belgian official to his daughter. He was incarcerated at the time on the charge of being a witch, and he was subsequently executed. The letter, apparently stashed in a container in the cell before his death, gave gruesome details of his imprisonment and trial.

Sara, along with her mother, was glued to the computer screen. Here was a primary document verifying much of what she had reported in her paper. But her paper had been dependent on secondary sources. She was mesmerized. Here was something "real." Here was a farewell letter from a condemned man to his daughter. He was about to die, but he cared a great deal that she would not believe the accusations against him. He described the beatings others had suffered to get them to confess what the magistrates wanted to hear. He told her he held no malice for them. He told her he loved her. The letter continued for two pages and at times was not easy to read. The translation offered an awkward sentence structure. Despite this challenge and the gruesomeness of the content, accessing this letter was a powerful experience. The retrieval of this firsthand confirmatory evidence enhanced the research experience considerably. She achieved momentum toward the efficacious outcome I had considered: accessing a variety of resources to retrieve information for her assignment. She had just tapped into the World Wide Web!

When I queried Sara about how she felt after she completed the letter, she said she was remorseful. "This is an amazing letter, and I feel terrible."

Needless to say, this was not the response that I anticipated. "Why terrible?" I asked.

"Don't you see, my paper would have been so much better with excerpts from this resource. This letter verifies the speculations that were made by the writers I read. It doesn't matter that this was Belgium. These same tactics were used in Salem." She went on to say, "Maybe I could have compared the witch hunts in Europe with those in Salem."

The efficacy seeds toward tapping a variety of resources were initiated. Although she certainly was not exhibiting technological efficacy at this point, a whole new world was opened up for Sara and her research.

I pondered Sara's simultaneous excitement and disappointment at missing the opportunity to include this newfound information. If I wanted to pay attention to a student's sense of self-efficacy, what would I build into this assignment? This question would lead me to approach the rehearsal stage of the writing process in a particular way, with careful thought as to how students should go about retrieving the information to be used in their assignment. The issue of efficacy about tapping a variety of resources would guide some of the design of my assignment.

A Reworked Assignment

After this experience and my reflections on the **efficacy** of the assignment, I began to wonder how Sara might have experienced the other four mental dispositions during this exercise if they had been consciously built into the initial assignment. What if the assignment had been constructed in such a way that rehearsing, drafting, and revising (the principal components of the writing process) were intentionally merged with expectations highlighting the mental dispositions of consciousness, flexibility, interdependence, and craftspersonship?

When I think about the mental disposition of **consciousness** and how it might have been deliberately brought into this writing assignment, I'm drawn to propose several possible routes. Sara needs to analyze and synthesize her own model of the writing process. This raises several questions: What specifically did she do during the rehearsal stage? What was involved in her initial consideration of the Salem witch trials? How did her thinking about that topic change? How did her approach change as it progressed through the writing process? These issues are important because the process is recursive. Each such decision feeds into the next, and each is then reconsidered in light of the new vantage point. By challenging Sara to focus on such questions, she can begin to understand the process with greater clarity.

One way to get at this issue is to have students think through the strategies they use when they work through their own writing process. If students can "rise above" their own thinking and "look down on" the process they are engaged in, they will develop approach ramps and strategies to attack future writing exercises. Often we teachers tell our students every move they are to make, and we offer them little or no opportunity to reflect on the skills and techniques they have already developed. This effectively leads them to assume that their prior experience is of little account and to look to others for direction about the "right" way to carry out their work.

What learner outcomes might I include if I were looking for **flexibility** of thinking in the midst of this writing exercise? One outcome might be for Sara to use her research and create an alternative piece on the Salem witch trials in another writing genre (other than a straightforward, prose report). I imagine a play or a poem or a news broadcast or news article. Or how might this paper look if it were to reflect the perspectives of the families of the accused rather than that of a detached, "objective" observer?

Another way to elicit flexible thinking would be to ask Sara to synthesize the insights she gained from her research and relate them to her present life. Has she ever experienced anything like an unfounded accusation? What did that feel like? What were her responses?

For the most part, Sara's paper synthesizes her findings into a descriptive piece. Her last paragraph, which brought applause from her teacher, began to suggest this dimension of flexible thinking: "There will always be conflicts in the world, and the Salem Witch Trials are good examples of religious disputes in a world of different perceptions of 'good and evil.' People in today's society still can't always discern what is good and what is evil."

Either of the aforementioned alternative tasks would involve different types of thinking, thereby calling on considerable flexibility from the student-writer. They would also call for flexibility from the teacher, as the latter would have to craft the assignment to raise expectations that would generate student flexibility in thinking.

The mental disposition of **interdependence** is a crucial stage of thinking in the writing process. As suggested above, it is typically associated with conferencing, whereby an author and a reader discuss the intentions, content, and composition of the written piece. It is a conversation with a critical friend, a peer, a teacher, a family member, a friend, and—eventually—oneself that moves the thinking of the author beyond simple consideration to more complex reflection and writing. The conversation is not unidirectional—from expert adult or teacher toward novice student—but is dialogic, with the student's intentions held foremost in mind. The interdependence is further enhanced because the conversation between writer and teacher takes place within a context that raises nonjudgmental questions and elicits points of clarification.

One approach to facilitating interdependence for Sara would be for her to work with a peer, "a writing buddy." They would need to be coached in constructive ways of dialoguing with each other and designing nonjudgmental questions to elicit Sara's analysis of her intentions. The note of reciprocity that this exercise includes serves to underscore the importance of the audience and its perspectives in the reception of any written piece.

The mental disposition of **craftsmanship** is probably the one that Sara—and most of us who have been trained in traditional writing approaches—most fully developed. As I watched Sara work and ponder about her paper, what she appeared to love best was tinkering with the language and the sentence structure as she wrote. She reworded the lead sentence a number of times until it pulled the reader into the piece: "Witchcraft is a word mainly associated with broomsticks, black cats, flying books, scalding cauldrons and magic potions."

Her outline, her draft, and the technical correctness of her final piece are notable exemplars of this mental disposition. Indeed, this disposition dominated the activity. She effectively learned how to gather information, compose note cards, write accurate bibliography citations, develop an outline, synthesize her research findings, and revise her paper for technical and stylistic accuracy. All these learner outcomes represent the craft of writing, and they were definitely the outcomes into which Sara put her energy. Although not inconsequential, they would have been enhanced had she also been called on to recognize the efficacy of her own learning, been conscious of the process she was going through, been called on to show flexibility in her writing and thinking, and had understood the interdependence that the writing process entails.

A Final Comment

The craft of writing is an exercise in thinking. It requires careful rehearsing, drafting, and revising in a continuing process of dialogue between writer and real or imagined readers. This chapter argues that the *process* of writing is a *product* that has not been fully considered in the teaching of writing in schools. Instead, most students find themselves challenged on only one mental disposition—that of being craftspersons.

Nevertheless, the writing process is most valuably experienced by students if this traditional mental disposition is complemented with careful attention to matters of consciousness, efficacy, interdependence, and flexibility. Keeping them in mind in the creation of writing assignments provides teachers with a platform for enhancing and verifying students' thinking-writing. When the five mental dispositions are fully folded into the writing process, budding writers will be able to extend their skills to the fullest.

References

Atwell, N. (1987). *In the middle: Writing, reading, and learning with adolescents.* Portsmouth, NH: Boynton/Cook, Heinemann.

Calkins, L. M. (1983). *Lessons from a child: On the teaching and learning of writing.* Portsmouth, NH: Heinemann Educational Books.

Costa, A., & Garmston, R. (1994). *Cognitive coaching: A foundation for renaissance schools.* Norwood, MA: Christopher-Gordon.

Costa, A., & Garmston, R. (1995). *Five human passions: The origins of effective thinking.* Xeroxed revision of a paper first presented at the 6th International Conference on Thinking, July 1994, Boston.

Elbow, P. (1973). *Writing without teachers.* New York: Oxford University Press.

Graves, D. H. (1978). *Balance the basics: Let them write.* New York: Ford Foundation.

Murray, D. (1987). *Write to learn* (2nd ed.). New York: CBS College Publishing.

Murray, D. (1989). *Expecting the unexpected: Teaching myself—and others—to read and write.* Portsmouth, NH: Boynton/Cook, Heinemann.

Romano, T. (1987). *Clearing the way: Working with teenage writers.* Portsmouth, NH: Heinemann Educational Books.

12

Learning Creative Process

A Basic Life Skill

Alison G. Strickland
Louis T. Coulson

A Prologue

On a Sunday morning during the time we were gathering our thoughts and outlining this chapter, a headline announcing the lead story in the editorial section of the *St. Petersburg Times* caught our attention: "An Inside Look at Classroom Realities: Reader Responses Show a Public Education System in Crisis." The editor of editorials for the *Times* had put out a call for teachers and parents to tell him what was going on in the local public schools. Responses flooded in. His conclusion? "If the public school system were an airplane, alarm systems would be going off in the cockpit" (Gailey, 1995, p. 1).

Reading the letters that followed depressed us. One accusation followed another. Teachers felt that administrators didn't support them in their struggle to maintain order in their classrooms. They claimed many covered up failures in their schools while currying the favor of county administrators who had more power than they deserved. They cynically mocked school reform programs mandated by state and local administrators. They expressed disgust with parents who acted as though schools were a day care service rather than a place for learning.

Business people and college professors wrote to complain that graduates hadn't grasped basic reading, writing, and math skills. In addition to concerns about the quality of education their children were getting, frightened parents said that the schools were increasingly violent and that they feared for their children's safety. Some had transferred their children to private schools. Others said they would if they could afford to.

All the letters expressed varying levels of frustration, anger, and confusion. Everyone complained about what was wrong. Most blamed someone else. Most wanted things to be as they remembered them in some happier past. No one approached the issue from a creative problem-solving perspective. No one offered a vision of a better future. Nowhere in pages of letters could we find any sign of imagination at work.

Then a familiar pattern emerged, and the recognition restored our energy. If years of teaching creative process and facilitating creative problem-solving meetings have taught us anything, it is this: When people get bogged down in complaining about what they don't want, they can't make the crucial shift into imagining how they want things to be when they have created a better way. Furthermore, all the blaming embedded in the complaining poisons the climate, making it hard to work with others to create innovative alternatives. This means their solutions are typically "fix it" strategies designed to take away the pain and restore what was. In the process, those judged responsible are often overtly or covertly punished.

Something else was clear. These letters so full of complaint and blame said as much about the writers as they did about the schools. Those who wrote them may have learned the basic skills of reading and writing, but they showed no sign of having learned the creative thinking processes they needed to respond effectively. The crisis in the schools these letters described doesn't call for fixing; it calls for transforming. The solution isn't, as many suggested, going "back to basics." (Translate that to read doing more of what didn't work in the first place and helped get us in the mess we're in.) Instead, consider what would happen if people began working together creatively to invent better ways to teach children in safe (dare we dream of nurturing?) environments that stimulate real learning—and then got busy working together to make it happen.

We don't need to start from scratch. *A growing understanding of creativity, creative process, and successful innovation not only can help us invent and implement better ways but also can become a core part of a renaissance curriculum.*

Educators can learn and teach creative process as we use it to create a new curriculum that nurtures and strengthens the innate creativity of each child. We can learn and practice the principles of creativity as we work together to create schools that work for kids, teachers, and parents. Of course, the process won't be neat and tidy and will never be complete. All we can do is begin.

Following are our thoughts about why creative process deserves a place in a process-centered curriculum; then we explore the underlying principles of creativity in action. We have interwoven the discussion of each principle with easily adaptable practices and have illustrated them with examples drawn from our own experience in classrooms both public and corporate. At the end, we'll share some thoughts about how to get started right away, with or without a mandate. As you read, we hope you'll make your own connections and invent new ideas you can try in your own setting.

Our thinking is based on many years of researching and teaching creative process. It is impossible to separate our experience from the influence of a number of scholars, colleagues, and friends who have shared our journey. Among them are J. P. Guilford, Robert Fritz, Ned Herrmann, Sid Parnes, George Prince, and Paul Torrance, who have contributed significantly to our understanding of creativity and creative process.

We have chosen to speak in a personal rather than academic voice because our journey, which began as an academic interest, has become a way of life and has touched not only our intellect but our hearts and spirits as well. We hope our passion for creativity will prove to be contagious!

Defining Our Terms

Because we so often encounter confusion about what is meant by creativity and creative process, we want to clarify both terms.

Creativity

Typically, people believe that creativity is a talent we are either born with or not. They usually connect creativity with gifted artists and writers. Some include scientists or mathematicians who make breakthrough discoveries. This notion takes most of us right out of the game and leads to the proverbial "I don't have a creative bone in my body!" response. It stifles our creativity and thus ourselves.

One of the most useful definitions of creativity we have found is one Bill Moyers used when he summarized his findings at the end of his PBS series on creativity: "Creativity is the ability to challenge assumptions, see in new ways, recognize new patterns, make connections, seize opportunities and take risks." Think of a time when you did any of those things, and you will find your creativity at work. When we define creativity this way, it brings it into the realm of our everyday lives. We call it ordinary creativity—a phrase with a nice paradoxical ring. We are fond of Abraham Maslow's remark—a first-rate soup is more creative than a second-rate painting—because it illustrates that creativity can infuse our everyday lives when we take it out of the realm of genius and connect it to ourselves as we recognize the small things we do all the time that demonstrate the creative process at work.

This is a crucial shift because the first step to purposefully developing creativity is believing you can be creative and connecting your understanding of creativity to things you have already done. Once recognized, you can enhance your creativity every day.

Creative Process

Scholars studying creativity have long agreed that there is a recognizable creative process with identifiable stages. Although the labels they put on these stages vary, the stages are described in quite similar ways. The creative process is universal, regardless of the arena or discipline in which it is applied. We were delighted to discover that ancient Peruvians had a single word, *hamavec,* for both poet and inventor because it tells us that the ancients sensed the creative process at work long ago.

Late in the 19th century, German physiologist and physicist Hermann Helmholtz described his process as *saturation*, during which he actively researched the problem; *incubation*, a more passive reflective stage; and *illumination*, the "aha" moment when the solution suddenly emerged. Later, others added additional stages. Early in the 20th century, French mathematician Jules-Henri Poincaré described *verification*, testing the solution to see if it works. Around the same time, American psychologist Jacob Getzels identified a stage that precedes Helmholtz's saturation—*problem finding*, when a person discovers an intriguing challenge or opportunity to work on that she or he hadn't been aware of before (see Edwards, 1986, pp. 3-5).

At this point, researchers were observing creativity at work in its natural state. People may or may not be aware of their process. Today's rapidly changing world calls for faster and more innovative responses and understanding, and purposefully using creative process when we need new insights and ideas helps.

Now, many people work consciously with creative process, and so our collective understanding of it is evolving. Along the way, many have developed deliberate strategies for stimulating new insights and ideas. The incubation stage has become more purposeful. We can intentionally let go and do nothing, trusting the process to continue outside our conscious awareness. We can purposefully use meditative states that shift our consciousness into a more relaxed state to invite new insights. This is the same state many scientists through centuries have described being in when they made the connection that led to their breakthrough insights and discoveries. We can increase the probability that "ahas" will occur by using various creative thinking skills that invite new connections.

Underneath the creative process described in linear terms as *preparation*, followed by *incubation*, which leads to an *illumination*, which we then test during the *verification* stage, we sense a system that works somewhat as a hologram because each part of the process has the whole embedded within it. We may begin by gathering information about an issue, find a key piece of data we were unaware of that sparks an idea worth trying, and leap ahead to implement it. Conversely, we might think we have reached the end as we implement an idea; then, once in action, the idea produces an unexpected result—and we find ourselves either back at the beginning reformulating the problem or struck by a brand-new insight that changes what we do next.

Why Teach Creative Process?

In the midst of the talk of "back to basics" that has permeated education for years, one basic skill has been largely overlooked. It is perhaps the most crucial of all—the ability to think, work, and solve problems creatively. There is no need to list the myriad crises crying out for creative solutions. They are everywhere.

As we consider why creative process deserves to be learned, let's begin with some practical curriculum issues:

• What skills will people need to succeed when they leave school?

- What must they know how to do to satisfy their employers?
- What must they know how to do to lead successful lives in the 21st century?

What do creativity and creative process have to do with these issues? *To succeed today, people must know how to deal with a constantly shifting, extremely competitive world driven by rapid change that will only accelerate.* Few people will reach the end of their working years doing the same job with which they began. Even if their profession remains constant, the way the work is done will surely change. If a computer or a robot can do what they do, they won't be doing it for long. One ability that will never be obsolete is thinking creatively. It's a life skill, and there's no place in which it doesn't apply, no arena in which it is inappropriate. Skilled creative thinkers will never be out of work. If not at work in an organization, they often become entrepreneurs who create their own work.

It's insane to continue to structure schools as though their major function is transferring knowledge because knowledge expands and changes faster than we can make meaning out of it. In this century, a good memory could put you on the honor roll because schools have traditionally pushed memorization over imagination. It is easier to measure what students have memorized than what they imagine and create, and too often good scores on standardized tests are confused with real progress and growth. Of course, knowledge makes up the building blocks with which people create; it is what people create from what they know, however, that truly matters. Working effectively with creative process as we live the few remaining years in this century can help ensure our survival in the next.

Today's businesses are demanding a different type of worker: workers who can think for themselves instead of waiting to be told what to do—workers who can continually invent new ways to improve things. And more and more people at all levels are being asked to create entirely new ways, not just fix or improve on what is.

Recently, a woman responsible for management development in one of our nation's largest electronic businesses attended a weeklong creative thinking workshop we lead. She came because her CEO kept challenging people to unleash their imaginations and think outside the box. "For the most part," she said, "they're willing. They just don't know how. I came to find out how." Her CEO is one of many who recognize that creativity and innovation are the lifeblood of any business—from the corner grocery battling to compete with chain stores to huge companies such as IBM that have learned the hard way that they cannot rest on laurels won in the past.

Tom Peters (1994), in his recent book *The Tom Peters Seminar: Crazy Times Call for Crazy Organizations*, repeatedly exhorts people to unleash their imaginations and make innovation a way of life. To support his case, Peters quotes *New York Times Magazine* writer Fred Moody's comment about Microsoft, a company that has eclipsed the mighty IBM. He wrote, "Microsoft's only factory asset is the human imagination" (p. 11). Companies have begun to value intellectual capital and recognize that their employees' ability to create and innovate adds more value to their net worth than anything else.

It is not only the business world that needs creative thinkers and problems solvers. Our nation's citizens need to be them as well. Peter Senge (1990), author of *The Fifth Discipline*, has said, "The new challenges of the Information Age demand that not only business, but schools and governments radically transform themselves." That cannot happen without people who know how to create. As citizens demand that government be pushed down to more and more local levels, those to whom the problems and·challenges are pushed down must know how to invent creative solutions and create new programs that work.

It is clear that people who understand creative process and know how to think creatively are vital to success in businesses, organizations, and governments today. The need grows more critical every day. Nowhere are the old ways working. We must work together to find new and better ways.

Beyond the need to live successfully in the midst of breathtaking change and to answer the call for more creativity and innovation in both the private and public sectors, there is a more basic and compelling reason. *People who are in touch with their innate creativity and know how to think creatively not only are more productive but also lead richer and more satisfying lives.* When Abraham Maslow described self-actualizing people, he was also describing creative people.

Creative people have internal loci of control built on confidence in their creative abilities and their ability to act, rather than just react, to the problems, challenges, and opportunities that come their way. They have curious, flexible, imaginative, and intuitive minds that help them see opportunities where others see only problems.

Developing our creativity is like teaching our minds to be on our side. In classrooms and business units, when people reconnect with their ability to create, apathy and burnout disappear as they come alive with new energy, excitement, and purpose. Although they can't control what comes along, they can control their responses to it and live with the confidence that they can trust their creative process not just to pull them through but to move them ahead. Children today face a shifting, changing uncertain world. Understanding creative process and knowing how to think creatively can help them face it with confidence and courage.

People who purposefully pursue their own creative development wind up changing who they are. Many with whom we have worked through the years have said they began developing their creativity so that they could be smarter and more competitive and wound up discovering creativity was also about the heart and the soul and that they had created a new way of life. Ultimately, what we all create is our own lives. What could be more relevant?

The Question of How

How do we do this? How do we teach our children and ourselves to be more creative?

We typically answer such questions with a model Alison developed 20 years ago (Figure 12.1). It still guides us as we design workshops and develop materials. We include the story of how the model came to her in her words because it illustrates firsthand the creative process in action. Because she lived

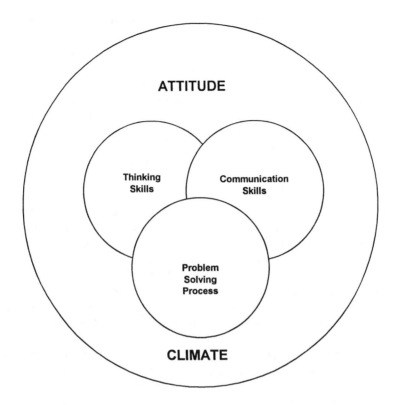

Figure 12.1. Creativity Model
Copyright © 1981 Applied Creative Learning Systems, Inc. (now Applied Creativity, Inc.).

it and remembers it clearly, we need not speculate about what happened in her mind, as we would with an example from someone else's life.

I began studying creativity in the early 1970s when I returned to graduate school. Then, I was one of those who said, "I don't have a creative bone in my body." I knew I was a competent person, successful academically and professionally; however, I would never have described myself as creative. I started exploring the field because as a teacher and a middle school English department chair, I wanted to learn how to spot and nourish creative talent in others. When I discovered evidence that we all have innate creative ability that we can purposefully develop, I was thrilled. I unknowingly made a decision that changed the course of my life—I decided to focus all my elective work on the field of creativity and creative problem solving and to put what I learned into practice. I became my own research subject.

After spending a summer immersed in the literature, I began work on a research paper to prove the hypothesis that creativity can be purposefully developed. Now I had to begin writing, and I had no idea how to pull all that I knew together into a coherent whole. This surprised me because research papers were something I normally did easily and well.

At the same time, I was searching for a quick way to answer the question, "How?" I often shared my excitement about developing human creativity with friends and colleagues and "How?" was the first question they asked. I could talk to them for hours about the different ways I was exploring, but I didn't have a clear and concise response I could offer in 60 seconds or less that would entice them to listen to more.

Then early one morning, I was standing in the shower, not thinking at all about creativity, the paper, or anything else, when I saw an image of three interlocking circles on the shower wall. In the interface of the three circles, tiny pinpoints of light sparkled. Before I could ask myself what this was, I heard a voice inside my head that explained to me what the circles meant—and it didn't sound like my voice! It said, "You can be more creative if you practice and attend to creative thinking skills, communication skills, and a creative problem-solving process."

I understood instantly. I knew what the sparkling interface meant, too. It symbolized the energy created when those three elements interact fluidly to create a synergistic whole. I also knew this unexpected flash of creative insight would quickly evaporate if I didn't capture it. I jumped out of the shower. There wasn't a piece of paper or a pencil in sight, so I grabbed a lipstick from the counter and drew the image on the bathroom mirror. Because I knew it was the organizing principle for my research paper and the quick response to "how," it was worth the greasy mess I created.

As I drew and labeled each circle, its implications were clear. Creative thinking skills was easy. I'd already made a metaphorical connection between training for an athletic event with physical exercise and training for the creative moment by practicing creative thinking skills that can increase the probability that you can invent a good idea when you need one.

I knew the communication skills circle represented two levels of communication. First was inner communication or self-talk—the messages we send to ourselves as we work on a challenge. I'd already found research that suggested that those who talk positively to themselves as they worked with challenging puzzles were much more likely to solve them. Those who said negative, even punishing, things to themselves were much less likely to succeed. The second level was intercommunication—how we talk with one another about issues and ideas. There are creative communication skills we can learn to use when we discuss new thinking with others that increase the probability that we can develop a fragile new idea into an implementable plan. Unfortunately, few people were ever taught to use them, as anyone who attends meetings can testify. Thousands of potentially useful ideas die a premature death everyday in classrooms and meeting rooms around the world because of a colleague's caustic comments or a frown on a power person's brow.

The last circle represented learning and using a creative problem-solving process. Creative process is like a road map that we can carry around in our back pockets. When we're rolling along getting easily to where we want to go, we don't need it. But when the road gets dark and we're feeling confused and unsure where to turn next, we can stop, pull it out, and locate our whereabouts.

That evening when I sat down to work on the research paper, it seemed to write itself. And I discovered in the process that the "the voice" had left something out. Surrounding the interplay of thinking skills, communication skills, and a problem-solving process is a subtle atmosphere. On an individual level, I called it attitude—beginning with our attitudes about ourselves as creative individuals. On an organizational level, whether it is two people working in partnership, a small group, or an entire corporate body, it is climate—how new ideas are treated and to what degree innovation is invited and valued. So I surrounded the three smaller circles with a larger one containing attitude and climate.

Alison's "aha moment" illustrates key aspects of creative process. First, she was looking for a way to organize her research paper and also wanted to communicate quickly and clearly ways people could develop their innate creative ability. She was highly motivated to find an answer. She'd done all the preparation work she knew how to do. She had saturated herself with information. Out of frustration, she'd put the project aside for several days and purposefully hadn't thought about it much. Then, when she wasn't thinking about it, the answer came to her full-blown in an image along with a voice telling her what it represented.

Research into the specialized functions of right and left hemispheres of the brain suggests that "the voice" was a product of the less verbal parts of her mind—the intuitive right brain that speaks in images and weaves pieces together in conceptual wholes that come in a flash of insight. Without intense preparation and eagerly seeking an answer, the model never would have appeared. Once it did, she recognized its usefulness immediately and captured it. Then she tested it out and elaborated on it as she worked.

Later, she put the model to work organizing an interdisciplinary creative thinking unit for middle school English and social studies teachers that eventually reached more than a thousand students. It involved learners in numerous creative thinking exercises designed to help them develop mental flexibility and stretch their imaginations. Each exercise was followed up with discussion of how the skill worked and how they could apply it in other situations.

Students talked about times when they had kept creative thoughts to themselves because of fear of being teased or put down. They developed strategies to make it safe to share creative ideas. They led small-group brainstorming sessions, practicing both creative thinking skills and communication skills that created a climate in which ideas could flourish. They processed each meeting to identify things that had worked well and things they wanted to do better the next time.

Students looked at the processes used by famous inventors, writers, and artists. They read biography and fiction, looking for the creative process in action, and assessed how effectively the people they'd read about worked with the challenges they faced. They kept journals filled with their observations and thoughts about what they were learning and their successes and frustrations with the processes they used to invent ideas. Students worked on projects in areas they chose that demonstrated their own creativity.

These are simple examples of ways that creativity and creative process can be introduced to students. Once the principles and practices of creativity are understood, the possibilities for involving everyone in a school are endless.

Principles of Creativity

Intensely interested in creative leadership, we read Steven Covey's (1989) best-selling book, *The Seven Habits of Highly Effective People,* soon after it was published. Covey's introductory chapter includes an idea that forms the core of his work—that natural principles govern human effectiveness. The principles concept sparked a connection that struck us with what we now consider a blinding flash of the obvious: If there are natural principles governing effectiveness, there must also be principles underlying creativity. What are they? Our search began.

First, we drew up a preliminary list. Next, we turned to the extensive journals we've each kept to track our own creative process and record the successes and frustrations of people we have worked with through the years. We looked for a match between each important observation and one of the possible principles we had identified. Each connection validated the corresponding principle. When we couldn't find a connecting principle, we knew we'd missed one, so we added another. Eventually we synthesized our beginning list to seven key principles that have stood up well. We continue to validate them against everything we learn and discover about creativity in action.

We approach this task with a lot of humility. One thing we've learned about creativity is that we never completely "get it." Creativity is surrounded by a mysterious, even magical, quality that lures us on to discover more, and now we know we never will completely understand it. That's what makes it intriguing!

In the spirit of exploring, we offer these principles of creativity. They are definitely work in progress. We know these principles are there because we sense their dynamic presence all the time. Only the words we use to define them will change as our understanding grows.

Creativity Is Developmental

Purposefully developing creativity is a lifelong project. No matter where we place ourselves on a continuum of "not at all creative" to "perfectly creative" (both impossible states), we can, with focused intention and practice, get better at it all the time. Once we commit ourselves, it's easy to do because unlike most other skills, we can practice anytime and anywhere we like. Stuck in traffic? Practice connection making. Pick two objects that attract your attention and see how many ways you can think of that they are alike. No matter where you are, challenge your assumptions and see what new ideas emerge. Looking at familiar things as though you've never seen them and ask yourself, "What would happen if . . ." Keep at it, and you will internalize creative thinking skills so that you find yourself using them naturally without consciously evoking them.

Developing creativity for adults and for children much beyond the early primary grades is like a reclamation project because we are working to regain what we once had in abundance. Among our collection of creativity quotes is this favorite written in the last century by French essayist Charles-Augustin Sainte-Beuve. It makes the point well.

> With everyone born human, a poet . . . an artist is born, who dies young and who is survived by an adult.

Creativity Is a Process

Creativity flows through a clearly identifiable process that can guide us whenever we want to create. Although creative process has much in common with analytical problem solving, there is an important distinction. Analytical problem solving involves identifying causes and taking appropriate actions on the basis of a linear cause-and-effect relationship. The answer is out there, and it is our job to uncover it. Problem solving often involves fixing something that has gone wrong so that it can return to its former state. Creative process involves creating something novel. It's an innovative response to a situation in which there's not one right answer but a multitude of possibilities. Its only limits are the limits of our imagination.

We have already described classic stages of creative process that people have observed through time. We also compared the creative process to a road map we can use to locate ourselves on our journey toward a creative solution. Here is the road map we carry, one we have synthesized from many different versions of creative process. It's as useful on a school playground as it is in a corporate meeting room.

The process begins with a stage we call *exploring.* As soon as you are aware that a problem, challenge, or opportunity you want to do something about has come your way, you have begun exploring. It may be a problem that confronts you demanding action, and no known and readily available solution exists. Sometimes a challenge comes along that you choose to work on rather than dodge. Sometimes you recognize an opportunity that intrigues you enough to pursue it.

The key issue in the exploring stage is *what,* not *how.* What do I know, and what can I find out about the current state of things? What do I want in place of what I have? Problems are essentially the difference between what you have and what you want. Taking time to clarify and articulate your understanding of these two elements is a crucial and often overlooked stage of creative process.

Often people can say more about what they have—much of which they don't want—than about what they want. Like those who wrote to the editorial editor about what they think is wrong with schools, they get stuck in complaining about what *is* rather than imagining what might *be.*

One way to clarify both questions is to brainstorm different ways of defining the problem and describing the ideal outcome. The challenge during exploring is to stay open and to look at things flexibly from a number of angles until a clear picture of both the current state and desired outcome emerges. Once you understand where you are and know where you want to be, a tension is set up between the two states that will pull you toward what you want. Then you are ready to move from *what* to *how*.

We call this stage *inventing*. Here you are looking for ideas that can close the gap between what you have and what you want and take you where you want to go. Too often people settle for the first idea that comes along rather than exploring further to discover new options. Resist this impulse. Stay open and flexible as you invent lots of ideas that might create what you want. This increases the probability you will get to ideas that are both novel and implementable.

When you have alternatives that are worth pursuing, you can move on the next stage: *choosing*. Here, judgment comes into play as you select the best idea or combination of ideas to implement. This shift can be tricky because once you bring judgment into play, you may abandon an idea with enormous potential because you see flaws in it. Here's a way to avoid this danger. Focus first on the positive aspects of the idea and identify everything it would do for you if you could figure out how to make it work. This strengthens the idea by articulating aspects that make it worth pursuing. Then shift your attention to your concerns. State them in action-oriented, how-to, problem-solving language. This turns a roadblock into a challenge and invites ideas for overcoming those concerns.

Now you are ready for the final stage: *implementing*. Here you plan your next steps, try the idea, and evaluate results to see if it worked. This stage sometimes takes you on another quick trip through creative process as you identify opportunities and invent innovative ways to make things happen.

You can lead even young children through creative process. A corporate attorney who attended one of our workshops decided to involve her 6-year-old daughter in creative process. Her goal was to help her daughter learn to solve her own problems instead of continuing the familiar pattern of listening to her daughter's troubles and then telling her what to do. Her daughter was upset because she and her best friend were quarreling. She began by asking her child, "How would you like things to be between you and your friend? How could you tell that you two were really getting along well and having fun together?"

Next she asked, "How many things can you think of to do that might make things more like what you want?" After they made a list of ideas, her daughter decided to call up the other little girl, tell her she wanted to be a better friend, and share some of her ideas to see which ones her friend liked. Of course, as they talked, the disagreement and hurt feelings were quickly forgotten, and, on the other hand, there's a good chance she'll remember some important learnings. This little girl had been involved in exploring what she wanted to create and inventing ways to make it happen. Then she got to choose what she wanted to do and do it on her own. In the process, she experienced being proactive (rather than passively complaining to her mother and looking to her for the answer) and learned she could change a troubling situation.

There Is Power in the Positive

This was one of the easiest principles to identify because so much of what works as people move through the creative process is connected to this dynamic. We are not talking about blind optimism that masks real problems or going through life passively, wearing rose-colored glasses. We are talking about using positive energy all the way through the process to move ahead. It starts with learning to trust the creative process to carry us through and then getting out of our own way, knowing that sometimes the best thing to do is let go and take time to incubate awhile, allowing the process to work outside our awareness and knowing eventually the "aha" will come.

As people begin exploring a challenge, the purposeful shift to thinking and talking with others about what we want, rather than about what we don't want, evokes creativity. A communication skill we've taught to children as easily as we have to adults is stating problems in positive, action-oriented language. Typically, people define problems as what's wrong—what they want to get away from. Instead, try beginning problem statements with "How to . . ." or "How might we . . ." and finishing them by talking about what you want. Thus, "My brother always argues with me" becomes "How might I get along better with my brother?" or even "How to have more fun with my brother."

Shifting to forward-moving, action-oriented language invites new thinking instead of habitual reactions. It seems quite simple—and it is, yet few people have discovered its power. When teachers and children learn how to use this dynamic communication skill, we've seen the climate of classrooms and entire schools change. Try it yourself. The next time someone comes to you with a complaint, listen until you can paraphrase it for them in positive problem-solving language ("Sounds like we need to work on 'how to' ") and watch what happens. You have invited creative thinking instead of complaining and helped people shift from a negative, reactive posture into a positive, proactive stance.

The power of the positive is at work when we imagine ideal outcomes. Too often, people drain their energy by imagining the worst and dwelling on what they don't want and what can go wrong. The more they practice creating images of ideal outcomes, the stronger their imagination gets and the more likely they are to realize the future they want for themselves. Encouraging students to verbalize what they want to achieve before they go to work on a creative project is one way to do this easily.

Brainstorming, one of the early creative thinking strategies based on suspending judgment in the initial phases of creative process, draws on the power of the positive. When people get judgmental as they explore and invent, they not only shoot down other people's ideas but can shoot down their own. Because people have been rewarded for so many years for being right and punished for being wrong, the safekeeping part of themselves doesn't let go easily. People frequently censor their own ideas even more quickly than they do others' ideas.

Brainstorming encourages people to generate lots of ideas including far-out possibilities, assuming that something useful can come from them. Because it is experimental, brainstorming works best in a positive, supportive climate. Then people can let go of the need to be right and come up with really good ideas others will approve of; they can shift into an experimental, speculative mode and think approximately rather than precisely.

The power of the positive is the principle behind the strategy that we described earlier of evaluating ideas for their strengths before turning to looking at concerns. Talk about concerns first, as most people do, and the idea doesn't seem worth considering at all. Identify its strengths, and the idea often turns out to be worth working on further until it is developed into an implementable solution. An added payoff: When people know their ideas will be respectfully weighed, they will be more willing to share them.

You can adapt this creative communication skill to daily interactions with others. When people come to you with an idea, even if you have serious concerns about it, talk with them first about the strengths you see in their thinking, and then voice your concerns in problem-solving language. Even if you can't overcome the concerns, people will know they have been heard and their thinking has been respectfully considered.

Using this gentler form of judgment works wonders when evaluating student performance. First, comment specifically on what works and what the learner has done well. Then phrase any critical comments as action-oriented problem statements to be worked on in the future. "Let's work on some ways to better organize your thoughts next time" is much more motivating than red-penciling *disorganized* in the margin of a report.

An optimistic attitude is a key characteristic of creative people—one we can all nourish in ourselves and others. The many people we've known who have successfully developed their creative abilities, implemented innovative solutions successfully, and made a real impact on their schools or organizations have one thing in common—a strong sense of optimism coupled with an infectious enthusiasm. This is another sign of the power of the positive in action.

There Is Power in Vision and Purpose

Like many others, when we first began exploring creativity, we were interested in learning to invent more and better ideas. It worked. We were never at a loss for ideas in a brainstorming session. Yet we sensed that the power of creative process was about more than just randomly inventing clever, novel ideas. We began asking ourselves, "Creativity in service of what?"

The relationship between creativity and purpose and vision is synergistic. People and organizations with a meaningful purpose and a clear vision naturally stimulate creativity and focus it toward a common goal. At the same time, purpose and vision grow larger and more compelling when born out of the imagination of people thinking creatively.

Taking time to ask the larger questions that clarify purpose and vision moves creativity to new levels. It helps shift people from the "Band-Aid" approach to problem solving, in which they cover the problem with the first solution they think of and hope things will return to normal. Creativity aligned with purpose means evolving with intention toward a larger goal.

Imagine what might happen if everyone who lived together in a school came together to ask, "What do we want to be and have as we live and work and learn together?" "What kind of a school do we want to create?" and then, "What do we have to do as we work together to get there?" When there is a shared vision and purpose, each person in the group can make decisions and take actions that are aligned with the larger goal. Discipline problems can be discussed within the framework of the vision.

What if all the children were encouraged to create visions for themselves—something they wanted to create for themselves during the school year—and then invented a list of ways they might make it happen? From there, they could develop an action plan for the coming year. An art teacher we know did this with all her classes. Then the children developed symbols that stood for their goal and an illustrated map showing how they were going to travel toward it. It made such a difference in her classroom that the next year, the whole school developed a vision and purpose for the year. Then they had students illustrate their intentions and placed the artwork throughout the school to remind them of what they were creating together.

Schools are filled with problems, challenges, and opportunities that range from annoyances such as noisy cafeterias to the catastrophes of drugs and violence. Why not bring the power of vision and purpose into play? What if all youngsters experienced the joy of both working together to create the type of school they would like to have and using their creativity to create what they want for themselves?

Understand the Brain/Mind Connection

Knowledge about the human brain that has emerged in the last 20 years or so suggests new ways to develop creativity and use the creative process more effectively in working with others. Understanding the specialized gifts of the left and right hemispheres, differences in thinking style preferences, and the usefulness of different states of consciousness enhances creative process.

Roger Sperry (see Edwards, 1986) won the Nobel Prize for his groundbreaking research proving that each hemisphere of the brain has different capacities and that each hemisphere perceives, processes, and makes meaning out of information differently. He found during his now famous split brain experiments that the left hemisphere is good at analysis and is verbally far superior to the right. It operates in a step-by-step logical manner as it moves toward drawing rational conclusions from what it knows. The left hemisphere is also time conscious and is much better at planning, organizing, balancing checkbooks, and getting us to appointments on time.

Much of this was already known. Sperry's major contribution was discovering the unique abilities of the right hemisphere and proving it was much more sophisticated than previously thought. More visually and spatially adept than the left, the right hemisphere can see things all at once and connect parts to a larger whole. Rather than using a logical, step-by-step problem-solving process, the right brain makes intuitive leaps, understands things metaphorically, and connects things in unexpected ways that spark flashes of insight. Sperry not only identified these unique qualities but also made a strong case for purposefully developing and valuing them. He has often commented that the education system tends to neglect the nonverbal forms of intellect and that science has unjustly discounted its importance for too long.

Everyone with a normally functioning brain can use both hemispheres; just as we develop a preference for one hand more than the other, however, we also have mental preferences that profoundly influence the ways we like to think, communicate, and problem solve. Consequently, mental preferences influence us all the way through the creative process, affecting the types of problems and challenges we like to work on, the ways we go about exploring the issues, the ways we invent ideas, the ideas we choose to implement, and how we go about putting them into action.

Logical, analytical thinkers learn, work, and create quite differently from big-picture, conceptual, and intuitive thinkers. It's not an issue of good/bad or right/wrong. They are just different. It's also not an issue of right brain = creative and left brain = uncreative. Learning to use the right brain more effectively does provide more creative thinking tools; nevertheless, as with any complex intellectual activity, creating is a whole brain operation. The key issue is knowing which mode of thought is most appropriate in a given situation and allowing that hemisphere to take the lead. Helping youngsters to understand and appreciate their mental preferences so that they can leverage their strengths and develop their less preferred modes will enhance both creativity and learning.

When people with varied mental preferences can communicate effectively and have the flexibility to see the value in other ways of thinking about things, differences too often perceived as a threat can become a valued resource. The result?—a synergistic creative team in which each person contributes a unique perspective, and together the group creates outcomes that individuals would not been able to achieve working alone. That's why we encourage clients to invite people with varied mental preferences to participate in creative problem-solving meetings and to take time to explore the thinking style preferences present in the group.

Brain research has also offered an explanation for the mysterious phenomenon of incubation. The literature of creativity abounds with stories of break-through insights and novel ideas that occurred in an almost dreamlike state of consciousness. Even the scientific method was conceptualized in such a state; yet when we study science, it is easy to get the impression that discoveries were made in an alert state of mind following a logical, rational process that led step-by-step to the solution. That may be the case *after* the flash of insight when the discoverer evaluated and developed the idea further—but not when the "aha" moment arrived.

When the three-circle model came to Alison in the shower, she was in a dreamy state of mind. The insight came to her full-fledged and seemingly out of nowhere. The image of a model synthesizing the information she had gathered into a cohesive whole bears the mark of the right brain at work. When people are in an alert state of mind, the less verbal right brain is usually drowned out by the verbal left. When we shift into a quieter state of consciousness and the left brain relaxes its grip, the right can then get its message across to us. This suggests that stamping out daydreaming in classrooms, as has been the case for centuries, has done us a disservice by robbing us of the ideas and intuitive flashes of insight that can come to us only when we are more relaxed and receptive.

Because the right brain often communicates in images, we need to encourage visual thinking as a legitimate problem-solving tool. Students can learn to mind-map a problem or a project and represent concepts and ideas visually in two- or three-dimensional models. They can represent goals with symbols. Through the process, they and their teachers can learn to access the thinking this long-misunderstood and often discredited right hemisphere can do.

The Creative Mind Is Curious,
Flexible, and Imaginative

Curiosity, flexibility, and imagination are hallmarks of a creative mind. Watch a small child at play, and you can easily see all three in action. Why are they so rare in adults? A colleague of ours, Jordan Aryan, describes it this way: "We were all born with a box of 64 crayons and then, after years of schooling, come out with nothing but a black Bic pen."

Curiosity, flexibility, and imagination are among the brightest of those crayons that are our birthright, and we must keep them. We need them because they allow us to think approximately, challenge long-held assumptions, and see things from opposing points of view without slipping into either/or, good/bad, right/wrong mind-sets. When we can do that, our imagination grows stronger, and we can begin to sense new possibilities all around.

Regaining the ability to think flexibly helps people tolerate the ambiguity that comes with creativity territory. As Tom Peters (1994) writes, "For a long time to come a tolerance for ambiguity will be success tool number one for line workers, corporate chiefs, independent professionals, and politicians alike." We've found in our work with business people that ambiguity makes them uneasy. If people grew up understanding creative process and learned to trust it, especially when they encounter ambiguity, they would find their curiosity, flexibility, and imagination there to serve them as they work with the problems and challenges that bombard them.

Because young children typically bring lots of curiosity, flexibility, and imagination with them when they first walk into a classroom, the issue is now to ensure that they keep those precious attributes. One way is to create a learning environment in which the speculation, approximate thinking, and experimentation that fuel creative process are encouraged and in which children feel safe to risk being confused and uncertain. Because children in a school environment quickly learn that being right is what they get rewarded for, educators must make it clear that feeling confused and uncertain doesn't mean they are wrong. It's crucial when asking children to get involved in the creative process: Because confusion and uncertainty come with the territory when people go in search of creative ideas, they must learn to tolerate some ambiguity or they'll never try anything new.

Numerous thinking skill exercises and problem-solving strategies encourage us to look beyond the obvious, stretch the artificial boundaries we impose, and loosen the rigid categories we've erected in our minds so that our imagination can soar. Sadly, they are used mostly in programs for gifted and talented students or as short, change-of-pace classroom activities disconnected from the curriculum. They become much more powerful when teachers and children understand the mental processes involved and how they apply to thinking and problem solving creatively.

One of our favorite strategies for stimulating imagination is playing "I wish . . ." This is a wonderful way to figure out what you want in place of what you have in any situation. We find most adults have a hard time making wishes at first. They equate wishing with impractical, fuzzy, or just plain foolish thinking.

Young children don't. They typically wish with abandon. Then, by the time they are 7 or 8, children seem to repress the ability to wish—probably because they have been told that wishes such as "I wish my birthday came every day" are selfish or "I wish someone would kidnap my brother" are bad. Even best-intended wishes such as "I wish I would make straight A's" are met with comments such as "Wishing doesn't make it so." Once, when we asked some school administrators to do some wishing to help clarify their ideal outcome to the problem they were working on, one indignantly refused on the grounds that wishing was stupid and childish.

Students don't need to lose curiosity, flexibility, and imagination as education progresses—not if they are accorded the same careful attention and rewards that rational, precise, and linear thinking has gotten throughout the history of education.

All Things Are Connected

Developing a flexible mind leads to the discovery that all things are connected. Breaking down artificial barriers between disciplines and looking for hidden relationships between seemingly unrelated things are inherently creative. Once people understand that nothing is totally irrelevant in creative process, they can use their ability to think in images and metaphor to clarify problems and solve them creatively.

Metaphor, long considered the tool of the poet, is also the tool of the creative problem solver. Unfortunately, what most people learned about metaphor in school is how they differ from similes. Metaphor is consigned to English class, and few people ever learn to use metaphorical thinking as a creative problem-solving tool. That's sad—because through the years, thinking metaphorically has become one of the most effective strategies we know.

A group of people from a company we've worked with extensively were able to perfect a manufacturing process they thought they'd have to abandon because a nontechnical woman in a creative problem-solving session compared her understanding of the process in question to baking cookies. As she metaphorically described her connections, chemists and engineers listened carefully. Her metaphor sparked an idea that saved the process they were ready to scrap. It also saved the company all the money invested to date and resulted in millions of dollars in profit. Had these highly technical professionals been unwilling to consider the humble art of baking cookies relevant to their problem, the connection that unlocked the problem would never have been made and the project may well have been lost.

Discovering they can use metaphor to explore new concepts and invent new ideas is a revelation to most adults with whom we work. Moving away from precise thinking and making connections between the problem at hand and a metaphorical expression of it can deepen the understanding of the issue. Inventing a metaphorical expression of the ideal outcome can suggest new ideas for bringing it about.

For example, a woman in a recent workshop was working on the challenge of managing a sharply increased workload caused by a recent reorganization of her department. She chose "juggler" as the metaphor for her current reality because she felt as if she were juggling lots of balls and people kept tossing her more all the time. Catching a new one often meant she inadvertently dropped one or more of the ones she already had in motion.

Then she transformed the metaphor to describe her ideal outcome. Now she had found a rhythm that allowed her to easily juggle different types of balls—some sturdy rubber, some fragile glass. When someone threw her a new ball, she made sure that if she had to drop one of the old ones, it would be a rubber one and not one made of glass.

Playing with this metaphor suggested a couple of quick ideas that could help her move from her beginning metaphor of frantic juggling to her ideal state of confidently juggling different types of balls easily. First, she knew she needed a fast and accurate way to tell which of the balls she was juggling were rubber and which were glass. This suggested establishing goals and priorities that could tell her which tasks were crucial and would break if they were dropped and which would bounce and could be picked up later undamaged. The metaphor also told her the first thing she had to do when she caught a new ball was determine what it was made of.

This fast metaphorical exercise helped her discover she didn't need to give up her juggling act as she had thought. Instead, she decided she could juggle quite well when she knew what types of balls she was working with and understood that dropping a ball wasn't a disaster as long as it was a rubber one. She also decided a key step in creating her ideal outcome was setting clear priorities for herself that would give her the confidence that she would no longer confuse a rubber ball with a glass one. Juggling became a clarifying image that she can call on during a hectic day to help her remember what she wants to create and decide what to do next.

"All things are connected" is also a key principle to hold in mind as people refine and implement new ideas. Everything we think or do takes place in a larger context. Considering possible effects on the big picture brings responsibility to creativity. Discussing possible far-flung effects helps us learn to act with intention. A science teacher got this principle across well by involving students in a study of the unanticipated effects, both positive and negative, of technological advances. That all things are connected also comes into play when we work to align what we do with a larger vision and purpose and ensure that we are "walking our talk."

Getting Started

The easiest way to begin is incorporating creative process into what you are already doing. You don't need to wait for a mandate from someone else. Simply begin where you can. Adopt a creative mind-set by continually looking for creativity in action and acknowledging and rewarding it any way you can. Use creative thinking strategies such as connection making and metaphorical thinking to teach what you are already teaching. Encourage youngsters to look at their problems from different viewpoints and demonstrate how creating what you want in place of what you have turns problems and challenges into new opportunities. Examine issues for what's working and what things people wish were different. Use those wishes to figure out ways to make things better.

These are strategies no one need justify. They demonstrate sound teaching and learning. If you find yourself in an environment in which creativity and innovation aren't encouraged, call it "effective thinking." People may think teaching creative process to children is suspect, but who would challenge you for teaching effective thinking? When you move beyond simply acquiring facts, there are so many correlations between learning and creative process that it's hard to tell the difference. Students learn as they create, and they create as they learn.

There are other similarities. Real learning involves making new connections and creating new meaning. So does creative process. When people are truly learning, they are not bored; they are excited and involved, as they are when they create. Facts that seemed boring take on new meaning when studied in the context of a creative project. (It happened to us while working on this chapter. One evening, we came across a school board meeting on our cable community access channel. On the surface, the meeting was dull as dirt, but because we were looking for connections with the ideas we were developing, we found ourselves listening intently.)

Creative thinking skills are also good learning tools. Teaching children to think metaphorically directly enhances learning, which makes sense because a key part of learning is connecting new information to what they already know. Research conducted in a Title I program in the middle 1970s by William Gordon and Tony Poze (1978) of Synectics Educational Systems (SES) was based on the hypothesis that simple connection making is an innate skill in normal K-3 students. When youngsters say things such as "rain means the clouds are crying," they are naturally building a bridge between what they already know and what they are trying to understand. They found, however, that the Title I children could not make even the most obvious associations.

The researchers approached this problem by developing exercises to teach children to make explicit associations between their personal experience and new concepts they were learning. They trained the teachers in facilitative responses that credited children when they made connections and helped them discover new ones as they talked about their thinking. This allowed these children who came from impoverished areas to talk about what was really going on in their lives, something they'd been reluctant to do with less accepting teachers.

Here is a striking example of a child thinking metaphorically while his teacher supported him, using facilitative responses that help create the type of safe classroom climate in which creative thought can flourish. The class was exploring the concept of erosion, and the teacher was encouraging her third graders to give examples from their personal experience. One withdrawn little boy tentatively raised his hand, lowered it, and then slowly raised it again. The teacher called on him. "Erosion's like the garbage outside my house," he said quietly. The teacher at this point hadn't a clue what the little guy was thinking. "Can you tell us more about that?" she asked, using an eliciting response to draw out highly individual connections based on personal experience.

"Well, the garbage just sits in the gutter where people put it down. When it rains, the water runs down the gutter and hits the bags of garbage and pushes them into a real big pile. Then the water is stopped up and there's a dam there. But the water keeps hitting the pile until it makes a hole in it and the hole keeps getting bigger and bigger until the bag breaks open and the garbage washes down the street." That was clearly erosion in action right there in Roxbury, Massachusetts.

Once the children knew how to purposefully search out such connections, they made dramatic improvements on standardized test scores. For instance, first graders showed a 273% gain in word recognition and an 84% gain in comprehension. Oral comprehension improved 286%. These impressive results came after just 30 hours of classroom practice during several months.

Recent brain research may explain why these children made such enormous gains. Ronald Kotulak (1995), in a nationally distributed article, reported that neuropsychologists are finding that when people think of a new connection between things, they are actually physically altering their brains. Brain scans have provided biological evidence that mental exercise causes the brain to grow by strengthening connections between brain cells called *synapses* and building new neural networks. (This brain growth occurs in persons of all ages and appears to help prevent or slow the onset of Alzheimer's disease.)

If metaphorical thinking alone helped disadvantaged youngsters learn so quickly, we are convinced that involving children in the principles and processes of creativity as they learn can, too. Imagine the brain growth that can happen every day while children are engaged in thinking and learning creatively.

Creative process can also form the structure of how people live together in a school and classroom. An innovative middle school principal who has transformed schools for the last decade has an unusual strategy for infusing creative process. She teaches groups of children to use creative process, brainstorming strategies, and creative communication skills. Then she turns them loose to use their skills in school activities such as student government, school improvement committees, and conflict resolution projects. She draws the faculty's interest by letting the kids lead the way.

Teachers with whom we have worked have taught their students to use creative process to plan a unit of study together. They begin by brainstorming a list of things they already know about the topic and developing a list of what they want to learn next. Then they generate ideas for learning activities and projects that can help them learn what they want to know.

Only when enough people recognize its true value will creative process take its rightful place in curriculum. Beginning where we are will help make it happen. The stakes are high. We can't afford to wait.

We believe wishes have the power to create new possibilities—so we conclude with a wish list. We wish for a day when we watch children begin school knowing that all 64 of their crayons will be safe. We wish every student could experience the joy and the responsibility of creating throughout the school years. We wish every school held fast to a vision of enhancing the creative potential of each youngster there. We wish that young people graduated with the confidence that they know how to meet their problems, challenges, and opportunities with creativity and imagination. And finally, we wish that someday schools will do such an incredible job of nurturing and developing each youngster's innate creativity that our work with adults will become totally obsolete.

References

Covey, S. R. (1989). *The seven habits of highly effective people: Powerful lessons in personal change.* New York: Simon & Schuster.

Edwards, B. (1986). *Drawing on the artist within.* New York: Simon & Schuster.

Gailey, P. (1995, March 19). An inside look at classroom realities: Reader responses show a public education system in crisis. *St. Petersburg Times,* p. 1.

Gordon, W. J. J., & Poze, T. (1978, March). Learning dysfunction and connection making. *Psychiatric Annals, 8*(3).

Kotulak, R. (1995, May 16). Inside the brain: Use it or lose it. *St. Petersburg Times.*

Peters, T. (1994). *The Tom Peters seminar: Crazy times call for crazy organizations.* New York: Random House.

Senge, P. (1990). *The fifth discipline: The art and practice of the learning organization.* New York: Doubleday.

13

Historical Inquiry

Martha I. Turner
Merv Akin

A key question to ask of students is, "What do you do when you want to learn about something you don't know?" The answers to that question reveal the inner workings of the learners' minds, their strategies for figuring things out, and their capabilities to cope successfully with the inevitable explosion of new unknowns to be encountered throughout their lives. Going from not knowing to knowing is a survival skill that applies to all areas of learning and one that increases in importance in the face of not only an expansion of new knowledge every day but also an expansion of the avenues of widespread dissemination of that information in the future. How do people distinguish fact from fiction? How do we decide what information is important or even relevant? How can we determine whether it is accurate? What do we do when we come to some information we don't understand? And what do we do with the knowledge we acquire? The additional acceleration in the passage of events puts a new pressure on historians to document it all and interpret the significance and impact of these events. That pressure extends to the classroom as well, as students are expected to master more—more complicated knowledge and more sophisticated forms of encountering new information.

Most students encounter history through the printed page or through the presentation of teachers. Both teachers' words and textbooks are replete with the conclusions that have been drawn by others considered authorities in the field. Students suffer from the experience of having history taught to them as an accumulation of facts and conclusions and not as a dynamic, integral force in their daily lives. The authority accorded the conclusions being taught has led to a regard for history as a cumulative story or set of understandings not subject to any continuing argument that may significantly change its impact on their own lives. It is not surprising, then, that studies of students' attitudes toward their subject matter in school have consistently reported social studies as one of the least-liked subjects in the curriculum. Students see history as irrelevant and having little value in preparing them for a rapidly changing world (Shaughnessy & Haladyna, 1985). They do not see a role for history in their day-to-day lives. And yet their lives are a veritable world of historical data. Every day, students come into contact with the information of other places, other times, and other people. They are surrounded by references to the past as changing information is reported in the present. They see it in the television, they hear it on the radio, they read it in the newspapers, and they access it on the computer.

Despite these attitudes toward history, its study has an important place in the curriculum—not the history of the textbooks but the processes of historians. Although students in school "do many things that are labeled 'study,' they seldom engage in an activity that . . . a scholar might recognize as study" (Clements, Fielder, & Tabachnick, 1966, p. 17). History also does not divide the curriculum into discrete disciplines. It is integrative. All disciplines and there-fore the processes of all forms of inquiry are part of the study of history. The processes historical scholars use to draw conclusions can inform educators about how to encourage students to develop ideas about the implications of the record of past places and events. The essential nature of knowledge is that it is constantly changing. History itself is the story of changing knowledge. "In the midst of a knowledge explosion, each of us must either know how to build new generalizations or be content to live in tomorrow's world with yesterday's knowledge" (Fenton, 1967, p. 13). When history is taught as only the interpre-tations of others, the vitality of learning history is compromised. Students need to learn to interpret the records themselves. They need to ask the questions the historians ask.

History is not the "past." History is not a record of past events. History is not an existing body of knowledge to be learned to become an authority. Yet in classrooms, history has been taught as such—as a narrative of a past life that yields to us the "lessons of history." But what are the "lessons" being learned? They can range from a blind acceptance of the interpretations put forth in the textbooks to an unrelenting disregard for history as irrelevant and vapid. Even with the naive belief of history as an account of the record of past events, we will see that the answer to the seemingly simple question, "What happened here?" reveals a host of underlying processes that contribute to the construction of the stories that constitute the "lessons" of history.

Through time, the stories of historians became the facts of history and accepted as truth. It was not until those narratives became subject to questions of evidence that history was acknowledged to be essentially a process of interpretation. And so it stands today that history is an inquiry—an inquiry into the human story and the record left by humans for historians to interpret. At the core of its focus are the facts—the evidence of history. As such, it continues to be a discipline of investigation, of interpretation, and of reflection. One group of social scientists has called what historians study the "residue" of human life and the processes of investigation they use "the scrutiny of things" (Clements et al., 1966, pp. 21, 22). We have residue, the remnants of "what happened here," in the forms of journals, artwork, newspapers, and photographs—those artifacts of social life that can be seen, or read, or touched, or heard. But nothing of the residue comes to life if it is not confronted with questions and the answers to the questions presented in some form for others to consider. We also know, however, that the nature of knowledge is not static. History is the study of that changing knowledge. So how can we relate the study of history to present classroom practices? As Richard Pascale (1990) has noted, "The essential activity for keeping . . . current is persistent questioning. I will use the term inquiry" (p. 14). And as Michael Fullan (1993) commented, Pascale has captured the essence of inquiry precisely in his assertion that for educators the "question is the answer" (p. 15).

The Craft of Historians

Historical facts do not define the nature of history. The historians' craft involves transforming the facts of history into answers to the question of "What happened here?" The interpretation of those facts can be hotly contended as they are selectively organized and fashioned into a reconstruction of the past. This continuous confrontation with the evidence means that history is constantly being rewritten, that subsequent generations interpret the past anew in light of the current knowledge available and fresh insights into past experiences.

> The same series of vanished events is differently imagined in each succeeding generation. . . . Our imagined picture of the actual event is always determined by two things: (1) by the actual event itself insofar as we can know something about it; and (2) by our own present purposes, desires, prepossessions, and prejudices, all of which enter into the process of knowing it. (Becker, 1958, p. 57)

For a subject matter that has been seen as stable and solid, the definition of history as a questioning of the past may be unsettling unless one comes to terms with all knowledge as a product of the human mind. Therefore, history is a growing, learning process that one can construct and label as historical knowledge. The historian then is a craftsperson who builds knowledge as carefully as a carpenter follows the steps in the process of constructing a building.

How does knowledge of history come into being? What are the steps involved in piecing together the facts to construct a picture of the past? Historians begin their craft of creating historical knowledge through processes that are fundamental to all inquiry—posing questions, confronting evidence, interpreting data, and communicating findings. The statement "Let the facts speak for themselves" is misleading because there are no facts that "speak" their meaning without some human interpretation. And the process of interpretation is at the heart of historical inquiry. As a result, facts may have many meanings, depending on the questions that have been asked of them. All the facts that make up the historical knowledge base come from a rather frail source—the human "voice" of those facts, the very mind itself. One historian coined the phrase "Everyman is his own historian" to emphasize that our knowing of the past is what we think it to be and this "thinking history" becomes "what we know it to be" (Becker, 1935/1966, p. 234). History comes from the questions and answers in the conversations professional historians have with the facts and with each other. Students of history have to learn to ask these questions to know for themselves the stories of the past. Yet these stories, too, are interpretations—interpretations that are continually open to question. And so the process of inquiry never fully stops. In that sense then, the known facts of history are only tentative conclusions, known as of the current time and open to further questioning, discovery, revision, and interpretation as new facts emerge and others continue to investigate the findings of the past.

In fact, let us follow a young historian around for a while to help us gain some insights into the processes students of history can use to know about the past. As we trace the steps of Anna Rosmus, a student who set out on a journey of historical inquiry, we will find her encounter with the "facts" to be the embodiment of what it means to be a historian, to be an active participant in the conversation about "what happened here" and in the necessary questioning about the meaning of the past in lives today. As a high school student in Passau, Germany, Rosmus entered an essay contest on the topic "Life in My Hometown Between 1933 and 1945." Expecting to find recollections about the town's resistance to the Nazis, Rosmus was surprised to find that the older residents were uncomfortable with the topic and put up some resistance of their own to her efforts to find out the truth. Her discoveries that some local leaders were Nazi sympathizers and that a concentration camp had been located nearby elicited enmity from the very people she was studying. Their anger was demonstrated not only with lack of cooperation and refusal to share information but with threats of vicious slander and physical violence. "For a long while, I received threatening and obscene calls virtually day and night. I was spat upon. . . . [Later] when I gave birth to my daughter, Salome, the location of my hospital room was kept secret because of the threats that my baby would be killed" (Allis & Spelman, 1991, p. 80). Rosmus's research overturned one deeply held conclusion about the role of the mayor as the town's only Nazi. She discovered that he was one of the few who actually helped the Jewish population in Passau. Uncovering this act of heroism, coupled with the findings about the hypocrisy of the activities of the townspeople during the Third Reich, caused Rosmus to be both vilified and honored. She was labeled "the nasty girl" in her town and yet received a prestigious award for the book she subsequently published from her research.

The confrontational nature of historical inquiry gives rise to a constant revisiting of the conclusions that were drawn through prior study. Historians must have a tolerance for the ambiguity of the tentative nature of knowledge with which they are working because the task of writing history is never done. Sometimes scholars discover that conclusions drawn in years past are found wanting today. Such was the case of the villagers of Passau, who had defined themselves as resisters to Nazi influence. Having to confront their past as a complex intermingling of resistance and collaboration made their story more complete, but this story still cannot be claimed to be the final word on "what happened there." This process is not historical revisionism but a contribution to the refining and updating of knowledge that takes place in all fields of inquiry. History is constantly being rewritten, and that trait need not disturb those who revere the story. We need to recognize that the changing nature of history fits in with the changing nature of knowledge itself. It follows, then, that if students are to be truly educated for a rapidly changing world, they must be prepared to manage this condition intelligently with the skills of inquiry. The continuity of history comes not only from looking at the present as a product of the past but also from looking at the past with the knowledge, values, and perspectives of the present.

So what is inquiry itself? It is both an art and a science. It is an art in the curiosity behind the questioning, the carefulness behind the observing, and the intuition behind the noticing of patterns. It is a science in its method of constructing meaning, testing for validity, and putting pieces together into a coherent whole. The historian must have the qualities of persistence, of openness to new ideas, of tolerance for ambiguity, and of appreciation for tentative but well-founded conclusions. The historian has to be able to communicate the results of inquiry effectively for understanding to take place. In this way, the inquirer into history can reflect not only on the final work but on the process as well, allowing others to contribute to the continuing nature of the inquiry itself.

Posing Questions

The beginning of the inquiry is questioning. But inquiry is not questioning alone. If the process of inquiry begins with questions, then it can be said that it ends with interpretation. Posing questions about the past, conducting research through careful observation and analysis, and formulating interpretations and explanations are all part of the craft of historians. Teaching students to ask productive questions requires a continual relation back and forth between the data through inferring and hypothesizing, then formulating more deliberate questions to confirm, deny, or refine the interpretations that are emerging. Teachers can model this process of wrestling with problems of history and formulating questions in front of students to provide examples of the skills that characterize scholarly endeavor.

Scholarly inquirers may also find themselves posing questions that may lead to controversy. In the case of Anna Rosmus, when she interviewed the people of her town, she found their reactions led her to formulate an unexpected set of questions leading to unwanted interpretations. In fact, Rosmus acquired her label "nasty girl" as a result of her questioning. "Several of them used even the word, 'shut up,' and 'don't ask any more questions about this time. Don't you think you ask nasty questions?' " (Safer, 1994). Questions form the basis of interpretation. "Every step in the argument depends on asking a question" (Collingwood, 1946, p. 273). The questions the inquirer asks shape the answers that are found. History then becomes an argument for a set of conclusions, for a particular point of view about what the data say. The results are conflicts over varying interpretations of the data and problems with the way data are fashioned into an organized pattern.

Problem finding itself can be an entry point for historical inquiry. It can start with noticing a discrepancy. "Problems" with information, however, cannot begin without some background in the regularity of the data. For the discrepancy to be noticed, one has to have studied the familiar pattern. This background is the role of a knowledge base in studying history. For students in the classroom, the doing of history takes place at the same time they are collecting a background in history. Problem finding will also take place when one is not consciously seeking out a problem but discovers it once questions are asked. Such was the case with Anna Rosmus. She was asking the question of what happened here and discovered a pattern of cover-up in the responses she was getting because they did not fit with the traditional story being told the younger generations. She noticed a discrepancy in what the proud tale of her town's past had been and the reluctance of her sources to talk about specifics in the case. She had to work through the problem to construct a coherent story. Such problem finding is deceptive in historical inquiry because the "solution" to a problem lies in an explanation and not necessarily the definitive answer to a specific problem. It is also in problem finding that the inquirer can get some resolution by explaining a puzzle or contributing focus to an unclear picture of the past. The problem-finding aspect may be deeply personal because the rewards for such endeavors are often not public or appreciated by others. When asked about her own reactions to the findings of her study of the town's past, Anna Rosmus replied, "I never regretted, and I never felt sorry. I remained cool. I didn't oblige my attackers by permitting them to see that I was hurt" (Allis & Spelman, 1991, p. 79). Problem finding in historical inquiry is not meant to offer solution to the ages.

Confronting Evidence

As evidence is being collected, historians are inevitably confronted with the realization that not all the data will ever be gathered. Historians must contend with the given that they will never know the whole story. They will be able to work with only a sample of the available data because information about the past is recognizably infinite. The past is knowable with the understanding that it is never fully known, never finished. In the process of collection, selection also inevitably takes place. And in the dynamic interaction of collection, selection, seeking new evidence, and organizing it, historians begin to formulate inferences about the meanings that are emerging. They make hypotheses that lead to further evidence gathering that may confirm, deny, or change their evolving hypotheses. They may begin to recognize some implications from their hypotheses that compel them to continue in this cycle of data gathering and inferring until a clearer definition of the scope of their study becomes clear. Historians realize that the most rigorous adherence to collecting a great amount of data will help to form more robust hypotheses. But even after all that work, they must find a place to stop at some time and come to terms with the reality that their conclusions will never represent the only way a set of data can be interpreted.

Constructing the interpretation, the meaning of an event, involves reconstructing relevant data. Whether evidence is relevant must be subject to a test of validity as well. This emphasis on relevance and validity of data can serve to promote an attitude of healthy skepticism among the young consumers of historical fact. Students need to, in a sense, cross-examine the witness to history and the interpreters themselves. Asking questions about the background, the expertise, and the completeness of a story is not questioning whether a given set of data exists but only setting the foundation for further inquiry and examination by student scholars. As new information is considered, weak or invalid evidence needs to be shown for what it is. But if students do not know about or practice the tests of relevance and validity themselves, how can they be critical consumers of newspaper accounts or television reporting when they become adults? Doing historical inquiry teaches them to hold their sources of information accountable.

Confronting evidence also means looking at contexts. The relationships among the data may drive the course of inquiry, informing historians about what paths to follow, what type of information to look for, and what data are misleading or irrelevant. Some data may have to be discarded. Conversely, the noticeable absence of data may have to be explained. As the fragments come together, a story of what happened here or why this is so may take form. Historians also must know the techniques of examining the sources from which data are obtained. The ability to access good sources is one thing; another is the ability to check the background of a given source of data and weigh it against criteria of soundness. What criteria usually constitute a sound source of data? Primary sources are always cited as close to the event as one can get, but the inquirer into history has to take into account the unique perspective and, thus, the idiosyncratic interpretation a primary source brings to reporting the story. This aspect requires that the inquirer seek out multiple sources of data to put together a picture of what happened. And those multiple sources must be put into a context in which the story unfolds.

There are times in the process that historians go beyond the more systematic and linear steps of identifying a story to be told or a problem to solve and "play a hunch" or act on their intuition about where their study is leading them. Anna Rosmus's discoveries began in the archives of the local newspaper. Following her hunches that something was being held back, she had to focus her efforts more on primary sources of data than newspaper accounts—the actual people of the time who lived through the Third Reich. She also had to have another quality essential for historians to confront evidence. She had to persist in the face of strong opposition in finding information, and she had to persist in the face of strong opposition once she had shared her findings. Historians must be prepared to be persistent in their research. This persistence is described as "that prime duty of the historian, a willingness to bestow infinite pains on discovering what actually happened" (Collingwood, 1946, p. 55). And, as we have seen, that "duty" may lead to a pain of another type once it comes before the court of public opinion. Thus, the "scrutiny of things" comes in many forms and turns up again and again in historical inquiry, exposing students of history not only to the operations in the process but also to the dispositions characteristic of scholars themselves.

Interpreting Data

Knowing that the task of interpretation is never complete, historians can claim to draw only tentative conclusions with the understanding that as new data emerge, generalizations may be subject to change. Thus, history is a study of change, of creating knowledge about change and letting it be subject to change. For students of history, the real learning takes place in this process of creating new knowledge and expanding the knowledge base already in use. Within the realm of this construction of new knowledge about history are some methods generally useful for the processes of constructing meaning: collaborating with others and reflecting on what has been learned.

Historical inquiry is not done in isolation. Even the most independent researcher needs to team up with others to accomplish the tasks of historical inquiry. This collaboration can take the form of feedback from other experts along the way. It ultimately is present in the response given once the research findings are presented. In a most unique sense, the historian "collaborates" with the sources of data themselves. The questioning turns into conversations, even if the "voices" of sources of data are dead. The historian can "listen" to data for answers to help in the formulation of further questions in the dialogue. They speak to one another in the true sense of a conversation, and one source of data can direct the historian to other sources of data to join in the conversation. Anna Rosmus sought help from archivists and elders in her town as she pursued her questions about the past. She followed up on leads that were given to her by others just as a sleuth goes about solving a mystery. Her sources of information were limited, and sometimes people would not give her needed data. Library officials refused to let her see town records. "At first I had to sue them to get access, then they told me they lost it. It happened over and over again" (Safer, 1994). Her course of inquiry was fueled at points in the process when things didn't make sense. She was determined to find the meaning of this puzzle. Others were inspired by her determination and helped her put together the pieces that did not seem to fit. She was able to confirm her findings as the facts unfolded, and her work subsequently contributed to the research of others. The teamwork of historian and sources results in a final "discussion" of the answers to questions asked. At that time, others join the discussion to the degree that researchers find themselves working together, maybe not always in agreement but as a "team" seeking the truth.

Learning comes both by active work with data and through reflection on the work done. Historical inquiry is essentially reflective inquiry. The conclusions that have been drawn in the past are revisited and evaluated in the process of reflection. Reflection also takes place as the questions are turned on the inquirers themselves and how their own perspectives affect the inquiry they do. Historians reflect on their work and the frames of reference they bring to their work. This process takes time. Ideas themselves require time to season, to cure, to incubate. Not all inquiry will lead to satisfying conclusions. It may lead to unexpected understandings that could be unsettling, disturbing, even disruptive of life itself. Anna Rosmus found this out for herself as she received reactions to her study in the form of threats and acts of violence against her. But the subjects of her inquiry were not just other people—she was just as much a subject of her study as she ventured into unknown territory regarding what it meant to be a citizen of a town with this dual legacy. "The people of Passau consider the kind of aggressions they have vented at me as a very welcome relief from their rather dull, provincial lives. If it hadn't been for me, they would have had to invent someone else in my place" (Allis & Spelman, 1991, p. 79). Her need to understand her roots became a quest into the background of a town's identity and, consequently, a personal quest into the meaning behind her own identity as well. Her own frame of reference and attitude played a part in the inquiry process.

Communicating Findings

Learning is entirely personal. No learning takes place without the active involvement of the learner in the process. So how do we know that a learner has learned? When a learner has communicated, when he or she puts into action the results of understanding, then the learning comes into reality and is added to the knowledge base. Therefore, the process of inquiry demands some sort of demonstration of understanding. This understanding can be communicated in various forms: through deeds, through writing, through art, and through speaking. When true understanding takes place, the learner is communicating the knowledge acquired through the process of inquiry. Knowledge comes into existence only with the communication of meaning. And all meaning is social—that is, it does not exist in a vacuum but must be constructed in relation to others for it to be "known."

The essay Anna Rosmus wrote for the contest was transformed into a book, *Resistance and Persecution: The Case of Passau 1933-1945.* She could have stopped there, but she set aside her fears to continue on the journey of discovery by starting again with new questions that were dredged up in the process of the first investigation. Her findings led her to ask more questions about the fate of the Jews in her town during the Nazi years and resulted in the subsequent publication of another book, *Exodus: In the Shadow of Mercy.* With this inquiry, she was able to give voices to some of the victims who might not have been heard if not for her efforts. The purpose of historical inquiry is for understanding—for understanding ourselves, our past, and our possible futures. In a sense, when Anna Rosmus launched into her study of the town's past, she was asking a question of understanding, that of understanding herself. As she uncovered that story of the place where she was born, she also uncovered part of the answer to the question, "Who am I?" We all gain a deeper insight into who we are as human beings when we seek to answer questions of our past. Understanding is the highest level of knowing something. It is putting knowledge to work for us in the best sense of the word. We are doing the work of understanding "what happened here" to better understand how things are and what they may become.

Students as Inquirers

Given that history is not an accumulation of facts but the act of creating knowledge that comes from asking meaning-filled questions, the construction of meaning is the result of scholarly pursuit and is the essence of real learning that should take place in our schools. " 'Learning from history' is very different from 'history teaches' " (Isenberg, 1985, p. 29). If educators teach history as simple facts or the conclusions of experts, we take the essence of real learning out of the hands of the learners. It would be like asking students to learn the answers to math problems without giving them the opportunity to pose and solve problems themselves; the process is lost, and so is the essence of its meaning. If we teach history as an opportunity for students to use historical inquiry just as Anna Rosmus did, we are being true to the purpose of learning from history. So, too, must students engage in the scholarly pursuit of the meaning of history and construct for themselves a scaffold of understanding that represents their knowledge. Attempts at dividing the process of inquiry into different academic disciplines, listing the sets of generalizations accumulated from those disciplines, and then testing for the recall of those generalizations by students of those disciplines are misdirected attempts at constructing learners' knowledge foundation. Learners must practice the skills of constructing and testing knowledge for it to become understood in their minds.

Just how do teachers translate the processes of historical inquiry into classroom practice? How do students grow from novice to junior historians following the processes that expert scholars use? The gradual sophistication that comes with practice can take place if educators base instruction in history on the types of questions and experiences the learners bring into the classroom in the first place. Students tend to miss the spirit of adventure and the passion that professional historians claim to experience when teachers present the study of history as a series of abstractions through abstract means. Even young children can work on the processes of historical inquiry given appropriate sources of information and experiences to guide them. We can make historical inquiry too complicated. As Seymour Papert (1993) has noted, "Rather than pushing children to think like adults, we might do better to remember that they are great learners and to try harder to be more like them" (p. 155). Young learners bring the gift of combining their imaginations with their experiences to construct knowledge. This link lends itself productively to a purposeful relationship between teaching and learning in the classroom. The means are there for it to happen.

What can be the beginning questions of inquiry in the classroom? According to one curriculum, there are several natural entry points for young students of history. Students have intrinsic interest in finding surprises or noticing oddities in information. They practice asking "How can we know that?" or "What has happened through time?" Young students also are curious about the causes of human events and want to know about the diversity that exists in life (Fielder, 1976). The wonder that the young children bring into the classroom about seemingly unrelated facts and their willingness to ask questions can be capitalized on by teachers. Studies of activities removed in time and place only make more dramatic the construction of concepts students derive as they make new relationships among the facts and build a foundation of knowledge. That construction of a knowledge base is important to a thorough understanding of any area and grows as students conduct their investigations. We must recognize, however, that they are building on a foundation already brought with them, which accounts for their ability to see how prior experience fits with the reality they are taught in school. In fact, this can be a driving force—that of separating fact from fiction, myth from reality, truth from fantasy. The questions the young historians ask are the very ones they need to practice to prepare for understanding future information. In their testing of the truth, they are establishing the habits of mind most useful in any investigation. They are beginning to answer questions through scrutiny rather than just through authority.

The job of students in the classroom is to learn. Their job skills are those of posing questions, confronting evidence, interpreting data, and communicating findings. For learning to take place, active involvement with the data is required. As students confront the residue of other ages, they may be able to develop fluency in the language of scholars and the skills of participating in a scholarly conversation. Students can read, react, and interact with each other. The residue can come from students' daily life. In fact, there was a time when members in a family household included several generations who were able to provide that bridge to the past with recollections and experiences that constituted readily available historical data in the home life of students. Today, we rely on the vast expanse of raw data available in the media. Students are able to develop an appreciation for the requirements of any vocation they may choose by asking questions about their own experiences, finding and solving problems about the data, and constructing answers through the processes of doing historical inquiry.

Schools as Places of Inquiry

Inquiry into history offers an opportunity to address the concerns of Howard Gardner that students do not understand most of what they have been taught in school (Brandt, 1993). The "multiple entry points" for study extend from the questions that are posed to the multiplicity of forms by which interpretations may be communicated. It is obvious that the role of teachers will have to change in a classroom that focuses on historical inquiry. Teachers themselves will have to be practitioners in the processes of inquiry. Gardner advocates apprenticeships for students. He encourages teachers to think of themselves as masters and to model what they expect from their students. "The master teacher thinks, 'I'm not just passing on the contents of a textbook; I'm modeling a certain kind of knowledge and standards for making use of that knowledge in daily life' " (Brandt, 1993, p. 6). For understanding to occur, teachers and students should be doing history together, with the teachers as master craftspersons and the students as apprentices.

As an example, one high school classroom organized itself as a community of historians who selected their own questions of history to investigate and, as closely as possible, followed the processes of historical inquiry to draw their own conclusions and present them to each other. Teachers asked students to keep three precepts in mind as they went about doing history. "Historians must have accurate information, they have to use that information in drawing conclusions, and they can't abuse the information they have by ignoring or contradicting it" (Kobrin, Abbott, Ellinwood, & Horton, 1993, p. 40). Students were given historical documents including the interpretations of experts to use in their investigations. These teachers recognized that students' endeavors in historical inquiry may not have all the requirements of scholarly pursuit, but students' experiences doing this will become a vital part of their developing a sense of craftsmanship.

> History is the business of writing answers to questions for which there
> are no answers in the back of the book. . . . The obligation upon the
> historian is that he must deal intelligently with the residue of that time.
> He must not ignore inconvenient residue; he must be an honest crafts-
> man. (Clements et al., 1966, p. 60)

By the familiar way educators go about teaching history as conclusions, we
perpetuate the ancient Greek practice of passing along the findings of experts
as logical, self-evident "truths" and disregard the importance of direct experience with the craft, the craft of "dealing intelligently with the residue of that
time." One becomes considered an authority only if one has gone through the
processes of testing one's own ideas with evidence. Learning is a result of
"study," and "study" is the process of constructing meaning from data.

Full scholarly control over any subject area requires mastery over its processes to handle the barrage of information. Because the process of inquiry is
also progressive, students should have continuing practice in school to improve
their skills of active interpretation of data. It is an important job worthy of the
time they spend in the classroom. For students to develop their understandings,
they must have time to go in depth. Gardner stated again that the implication
of this "is that we've got to do a lot fewer things in school. The greatest enemy
of understanding is coverage" (quoted in Brandt, 1993, p. 7). One of the keys to
understanding what every student should know is that knowing requires an
attitude of respect for inquiry.

Respect for inquiry leads to another aspect of doing history—that of the
notion of caring. If Anna Rosmus had not cared about her past, she would not
have had the impetus to begin and finish her journey. Her friends did not see
the importance of digging up the past and finding out what really happened.
They were living in the present and did not care or see the relevance of their
town's past to who they are. Representative of her fellow students were
Rosmus's brother and sister, whose reactions Rosmus described with the following: "They sympathize with me, but they feel it is enough for one of us to
hold up the flag" (Allis & Spelman, 1991, p. 80). It took courage for Anna Rosmus
to embark on her journey of discovery and persist in the face of adversity. She
established her authority and stood her ground as someone who had gone to a
depth of inquiry not done before. Ironically, these values of tough-mindedness
and independent thought are the very ones that are sought by those with a
concern for improving schools. Students rarely have opportunities to become
experts—authorities with an in-depth grasp on anything. As we see in our
examples of students doing history, however, scholarly inquirers start on a
personal basis—a curiosity about something, a unique take on a given set of
data—not on standards set by external forces. And so sincere inquirers may
have to end on a personal basis, that of knowing an accomplishment for
themselves alone. Such a process can contribute to students' consciousness of
their place in the world.

As described here, the adventure of historical inquiry is sometimes an
intellectual endeavor, a mental process based on a way of thinking. But it also
can be a process that can induce feelings of wonderment, sadness, and satisfaction. Reaching into the past can evoke in students images of the acts—sounds,

thoughts, and feelings—that bring that past to life. History is imaginative, looking into a mirror of the past to find out for ourselves what the dim and colorful reflections tell us. In the struggle to improve education, we have confused knowledge as external rather than as finding out for ourselves. This view has been greatly strengthened in recent years by reports about what high school graduates don't know and their alarming disregard for some of the most basic facts. But the most basic facts tell us that the picture is always changing—even our picture of the past.

What does history have to tell us about ourselves and where we are going? It is only in the process of inquiry that we can expect to answer those questions. Scholars from all fields reach into past practice to develop ways to encounter future possibilities. In the spirit of the process, those concerned with implementing this approach must respect the time it takes to seek answers to questions that are yet to be generated. As Fullan (1993) has indicated, "Lifelong inquiry is the generative characteristic needed because post-modern environments themselves are constantly changing" (p. 15). And so, if this is the state of the art, why not teach it in schools to students who are immersed in a world of data with which to inquire? If schools themselves are to be models of learning for students, then they have to be places of continuous inquiry and classrooms places for a community of learners.

Any push for higher standards in education needs to be focused on ways of knowing—not on what to know. The doing of history challenges even the highest-achieving students to go beyond the conventional "read to recall on tests" type of learning. As Peter Senge has asserted, "Really deep learning is a process that inevitably is driven by the learner, not by someone else. And it always involves moving back and forth between a domain of thinking and a domain of action" (quoted in O'Neil, 1995, p. 20). The doing of history affirms that sense of efficacy and resourcefulness that contributes to students' sense of self-worth. A sense of self grounded in where they have come from can ultimately lead to a sense of who they will be as contributors to society. The value of this need to establish learning identities is even more obvious to today's students because they are immersed in a world of change.

References

Allis, T., & Spelman, F. (1991, March 25). Scorned as the real-life nasty girl, Anna Rosmus forces her hometown to confront the shadows of its Nazi past. *People Weekly, 35*(11), 79-80.

Becker, C. L. (1958). What are historical facts? In P. L. Synder, *Detachment and the writings of history: Essays and letters of Carl L. Becker.* Ithaca, NY: Cornell University Press.

Becker, C. L. (1966). *Everyman is his own historian: Essays on history and politics.* Chicago: Quadrangle Books. (Original work published 1935)

Brandt, R. (1993). On teaching for understanding: A conversation with Howard Gardner. *Educational Leadership, 50*(7), 4-7.

Clements, H. M., Fielder, W. R., & Tabachnick, B. R. (1966). *Social study: Inquiry in elementary classrooms.* New York; Bobbs-Merrill.

Collingwood, R. G. (1946). *The idea of history.* London: Oxford University Press.

Fenton, E. (1967). *The new social studies.* New York: Holt, Rinehart, & Winston.

Fielder, W. R. (1976). Teaching toward inquiry: What is teachable and learnable? In W. R. Fielder (Ed.), *Holt databank system: A social science program.* New York: Holt, Rinehart, & Winston.

Fullan, M. (1993). *Change forces: Probing the depths of educational reform.* London: Falmer.

Isenberg, M. T. (1985). *Puzzles of the past: An introduction to thinking about history.* College Station: Texas A & M University Press.

Kobrin, D., Abbott, E., Ellinwood, J., & Horton, D. (1993). Learning history by doing history. *Educational Leadership, 50*(7), 39-41.

O'Neil, J. (1995). On schools as learning organizations: A conversation with Peter Senge. *Educational Leadership, 52*(7), 20-23.

Papert, S. (1993). *The children's machine: Rethinking school in the age of the computer.* New York: HarperCollins.

Pascale, R. (1990). *Managing on the edge.* New York: Touchstone.

Safer, M. (1994). Nasty girl. *60 minutes.* New York: CBS.

Shaughnessy, J. M., & Haladyna, T. M. (1985). Research on student attitude toward social studies. *Social Education, 49*(8), 692-695.

14

Above the Word

When Process Is Content in Foreign Language Teaching

Virginia Pauline Rojas

The Asking

> I attended your workshop and want to incorporate some of your ideas [the letter began]. I teach French and feel that I need to inject "new life" into my classes. Although I still have to follow the curriculum set down by my department, I would like some concrete activities to do in my classes that would allow more student involvement and steer me away from monotonous drills. Any help you could give me would be greatly appreciated.

My cognizance of the dramatic turnabout required to attain this goal was momentarily camouflaged by the seeming simplicity of this teacher's request. Wasn't her apparent receptivity to the replacement of mindless drills with motivating activities indicative of an effort to invite students' active participation? Didn't her desire to transcend regimentation resonate with a compelling need to reorganize her work? Or was her allusion to the conclusive issue of curriculum coverage a more revealing predictor of the omnipresence of traditional techniques in her practices? Indeed, did not her confession of celestial

199

compliance bring to the forefront many of the complex issues that eclipsed a movement thought to have brought fresh life to foreign language classrooms decades before?

Acknowledging that there is more to language learning than the mechanistic memorization of linguistic forms, the communicative movement tried shifting away from the behaviorist principles that dominated foreign language education for so long. Rather than positioning students as passive recipients of information, communicative language classrooms attempted the adoption of cognitive psychology and its view of learners as active participants in the learning process (Curtain & Pesola, 1995). The recognition that prolonged periods of drills are not the way to teach, coupled with an emphasis on language as a social encounter, called for a profound reconception of the foreign language classroom (Ramirez, 1995). Theoretically, foreign language teachers were free to design a wide range of interactional opportunities by focusing on real-life language events and appropriate corresponding phrases. Students were supposedly set loose to develop their own learning and to experience the euphoria of producing language as a tool for communication.

Despite these innovative attempts, significant progress has not been made in the daily practices of foreign language classrooms. The emancipatory potential of the communicative approach is lost in its sustained presentation of language as an existing body of knowledge. A static conception of language endures in canonized scripts and canned curriculum packages. Teachers continue to dispense an unyielding litany of linguistic "dummy runs," although now the content has changed from reified syntactic rules and grammatical norms to communicative menus (Barnes, 1995). Their talk seems dominated by the single-minded goal of sequencing tasks around explicit explanations of grammar. Time-worn texts and assessment models prevail in their classrooms even as fashionable labels disguise the reality of their ritualistic roles. Students passively ingest and regurgitate linguistic phrases on episodic tests or risk banishment to yet another level for those with little talent or motivation for language learning. Sadly, they are deceived into thinking that they cannot construct meaning in another language. Neglected is the core issue—the distinction between content and process—about the goals of foreign language education that inhibit "real life" from ever entering their classrooms.

Unbounded Visions

A process ontology of foreign language education celebrates the Vygotskian/Bakhtin rebellion against such a technical model of literacy (Clark & Holoquist, 1984). Communication is not mere verbalism nor a ping-pong of expressions and gestures; rather, it is a place of negotiation that is only sometimes predictable. In reality, mutual comprehensibility is rare in the day-to-day life of discourse. Learners of another language therefore require more than a naive reliance on the restricted meanings of fixed formulas: They must own the problem-solving capacity for interpretation and response. A process literacy enables foreign language users to understand and read lived relationships and cultures, to reflect on and make judgments about those relationships, and to select informed "ways of speaking" from an extensive linguistic repertoire (Hymes, 1972). Its development requires time, simulated practice with an element of the unforeseen, and reflective modeling between experts and novices.

A *process competence* involves the evolution of foreign language learners' communicative knowledge and abilities as they move from initial competence toward the target competence (Breen & Candlin, 1980). Its attainment is similar to the socially generative process responsible for cognitive or moral development (Habermas, 1971). As active seekers and processors of information, students must unearth the consequences of their own actions by engaging in the cycle of practice and feedback. When confronted with conversations in which there is no routine reply, they must persist in finding ways to communicate. Language itself is the medium for the construction of new knowledge. Students acquire communication skills and learning strategies concurrently as they struggle to make sense of and resolve unfamiliar situations. A process competence positions students as contributors and regulators of their language learning, allowing them to exercise a degree of control over the attainment of their foreign language proficiency.

This competence requires a reordering of the foreign language curriculum to emphasize the process of learning over linguistic content (Long & Crookes, 1992). Jacobs (1989) identifies these goals as complementary and therefore recommends a curriculum model that is both content and process oriented. The curriculum includes the substantive knowledge to be learned, whereas the metacurriculum incorporates the learning skills and strategies that help students acquire the content and develop the capacity to think independently. The latter helps students to unlock the former insofar as the skills are inherently connected to the concepts themselves. A foreign language curriculum consists of the structural elements of language that speakers use to put together appropriate expressions, but it is the metacurriculum that will provide language learners with the means of knowing when to use which and why. Ultimately, the synergy between the two guides students to explore effective options for learning the language, using the language, and enjoying the language (Galloway & Labarca, 1990).

Methodologically, this curriculum operates by engaging students in different performance behaviors through cognitive and affective learning activities. Of utmost importance is for these activities to approximate what is to happen in real-life communication situations. Initial activities engage students in the theme or content of the unit of study; open-ended questions or circumstances are symbolically codified to convey an aura of the unknown. Students are then immersed in a plethora of well-paced tasks requiring divergent thinking based on complex materials offering alternative possibilities. The next phase of activities allows students to make sense of the ideas and information by providing for rehearsal opportunities to show what they know. A variety of classroom organizational patterns enhances interaction and negotiation among multilevel language learners. Students have occasion to revise and improve their proficiency and performance on the basis of clear and consensually constructed criteria in the final stage of activities. Assessment resonates in a rational moment of intellectual fellowship between learners and teachers.

The extent to which this partnership triumphs depends for the most part on foreign language teachers. Process teachers are not dispensers of knowledge or guardians of reified norms; they are organizers of learning situations that encourage students' performance before their competence. Process foreign language teachers envision desired states of linguistic and cultural competence, but they grasp the heuristic truth of their attainment. As coaches, they devise overall strategies through which students will continuously move themselves toward those states and maintain faith in the potential of all learners to do so. Foreign language process teachers identify the knowledge of the curriculum and work out the skills sequence of the metacurriculum in a connected and scheduled way. They design authentic activities, using a model of cognition and materials to ensure the cultivation of higher-level thought processes (Jacobs, 1989). While language learners engage in the process of decodification and recodification with each other, foreign language process teachers are busy observing and validating sustained movement toward those desired states of linguistic and cultural competence.

Rites of Passage

This process approach to foreign language teaching might be viewed as an overwhelming task when compared with the intuitive appeal of its predecessor and its habit of breaking language down into seductively manageable bits. Ironically, so much time is devoted to these bits of form and function in regimented steps that little is left for what are surely every foreign language educator's greatest ambitions—to instill the dispositions for linguistic and cultural competence in preparing students for global literacy. As Brown (1991) so aptly reminds the profession,

> Language is a tool for overcoming powerlessness. Our professional commitment intrinsically drives us to help the inhabitants of this planet to communicate with each other and to negotiate the meaning of peace, of goodwill, and of survival on this tender, fragile globe. (p. 257)

Using the framework offered in Chapter 1 of this text, these dispositions are delineated below.

Efficacious Voice. The notion of voice has been little explored in foreign language education, although it has gained attention in second language literacy discussions as a problem-solving tool for social and political transformation (Freire, 1985; Pennycook, 1994; Simon, 1992). In the Vygotskian spirit, language possesses the theme of human agency as individuals struggle to negotiate meanings between cultures. Foreign language learners need to envision their success in acquiring and making knowledge in another world and to embrace a deep and abiding faith in themselves to do so. More important, they must see their own foreign language literacy as the medium that produces a lived experience between two cultures (Cummins & Sayers, 1995). Foreign language classrooms must convey to students that they are capable of this responsive posture that subsequently will enhance the development of their own self-efficacy. The choice of tasks that students perform, as well as the type of feedback they receive, is critical to their belief in themselves to make a difference in their new language (Schunk, 1989).

Flexible Empathy. Pennycook (1994) advises that the creation of voice reciprocally commits to the birth of "listening intellectuals" and quotes Roger Simon (1992) for a definition:

> What is not needed is the pretensions of empathy, the claim to share an understanding of the positions and feelings of others, but rather the recognition of the impossibility of such claims and hence the requirement that we listen and try to hear what is being said. (p. 72)

Many foreign language classrooms present culture as some abstract concept to be understood independent of human experience. Students, initially unable to transcend their own cultural boundaries, mistakenly see this exercise as one of interrogation. Lost is the cultivation of the self-reflection and rationality needed to resist imposing judgments on what may appear to be the ambiguous and paradoxical behavior of others. Because, ultimately, the nature of the foreign language classroom acts as the intervening variable in this development, teachers must avoid the pitfall of treating culture as if it exists in a vacuum. The classroom itself becomes the forum for teachers and learners to coinvestigate cultural experiences. Together, they must learn to listen if their own voices are to be heard (Pennycook, 1994).

Pragmatic Craftsmanship. This dialectical concept of cultural criticism as a position from which to communicate with other cultures is indeed useful in preventing discourse from becoming a battlefield. Nevertheless, it does not prepare foreign language speakers to parry the mutinous intentions of oppositional native speakers. A minimalist outlook of linguistic and cultural competence focuses on the form and sociolinguistic accuracy of style and referential meaning; a maximalist viewpoint goes beyond to penetrate the sociopsychological drama of communicative congruence or dissonance. Foreign language learners need to visualize themselves as sophisticated performers of elaborated metaphor and then to execute such speech acts with clarity and precision. Through the generative process of dialogue, students can work toward mastery of the ways in which to use structural features and contextual meaning to achieve cohesion and coherence with the most powerful political construct accessible to humanity.

Worldly Consciousness. The superficial mastery of linguistic and cultural competence is insufficient for global life (Cummins & Sayers, 1995). The skill of reading the sometimes hostile intentions of others empowers foreign language speakers with the influence to redirect the course of events. It is an experience that enables individuals to know themselves and situations through retrospection and thereafter to bring to consciousness the process of social transformation. Literacy in the discourses and counterdiscourses of worldwide voice is a critical means available to transform the possibilities of lives and the ways in which these possibilities are understood (Pennycook, 1994). Foreign language classrooms

can assist learners in this reconstruction by developing the repertoire of communication strategies that allows students to become conscientious multilingual authors.

Ethical Interdependence. Awareness of the proposition of "utterance as a contra-
diction-ridden, tension-filled unity of two embattled tendencies in the life of
language" amplifies the urgency for communicative ethics in global literacy
(Bakhtin, 1981, p. 272). Habermas's (1971) theory of universal pragmatics essentially does this by defining communicative competence as both a social and
interpersonal goal. Foreign language learners' rights translate into a social
obligation to use their proficiency for the purpose of forging consensus within
the power relationships framework of discourse. The emancipatory potential
for such conflict resolution carries evocative power for foreign language classrooms. They must unequivocally provide a learning environment supportive
of an antihegemonic and ethnocentric stance. Two examples are portrayed
below.

Cases in Point

Oh, They Could Tell Us Stories

Mrs. Yao came to the United States just after the Tiananmen Square incident.
Trained as an English teacher in China, she entered a graduate program to
recertify herself for public education in her new country. She was advised to
obtain her credentials in English as a second language and bilingual education;
to do so, she first had to retrain in elementary education. Ironically, after
graduation, she secured a position in a Foreign Language in the Elementary
School (FLES) program in a fairly affluent neighborhood. Mrs. Yao meets with
her students three times a week for a total of 90 minutes. The articulated aim of
the program is to develop positive attitudes for language learning through an
understanding of its impact on self and others. An ancillary goal is to raise the
cultural consciousness of learners by helping students become Chinese cultural
informants themselves (Kumaravadivelu, 1994). The program is content related
because it uses concepts from the mainstream curriculum.

Mrs. Yao follows the themes of the "whole language" arts program. She is
comfortable with the alliance between the principles of the whole language
movement and the goals of proficiency-oriented foreign language teaching
(Curtain & Pesola, 1995). Both share a view of language as a social process: It is
acquired as students interact within a given context with one another to make
sense out of the predictability and meaning of language. Learners are continuously encouraged to take risks in this quest and are therefore not punished for
making mistakes. The whole language movement—whether it is for first or
second language acquisition—advocates the following:

> The construction of meaning, wherein an emphasis is placed on com-
> prehending what is read; functional language, or language that has
> purpose and relevance to the learner; the use of literature in a variety

of forms; the writing process through which learners write, revise, and
edit their written work, cooperative student work; and an emphasis on
affective aspects of the students' learning experience, such as motivation, enthusiasm, and interest. (Bergron, 1990, p. 319)

Despite Mrs. Yao's traditional skill-and-practice foreign language learning memo-
ries, she is secure with the lack of methodological absolutes inherent in the whole
language movement. She prides herself, however, on her capacity for designing
classroom activities with a sense of principled pragmatism (Kumaravadivelu,
1994).

The current theme of the third grade is "Fables Around the World"—Mrs.
Yao's favorite. The Chinese language has a splendid collection of stories joining
fantasy and morality. Mrs. Yao borrows the semantic web that was completed
in the English language arts class to open her unit on fables. Speaking only
Chinese, Mrs. Yao reminds the students about all that they know. To introduce
a first fable about a king who likes to listen to flutists, Mrs. Yao puts together a
collection of artifacts related to the story. As the students identify the items, Mrs.
Yao asks them to predict the significance of each. Most do so in the form of
Chinese interlanguage, although two or three students reply in English. Included are flutes, sheet music, a crown, and pictures of a king and prince
listening to musicians. Students are encouraged to fill the box as they learn more
about this and other fables.

A group of high school students are brought into the class to read fables to
the third graders. They have created big books to share in Chinese just as the
mainstream curriculum does. As one reads, the others dramatize the events. In
the meantime, Mrs. Yao teaches Mr. Wu—the high school Chinese teacher—
how to assess his students' reading performance through the use of miscue
analysis. Mrs. Yao uses total physical response strategies to reinforce the actions
of the stories. Naturally, her third graders love to react as she signals the
commands. Later, she distributes fables to groups of students. Using the jigsaw
cooperative learning strategy, Mrs. Yao has each expert group illustrate story-
board graphic organizers to help students pictorially represent the information
(and to reinforce the concept of Chinese characters). She convenes each group
to record their descriptions and distributes the responses that she has tran-
scribed. Students give interrupted book reports—a technique in which students
tell about their stories until another group interjects.

The language arts curriculum is focusing on characterization, so Mrs. Yao
is using the opportunity to teach descriptive and causative language through
four activities. Students have the opportunity to think and talk about relationships between the characters in their fables as they prepare sociograms in
groups. Mrs. Yao models the concept using the fable about the musician for the
class; they divide into groups to complete their own. Mrs. Yao values the linguistic
and cognitive power of this activity. Students are also given shadow drawings of
particular characters; individually, they are to draft symbols to reveal what the
personality might be thinking about. In groups again, the students are provided
with roles as they prepare for Reader's Theater. Mrs. Yao later introduces the
technique of improvisation so that students can respond in new situations rather
than just reenact previous ones. Throughout these activities, Mrs. Yao allots

15-minute periods for interactive journals. Some students are able to flow naturally into writing in Chinese, whereas others sketch their words when characters stop coming. Mrs. Yao manages to have conferencing with each student at least once to offer some language learning feedback.

As a final project, Mrs. Yao leads the students in a book-making activity. Pairs of students are assigned a proverb from the earlier collection of fables and given the opportunity to write their own stories in Chinese. Each book includes a title page, illustrations, and notes about the authors. Beforehand, the students had codesigned a creative writing rubric with Mrs. Yao; these books are rated on the categories of ideas, organization, structure, illustrations, and mechanics. After the final edits, the books are placed in the multilingual section of the library. So is a copy of a journal in which Mrs. Yao had an article accepted for publication. Since the beginning of this unit, Mrs. Yao had been working on a teacher action research project with a third-grade Chinese as a foreign language teacher in a neighboring district. The focus of their investigation was on the use of the whole language approach for foreign language teaching in the elementary school. Like researchers before them, they found that "learners who receive grammar-based instruction still pass the same developmental sequences and make the same types of errors as those who acquire language in natural settings" (Lightbrown & Spada, 1993, p. 67).

The Long Way Home

Mr. Lopez, a Nicaraguan by birth, received a scholarship to study political science in eastern Europe. He is now quite fluent in Spanish, Polish, Czech, and English. While studying for the entrance examination to law school in the United States, Mr. Lopez volunteered at a nearby community center and found a vocation in teaching. He obtained emergency certification and a job as a bilingual teacher in a large urban middle school. For 2 years, Mr. Lopez attended classes to earn permanent certification as well as a graduate degree in language education. Soon after, he attended a recruitment fair with a girlfriend and landed a position as a Spanish teacher in an international school in Spain. During the interview, the headmaster reported some concerns regarding the teaching of Spanish at the school: It seemed that neither the American parents nor the Spanish parents were satisfied with the program.

At the heart of this discontent was the issue of "how and why students of varying backgrounds are separated or taught together, what kinds of materials are used with each group and what kinds of methods and approaches have been found to be effective" (Valdes, 1995, p. 319). The English-language parents expect their children to speak fluent Spanish because in many cases, they have been living in Spain and studying the language for 2 to 3 years. Their shock is loudly conveyed to school administrators when they detect the inability of their children to accomplish the simplest of tasks in local restaurants. Likewise, the Spanish parents worry incessantly about what they perceive to be the less-than-totally-native-like proficiency of their children whenever an English word finds its way into otherwise perfect Spanish discourse. When confronted with the criticism, the host-country language teachers politely remind American parents and administrators of their own inability to order a full order of *tapas* and magnanimously insinuate private lessons. The stirring response to Spanish parents' concerns unknowingly amplifies existent ambiguity over the selection of an English-medium school until, finally, they plea on behalf of the Spanish language itself for reduced tutoring rates.

Years ago, when the school exclusively catered to the English-speaking expatriate community, Spanish was offered as a foreign language. As student population demographics changed, a course for native-speaking Spanish students was created because the teachers "found that they could not mix fluent speakers of the language with students who were barely beginning to get their courage up to say a phrase or two in Spanish" (Valdes, 1995, p. 299). Another concern they held was that the Spanish students take a national examination for admission to university. The division, in fact, is not always so simple. Some English-background students come close to being fluent speakers of Spanish, especially those from mixed-national marriages. Some Spanish-background students, on the other hand, have lived outside their homeland and attended English-medium schools for so long that their bilingual skills are limited. Teachers and students alike are often quite perplexed with placement and instructional issues. The majority of the Spanish-language teachers are not trained to teach Spanish as a foreign (or second) language; indeed, some of them are not trained as language teachers at all.

Mr. Lopez is mesmerized with the language ecology of the school. Whenever these issues are discussed at departmental meetings, the staff spends time trying to conjure up yet another division. A consultant was once brought in to help, and the entire afternoon was spent reviewing psychometric instruments for constructing language proficiency levels for distinct populations. By the end of the session, the Spanish teachers established 11 program strands as well as the policy of absolutely no midyear entry. Unnerved by the acts of reification, Mr. Lopez remains convinced that these "current practices are not informed, in fact, by a coherent set of theories about language learning" (Valdes, 1995, p. 308). Synthesizing the academic literature from his research on the teaching of languages and reflecting on his middle-school exposure to hands-on and integrated instruction, Mr. Lopez volunteers to model the inconceivable: a mixed-proficiency language classroom.

Mr. Lopez draws from several domains to teach this class. First, he revives his stateside experience in a two-way language development program whereby the linguistic minority become literate in their native language and the linguistic majority develop proficiency in a second language (Curtain & Pesola, 1995). Although the international school populations are different, he finds the comparison conceptually useful, especially the content-based component. Second, Mr. Lopez delights in exploring the "anti-banking" language methods that seek to promote learner autonomy (Freire, 1981). He does so by facilitating negotiated interaction through group activities, inviting class discussion through referential questions, and generating student-selected topics (Pica, Holliday, Lewis, & Morganthaler, 1989). Finally, Mr. Lopez embraces the principles of transformative pedagogy and their commitment to literacy as a vehicle for personal and social change (Giroux, 1987). Simply put, he endorses the "strategic investment of learners in their own linguistic destinies" (Brown, 1991, p. 256).

The current theme of this pilot class is "Language Learning Without Boundaries." Not only does this theme tackle the core issues underlying the birth of the class, but also it establishes a space for collaborative critical inquiry between teacher and learner (Cummins & Sayers, 1995). Mr. Lopez opens the unit by putting excerpts of various authors' accounts of their own language learning experiences on an overhead projector. Students read these "in character" and, as they do, construct inferences on their relationship to the theme. Afterward, Mr. Lopez plays New Age music to create a meditative mood as students put to paper their personal thoughts. As their ramblings are strictly for the purpose of planning, no attention is given to correctness. Pairs of students come up with questions about the theme; the pairs become foursomes, and the foursomes eightsomes, until the entire class is editing the list of questions they want to investigate. Mr. Lopez shares an authentic list of his own.

Bilingual parents are brought in to detail their linguistic memoirs. Many carry props and visual aids to contextualize abstract concepts. The school librarian, an American who settled in Spain after meeting and marrying a Spanish lawyer, intones a lyrical ballad to tell her story. Some students keep track of assigned readings in the form of four-columned logs; these include the title of the reading selection, the date read, the reader(s), and comments. Other students take empathetic notes and afterward participate in conferencing with others who have taken the same identity. Six students have originated a reading circle that meets once a week to talk about their selections. To foster language awareness, Mr. Lopez distributes cloze passages and guides students through a problem-solving lesson in a "deliberate attempt to draw learners' attention to the formal properties of their L2 in order to increase the degree of explicitness required to promote L2 learning" (Kumaravadivelu, 1994, p. 37). Students are asked to reread texts, this time looking for one sentence—and only one—that speaks to them. In groups of five, students share the sentence they chose and explain why before putting the collection into an order that makes sense. Mr. Lopez is gently surprised by the sensitive environment these narratives yield.

Since the beginning of the unit, students have been keeping project journals with a specific task in mind. Mr. Lopez distributes to each student a graphic organizer for presenting chronological information and requests that they complete it with key events from their journals. Partners are assigned with the specific roles of speaker and listener. At the end of 2 minutes, the speaker tells the listener what it was like to be attended to. Roles are switched and the exercise is repeated. Using his own graphic organizer, Mr. Lopez models the writing of his linguistic autobiography in the form of a poem. Students are amazed to discover that despite his multilingualism, their teacher is self-conscious of his accent in English. Alberto, a Spaniard who has attended the international school since the age of 5, reveals his view of English as a stepladder language in the form of a letter he writes to his classmates 25 years from now (LaPonce, 1987). The update informs his friends that he has indeed reached his goal of becoming an ambassador. In a series of diary entries to her American mother and Spanish father, Laura hints at the subtle ways in which both parents have let her know of separateness.

Linguistic autobiographies, Mr. Lopez senses, dialectically extend into research projects. Students work in groups to formulate hypotheses about the issues they have identified through their readings and writings, namely, language and ethnicity, language and nationalism, language loss and retrieval, language maintenance, bilingualism, linguistic and cultural hegemony, language and inequality, and language and education. They create survey instruments under the guidance of Mr. Lopez and a colleague holding an advanced degree in research. For weeks, students collect the data using the broadest possible intercultural network available: the Internet (Cummins & Sayers, 1995). The stories they recover come from faraway places, and, when necessary, translators are recruited to assist. Although the students have the product requirements laid out for them, they add their own criteria for success in the form of a checklist of effective research behaviors. Three of the research papers offer the opportunity to initiate interschool exchanges and class-to-class partnerships in Spanish-language countries (Cummins & Sayers, 1995). Mr. Lopez is pleased with the success of the mixed-proficiency classroom that was "marked by a repeated rhythm of whole class preparation, review and sharing, followed by opportunity for individual or small-group exploration, sense-making, extension and production" (Tomlinson, 1995, p. 9).

Something We Can Count On

These two teachers are able to bring real life into their foreign language classrooms in complex and subtle ways. They hold no methodological absolutes but are constantly refining their own sense of strategic relativism in making the process of language acquisition the focal point of learning. They do not look for a prescriptive scheme or fixed package of ready-made activities but actively engage in planning and reflecting on the processes of learning and teaching languages. Both Mrs. Yao and Mr. Lopez embrace what others perceive to be a radical pedagogical structure by relinquishing their traditional roles of teachers as holders of exclusive rights to reified information. They give equal chance to language learners to participate in the decision-making process, to stretch their linguistic and cultural competence, to explore knowledge through modeled skills, and to partake in the documentation of their achievements. Beginning with the discourse around them, Mrs. Yao and Mr. Lopez manage to help foreign language learners not so much with individual narration of perfect form but more with the critical explorations of all the foreign language voices that are speaking around them. A curriculum that prepares learners for less does no one a service.

For Those Who Want to Know How. My response to the French teacher, as they are to you the reader, is that the overreliance on prescribed activities for new life in a classroom blinds teachers and students from realizing their own vitality in developing a strategic framework for foreign language teaching and learning (Kumaravadivelu, 1994). My journey as a critical language teacher has been mentored by the following messages of the educator Paulo Freire (1986):

- Take the risk to disrupt a passive education.
- Break free from the oppressive distortions of current classroom structures and develop a clear vision of emancipatory instructional practices.

- Gain competence in the aesthetic management of a process classroom.
- Persist in sustaining your vision in the face of resistance and condemnation.
- Cultivate the humility to generate student voice and then to listen to it.

I invite others to nurture a critical foreign language classroom and to share in its attainment.

References

Bakhtin, M. M. (1981). *The dialogical imagination* (C. Emerson & M. Holoquist, Trans.). Austin: University of Texas Press.

Barnes, D. (1995). Talking and learning in classrooms: An introduction. *Primary Voices, 3*(1), 2-7.

Bergron, B. (1990). What does the term whole language mean? Constructing a definition from the literature. *Journal of Reading Behavior, 22,* 301-329.

Breen, M. P., & Candlin, C. N. (1980). The essentials of a communicative curriculum in language teaching. *Applied Linguistics, 1*(2), 89-112.

Brown, H. D. (1991). TESOL at twenty-five: What are the issues? *TESOL Quarterly, 25*(2), 245-257.

Clark, K., & Holoquist, M. (1984). *Mikhail Bakhtin.* Cambridge, MA: Harvard University Press.

Cummins, J., & Sayers, D. (1995). *Brave new schools: Challenging cultural illiteracy.* New York: St. Martin's.

Curtain, H., & Pesola, C. A. (1995). *Languages and children: Making the match* (2nd ed.). New York: Longman.

Freire, P. (1981). The people speak their word. *Harvard Educational Review, 51*(1), 27-30.

Freire, P. (1985). *The politics of education: Culture, power and liberation.* Boston: Bergin & Garvey.

Freire, P. (1986, February). *Keynote address.* Paper presented at Workshop on Worker Education, City College of New York Center for Worker Education, New York.

Galloway, V., & Labarca, A. (1990). From student to learner: Style, process, and strategy. In D. W. Birckbichler (Ed.), *New perspectives and new directions in foreign language education* (pp. 111-158). Lincolnwood, IL: National Textbook.

Giroux, H. A. (1987). Schooling and the politics of ethics: Beyond liberal and conservative discourses. *Journal of Education, 169*(2), 9-33.

Habermas, J. (1971). *Knowledge and human interests* (J. Shapiro, Trans.). Boston: Beacon.

Hymes, D. (1972). On communicative competence. In J. B. Pride & J. Holmes (Eds.), *Sociolinguistics* (pp. 269-293). London: Penguin.

Jacobs, H. H. (Ed.). (1989). *Interdisciplinary curriculum: Design and implementation.* Alexandria, VA: Association for Supervision and Curriculum Development.

Kumaravadivelu, B. (1994). The postmethod condition: (E)merging strategies for second/foreign language teaching. *TESOL Quarterly, 28*(1), 27-48.

LaPonce, J. A. (1987). *Languages and their territories.* Toronto, Ontario, Canada: University of Toronto Press.

Lightbrown, P., & Spada, N. (1993). *How languages are learned.* New York: Oxford University Press.

Long, M. H., & Crookes, G. (1992). Three approaches to task-based syllabus design. *TESOL Quarterly, 26*(1), 27-56.

Pennycook, A. (1994). *The cultural politics of English as an international language.* New York: Longman.

Pica, T., Holliday, L., Lewis, N., & Morganthaler, L. (1989). Comprehensible output as an outcome of linguistic demands on the learner. *Studies in Second Language Acquisition, 11,* 63-90.

Ramirez, A. G. (1995). *Creating contexts for second language acquisition: Theory and methods.* New York: Longman.

Schunk, D. H. (1989). Self-efficacy and cognitive skill learning. In C. Ames & R. Ames (Eds.), *Research on motivation in education* (Vol. 3, pp. 13-44). Orlando, FL: Academic Press.

Simon, R. (1992). *Teaching against the grain: Essays toward a pedagogy of possibility.* Boston: Bergin & Garvey.

Tomlinson, C. A. (1995). *How to differentiate instruction in mixed-ability classrooms.* Alexandria, VA: Association for Supervision and Curriculum Development.

Valdes, G. (1995). The teaching of minority languages as academic subjects: Pedagogical and theoretical challenges. *Modern Language Journal, 79*(3), 299-328.

15

Humor as Process

John Dyer

Prologue: Humor Works!

Theory is when you know everything, and nothing works. *Practice* is when everything works, and nobody knows why. In this article, theory and practice are combined: Nothing works, and nobody knows why!

Recently, I was speaking with a colleague who had left the security of a position in the public sector and moved to full-time work as an entrepreneurial consultant in the private sector. He had told me that the good news was that he earned $400 per hour. The bad news was that last week he only worked 15 minutes. We both roared with laughter. Last week, a group of us went for lunch with a friend, Lynn, who uses a wheelchair as a result of advancing multiple sclerosis. As we walked past an outdoor ice arena, we stopped to watch the people skating. Lynn, with a twinkle in her eye, suggested that she would like

AUTHOR'S NOTE: There are many forms of laughter, some of which are cruel, insensitive, and destructive. Humor that is insulting or degrading is not defensible or acceptable. Laughing at the misfortune of others is a sign of shallow character, insecurity, and weakness. The references in this chapter do not support toxic forms of humor that (a) exist at the expense of others, (b) display a complete lack of compassion, and (c) are based on a lack of intelligence and common sense. All references to humor, laughter, and fun in this chapter relate specifically to the positive types of humor—humor that is sensitive, respectful, intelligent, motivational, and enjoyable to everyone.

to go skating. She then proceeded to suggest that we put skates on her feet and push her around the ice in her wheelchair—the image was so bizarre we were all out of control. We have a friend who is a recovering alcoholic. The first time we invited him to dinner after he had begun the program, there was a certain awkwardness. Do we serve drinks to the other guests, or do we avoid the issue? In the moment of uncertainty, our friend—in total seriousness—declared, "I have been reading so much about the evils of liquor and alcohol that I have decided to give up reading." These types of situations occur in our lives on a regular basis. I have learned from this that humor works!

We are continuously learning more about the value of humor in health. The relationship between state of mind and immune systems is clear. The connections between humor, laughter, and stress reduction are irrefutable. The correlation between being joyful and quality of life is self-evident. As Steve Allen Jr.—family physician, health educator, and son of entertainer Steve Allen suggests,

> The laughter and play workshops are preventive health education. . . . There is not a lot of hard evidence that "laughter is the best medicine," patients who laughed more did not necessarily live longer. . . . Most felt better throughout their illness. . . . Feeling better is the whole point of life. (personal promotional literature, 1995)

It is clear to him that people have to be proactive in their pursuit of laughter and play. Quality of life is too important to leave to chance.

Human reality is formed by our filters of perception. In recent times, there is increasing observable evidence of a growing sense of collective despair. A sense of futility is becoming pervasive. We are all trying to adjust to a complex society created by the increased use of advanced technology. We are learning to cope with the notion of a global economy. We are overwhelmed by the precarious state of the environment. Rapid communication systems bombard us with sensationalistic journalism, and media representation of the "worst of the world" is delivered to our homes. Death, destruction, violence, and brutality are presented as "entertainment" with unconscionable abandon. We have come to realize that the world is not like that. We have our problems that cannot be ignored. The world, however, is filled with kind, caring people who love their families, work hard, and optimistically pursue a better future. To keep thoughts in perspective, to keep a balance, we have to change our "filters of perception." One way of doing that is to honor our sense of humor: publicly celebrate the joy around us and share the laughter.

Economic shifts have resulted in many extensive changes within organizations. Careers are being drastically affected, and this has become a major source of stress. The following is one person's comment about his situation:

> I have reached the apex of my developmental mountain, and it is a molehill. This is tremendously freeing. I no longer have to worry about becoming the president of IBM. I imagine IBM can relax too. I seem to be traveling at tremendous career speed, albeit in a circle. I continue to arrive at the place where I started. My career ladder turns out to be step master. I'm a man whose time has arrived. It's just that the rest of me

> hasn't. I now find myself applying for a job I'm terrified that I might get. On the other hand, I'll be mortified if I don't make the shortlist. I'm only 5'1" tall; surely that must be short enough. Perhaps it is truly time to explore a new universe. A place where no one has gone before. But then, what kind of jobs would be available in a place like that. I spent yesterday working on my body language with my chiropractor. I'm hoping that it will improve my speaking gestures!

My guess is that this colleague will do well. One research study indicates that other things being equal, personnel managers hire the applicant with a sense of humor. A sense of humor is frequently listed as a quality that organizations identify as essential for leadership positions.

Dr. Kenneth Pelletier (1992), Stanford University Medical School, has been involved in corporate wellness and executive health programs for the past 11 years. He has learned that people who are survivors in times of upheaval have some common characteristics. These include (a) a persistent positive state of mind, a continual sense of optimism, a sense of personal efficacy—that they are in control, not victims; (b) a sense of humor; (c) participation in specific stress-reducing activities; and (d) collegial support in the workplace. Once again, it is obvious that humor does work!

Think about your response to this "pop quiz": Although the brain is only 2% of the total body weight, it consumes 25% of the body's oxygen supply. What does this mean?

1. If you feel short of breath, stop thinking?
2. People without brains need 25% less oxygen?
3. Our brains should be bigger!
4. We should spend 75% of our time doing something other than thinking?
5. The body considers our brain more important than our sex glands, so thinking about sex is more satisfying than doing it, but doing it requires less oxygen than thinking about it.

This might explain the recent phenomenon relating to "inner tennis" and "inner golf." I tried "inner golf" and lost my ball. It was inevitable. My brain was never meant to be a fairway, and so the ball is likely lying in a water hazard. If the water freezes, everything will slip my mind.

Sandy Queen, director of Lifeworks, Inc., Columbia, Maryland, says, "Lighten up! This is the only life you have" (personal promotional literature, 1995). Our sense of humor is one of our individual capacities for uniqueness. It becomes an essential ingredient for both motivation and self-esteem. We laugh at our own weaknesses, and the laughter becomes our strength.

The following quotation from a personal journal exemplifies the power of humor to keep things in perspective.

> I think I'll apply for the head of record services. It is right up my alley as I have always had a fascination with precision and perfection. The problem is I have no capacity for numbers and details. You see the

problem? Unless they establish a Ministry of Incompetence, I don't seem to fit the mold for what's happening. The world continues to become more serious, while I become more frivolous. They just don't take silliness seriously. I'm going to go and learn how to do something really well. I just have not determined what it is yet. Currently I am trying to convince my body that there is no crisis and it can slow down. I sit in mental neutral and rev my imaginary engine. Thank God I'm a prophet and know about these things. From now on I am going to try and make all my mistakes in the morning while I have a clear mind.

Bizarre imagination becomes a healthy antidote for the discouraged. The process of divergent thinking that is necessary to create humor frequently leads to imaginative, inventive, and original solutions or alternatives. Understanding humor is a cognitive process. It increases capacities for lateral thinking. Again, I am convinced that humor really works!

Arthur Black, CBC radio host and author, likes to think of himself as "comic relief for audiences that have just been bushwhacked by hours of seminars, workshops, lectures, solemn orations—or just a hard day at the office. . . . It's my job to make people relax, laugh, loosen up a little—and if I can, make them think a bit too" (personal promotional literature, 1995). His orientation is to make the world a better place. Shouldn't that be everybody's? And what better way to do it than to share our laughter with others.

If humor is truly a significant phenomenon, what can educators do to enhance the familiarity and use of the process? I have two projects in mind to help us achieve this goal. One idea is to write a short story about a guy who is cut off from his computer friends because he's used up all of the six-letter words in the English language and he can't think of a new password to get logged on to his computer. . . . This leads to an unhealthy relationship with a sleazy modem, and the inevitable tragic ending occurs when a virus-infected computer gives him a megabyte and he goes insane from an electronic form of rabies. (Okay, so humor doesn't always work.)

The second notion is to publicly recognize the importance of humor and with intentionality address the dimensions of humor as legitimate educational processes. The processes of humor become an integrated part of the school curriculum and a component of teachers' repertoire for facilitating learning.

Humor Is No Laughing Matter: Physiology and Humor

Humor does not diminish the pain—it makes the space around it get bigger. (Klein, 1994, p. 92)

The following are some of the physiological responses to humor, joy, and other positive frames of mind:

Natural Muscle Relaxant. It is impossible to keep your muscles tense and laugh out loud at the same time. This can be observed as four strong individuals are carrying something heavy. One of them starts to laugh; the rest get the giggles;

they have to set it down. Internal stress both causes and is aggravated by muscle tension. The release of this tension is healthy both mentally and physically.

Internal Organ Massage. Laughter results in a collection of physiological responses that can best be compared with internal massage. As a consequence, the heart, the lungs, the diaphragm, the liver, the kidneys—all are stimulated in a healthful way.

Increased Oxygen Intake. When you laugh out loud, there is a sudden expulsion of breath and carbon dioxide. The subsequent intake of breath brings a rush of oxygen that enriches the blood and distributes the required oxygen to the brain and other vital organs.

Decreased Blood Pressure and Pulse Rate. The immediate reaction to laughter causes an increase in blood pressure and pulse rate, but when the laughter subsides, both blood pressure and pulse return to a rate lower than they were before the laughter occurred.

Stimulation of Production of Healthful Endorphins.

> The brain is one of the most active and prolific glands in the body. Scientists have identified more than 2,000 substances that the brain secretes (and more are discovered each year). The state of mind influences which chemicals are secreted; it can produce biochemical changes in the human body. Thus Cousins correctly saw joyfulness, playfulness and laughter as conditions likely to bring about positive physical changes in the body. (Rogers, 1984, p. 47)

There is also clear evidence linking positive frames of mind to the immune system. Violent and stressful states of mind reduce the amount of serum immunoglobulin in our system and make us susceptible to disease, whereas positive states of mind such as love, joy, and safety increase the amount of serum immunoglobulin and result in improved personal health (Pelletier, 1992).

Once in a Laugh Time: Sociology of Humor

> You're only young once, but with humor, you can be immature forever. (Art Gliner, quoted in Klein, 1994, p. 87)

Social Lubricant. People get along better when they are in good humor. When you smile at someone, you tell them you care, you accept them, you understand, and you have affection for them. When people laugh together, a bonding force is created that cannot be duplicated in any other way. Humor is a strategic component of individuals with a highly refined capacity of interpersonal skills.

Safety Valve. Playfulness is a way of mastering anxiety. Humor is a defense against aggression, tyranny, conflict, and intimidation. Observe a meeting at which a disagreement breaks out and tension increases. It appears that there is going to be a serious conflict. Then someone makes a joke or says something funny, and everyone bursts out laughing. The conversation resumes at a much lower level of tension—a fresh new beginning.

Tonic. It is said that humor and laughter are the shock absorbers on the road of life. In everyone's daily experiences, there are times of trouble, obstacles to overcome, challenges, and disappointments. Humor helps us over these bumpy spots.

Energizes and Reduces Boredom. It is self-evident that individuals cannot apply themselves with full concentration for an entire workday. Fatigue sets in, and efforts become counterproductive. The faster we go, the further we get behind because of errors and poor judgment. Periodically, we need to refresh our minds and refresh our bodies. Laughter and humor provide an essential social, mental, and physiological release.

Molding the Mind With "Fun" Gas: Psychology and Humor

> We all need a sense of humor or someday we will wake up with no sense at all. (Melvin Helitzer, cited in Klein, 1994, p. 95)

Although humor and laughter have been given a great deal of research attention in the past two decades, they are still somewhat of a mystery. Part of the mystery comes from the observation that laughter is evident almost from birth.

> Most babies start to chuckle by the time they're only 9 weeks old, some when they're as young as 29 days. . . . At first a surprise or bodily sensation triggers laughter in the infant. At 4 to 6 months of age touch and sound typically produce giggles. By 10 months, the baby laughs at something visually provocative, such as a funny face or a parent's deliberately comical actions. When infants are about a year old they begin to instigate laughter themselves by playing games such as peek-a-boo and hide-and-seek or pretending to tumble down accidentally. By age 16 weeks, says Cohen, babies laugh about once an hour, and by the time kids are 4 years old—when they are particularly turned on by slapstick—laughter breaks out on the average of every four minutes. . . . The person who purposely looks for the element of humor in an uncomfortable situation is making use of an important emotional control procedure. (Allen, 1992, pp. 7-8)

It is the emotional context of humor that manifests its psychological significance and implies the importance of the process in teaching and learning in schools.

> Emotion also has an important positive side that can move life beyond mere survival into a much more pleasant sense of joie de vivre. Infants

are born with the ability to cry and smile, which they quickly develop, and they soon discover that smiling has better internal and social payoff. Many of our emotionally stereotyped facial expressions (such as crying and laughing) trigger the release of endorphins and other peptides that enhance the emotion in us and in those around us. We may accept grief, but we tend to move toward those things that give us joy—music, games, jokes, dances, caresses, sunsets, celebrations, vacations. By separating emotion from logic and reason in the classroom, we've simplified school management and evaluation, but we've also then separated two sides of one coin—and lost something important in the process. It's impossible to separate emotion from important activities of life. Don't even try. (Sylwester, 1995, pp. 74-75)

Almost every individual is carrying some type of psychological baggage with a corresponding emotional component. That is part of being human. It may be related to work, to family, to health, to finances, to marriage, to children, or to job security. We all carry stress in one form or another.

The situation is exacerbated by the rapid communication technology that has been developed and the lack of morality in the social conscience of the media. The news media celebrate the worst in our communities and sensationalize death, violence, abuse, and every perverse behavior imaginable. If there has been an assault, a robbery, a rape, or a murder in the community, you will hear it first thing in the morning as you wake up to your clock radio. It will be portrayed as the most important news event. If a mass murder occurs 3,000 miles from your home, you will hear about it in minutes. If a 2-year-old is murdered in a foreign country, you will see it on the local eyewitness news. Graphic pictures of wars, killing, and military uprisings will be displayed on the television screen as you sit and eat your dinner.

In discussion with news reporters, I am told that they report what the population wants to hear, see, and learn about. It appears that there is some basis for this argument. People, in general, will attend to those items that represent their worst fears.

> The right hemisphere processes the negative aspects of emotion that lead to withdrawal behaviors (e.g. fear, embarrassment), while the left hemisphere processes the positive aspects that lead to approaching behaviors (e.g. laughter, joy). Strong feelings tend to be negative, probably because it's more important for the brain to communicate that a problem exists than to say that everything is okay. (Sylwester, 1995, p. 51)

The impact of this distorted portrayal of the world, however, is at least twofold. Children grow up becoming desensitized to violence and, in some cases, modeling it and acting it out. What happens to adults is even more frightening. Adults start believing the world is like this. The world, however, isn't like this. We have our problems, but the world is filled with kind, hard-working people who love one another and support their communities. Sylwester (1995) identifies some significant implications for educators.

Conventional wisdom incorrectly sees the human race as principally competitive, probably because the mass media focus on such events as wars, competitive crimes, business acquisitions, and sports victories. The mass media focus on dramatically unusual, not the norm in human behavior, and so the news typically reports what's new and unusual— the distortions of normal human behavior. . . . Wars, assaults, child molesting, and cut-throat business practices aren't what the human race is about. They represent forms of human pathology, not the norm. . . . Consequently, one would expect schools to focus on the development of skills that are more definitive of our species, that encourage and enhance social and cooperative behaviors, especially since we educate students in group settings and assign them common problems. (p. 117)

The psychological need for humor and laughter is evident. It provides a balance in perspective. It prevents us from being extreme in our reactions to our problems. Through humor, we can maintain a healthy mental attitude that allows us to work more efficiently and effectively and live more joyfully.

Your Head Can't Work if Your Funny Bone Is Broken:
The Pedagogy of Humor

Debra Korobkin (cited in Zemke, 1991), a Kellogg fellow of doctoral studies in adult education at the University of Georgia, summarizes the findings of a number of studies in an article for the journal *College Teaching.* Her literature search revealed a long list of claimed humor benefits: improvements in retention of material, student-teacher rapport, attentiveness and interest, motivation toward and satisfaction with learning, playfulness, individual and group test scores, class discussion and animation, creativity, idea generation, and divergent thinking. Korobkin also notes claims for decreases in academic stress, anxiety toward subject matter, dogmatism, and perceived monotony.

Some of these phenomena relate directly to the climate in which learning occurs, as opposed to the actual pedagogical use of humor as an instructional strategy.

Motivates and Creates a Positive Atmosphere. People are attracted to humor and they enjoy an entertaining environment. Including humor in a learning situation attracts the learners and makes them want to be there in a receptive and cooperative mood. Research studies relating to teachers' use of humor suggest that this is the most commonly articulated reason for intentionally using humor.

Another interesting finding of this study is the listing of reasons teachers provided for using humor. Most teachers indicated that they use humor as a way of putting students at ease, as an attention-getter, as a way of showing that the teacher is human, as a way to keep the class less formal, and to make learning more fun—not as a pedagogical strategy for increasing student comprehension or learning . . . that high school teachers do not use humor as a learning strategy per se, but as a strategy that renders the classroom environment more conducive to learning . . . help communication researchers conceptualize classroom humor as a facilitating strategy to learning rather than an actual learning strategy itself. (Neuliep, 1991, p. 351)

Reduces Interpersonal Barriers. Appropriate humor stimulates cohesion and brings people together. Laughing together creates a bond with the group. It reduces self-conscious behaviors, withdrawal, and potential personal conflict. Humor stimulates interaction, discussion, participation, and cooperation.

Perhaps we can begin by recognizing that schools are places where "human beings" live, work, and play. As John Dewey was fond of saying, education is not preparation for life, but rather, life itself. So the people in schools—children and adults—must laugh, cry, feel anger, joy, elation, and disappointment simply because they are human. The expression of these feelings belongs in schools as much as in life outside of school. (Rogers, 1984, p. 48)

Increases Interest and Decreases Boredom. Is learning fun? Not always. Deep learning is hard work and frequently involves drill and repetition. It takes effort and concentration. Learning can be embarrassing and a threat to our self-esteem because it exposes our ignorance and acknowledges our incompetence. Frequently, we learn by failure. Failure isn't fun. From a learner's perspective, the intentional inclusion of humor is a refreshing necessity. All work and no play doesn't necessarily make a teacher a dull person, but it can make a dull lesson.

Because neurons thrive only in an environment that stimulates them to receive, store, and transmit information, the challenge to educators is simple: define, create, and maintain an emotionally and intellectually stimulating school environment and curriculum. (Sylwester, 1995, pp. 129-130)

Humor plays an important part in achieving this objective. The teacher's role is pivotal. There will be moments of spontaneous humor and fun in the classroom. The teacher's reaction will demonstrate approval or disapproval. Approval will affirm that playfulness is an acceptable and desirable part of learning. The child within is a joyful dimension of adulthood, and it is important to acknowledge and express that component of character. The teacher's attitude toward humor, laughter, and play is much more important than the teacher's comic talent. The teacher's role in this area is to establish a learning environment that gives permission for students to enjoy themselves and to help students to be in "good humor" while learning. Teachers demonstrate that appropriate laughter and learning are compatible partners. The teacher can also help students distinguish between appropriate humor and artful humor. It is this dimension of character that elevates an average teacher to an artful teacher.

Good teachers, then, are prepared to laugh at themselves, to share their own mistakes, to help children understand that teachers, too, are human. Good teachers also encourage their students to laugh at themselves, to relieve tension by allowing themselves to see the occasional absurdities, inconsistencies and some just plain foolishness in their day-to-day behavior. . . . Good teachers also have the courage to teach children not to laugh at the mistakes and misfortunes of others. Unfortunately there is no lesson plan, curriculum guide, or workbook that can help a teacher deal with this kind of "humor." It must be confronted directly and honestly through intelligent, informed discussion. (Rogers, 1984, pp. 48-49)

There are numerous strategies that teachers can use to become "environmental architects for humor." The following examples may be a catalyst for teacher initiative in this area.

1. Make bulletin boards playful with the use of cartoon characters, rainbows, and flowers.
2. Reserve a section of the bulletin board for cartoons and feature a cartoon of the day.
3. Post photographs of special school events and add comical captions.
4. Start each class with a humorous quotation or anecdote.
5. Use tapes of comedians or children entertainers as energy breaks throughout the day.
6. Show old silent film comedy videos in homeroom prior to the morning and lunch bells.
7. Structure special student events and activities just for fun—*and*, as the teacher, be an active participant (i.e., in lip-synch contests, guess the baby picture contests, Halloween costume parties, games, etc.).
8. Make entertaining announcements over the public address system.
9. Include comical items on examinations.
10. Display humorous art.
11. Keep a collection of humor magazines, joke books, and so forth in the room for student leisure reading.
12. Wear a mask, a costume, or some comical piece of clothing to class for no reason and with no explanation.
13. Include short, fun games as energy breaks during the day.
14. Decorate the room with helium-filled balloons and streamers for no special purpose.

These suggestions do not necessarily improve learning effectiveness. They convey to the students, however, that this place of learning is a place of joy and that it is okay to laugh and smile in the classroom.

In addition to the use of humor in supporting the instructional climate, there are specific reasons for including humor as an instructional technique or as part of an instructional strategy.

Creates Mental Images That Embed Learning. Retaining information, data, or concepts in long-term memory can be facilitated by the use of a dramatic hook.

Humorous portrayals of "content" create an intellectual disparity that reinforces longer retention.

Focuses Attention. Learning requires an active, inquiring mind. Humor is effective in focusing mental attention, creating interest, and stimulating concentration. The mind can give undivided, intense concentration for only limited periods of time. Estimates for the average adult are 7 to 12 minutes of deep concentration. Periodically, our thinking momentarily shuts down to refresh our brain. Humor spontaneously provides an opportunity for this phenomenon.

Recent literature on brain research and attention extends our understanding of how the use of humor (and other high contrast behaviors) support learning.

> While our attentional system has a built-in bias for high contrast, novelty, and emotional overtones, the curriculum presents a predictable universe. . . . We want students to solve such problems automatically and unemotionally—to achieve mastery—but mastery reduces students' need to actively attend to a process. It's a dilemma: the effective teaching of skills can reduce students' active attention to the process. Moreover, routine, low-contrast curricular tasks tend to bore students who spend hours with video games, and TV programs which too often emphasize the bizarre and violent—high contrast behaviors that attract attention. . . . Again, teachers have creatively responded at the practical level by adopting new (and, likewise, somewhat bizarre and violent) instructional methods: offering skill master games and scolding inattentive students are both ways of artificially increasing students' attention in otherwise unemotional, low-contrast learning tasks. . . . Such games artificially enhance attention-getting excitement through rapid action, and teachers have intuitively used them to adapt their instruction to the processing realities of their students' stable attentional mechanism. (Sylwester, 1995, p. 83)

Humor is an example of high-contrast behaviors. The use of bizarre or unusual perspectives and the unpredictable, erratic, impulsive, spontaneous nature of humor automatically attract and refocus our attention.

Humor as Content. The use of humor as an instructional strategy differs from the use of humor to maintain a positive learning environment. As an instructional strategy, the teacher can intentionally incorporate humor as content and/or humor as process. Humor as content is the easier of the two to identify, plan, and incorporate in a lesson. Any use of humorous material that relates directly to the subject being taught is an example of humor as content:

1. Acknowledge the writings of humorous authors in the study of literature.
2. Analyze styles of humor and use these styles in language composition assignments.
3. Discuss political cartoons as part of social studies or political science classes.

4. Review entertaining commercials in business education and marketing classes.

5. Include examples of political satire in history class.

6. Identify historic examples of errors in scientific thinking that are humorous in retrospect.

7. Incorporate films of early attempts at developing aircraft.

8. Use sitcoms and other examples of humor in television in the study of mass media.

9. Use the writings of authors such as Ogden Nash and Shel Silverstein when studying poetry.

10. Capitalize on materials intentionally designed to communicate serious issues in a humorous fashion. Examples are the satirical videotapes on management and customer relations that feature the British comedian John Cleese.

11. Produce comical plays or musical comedy as school productions.

12. Practice punctuation in "unpunctuated" jokes, humorous anecdotes, and so forth.

Humor as Process. This is the intentional structuring of a learning process in which humor becomes a vital component. The following examples are instructional strategies that show how humor can be used as process in learning:

1. When using the brainstorming process, emphasize that humor is encouraged and that no idea can be too outrageous—that comical responses require the most divergent thinking.

2. Write comedy in the form of short stories, poetry, skits, plays, satire, scripts, and so on.

3. Produce comedy through drama or video presentations.

4. Write captions for cartoons.

5. Draw caricatures in art class.

6. Create parodies on fairy tales, classic literature, or news stories.

7. Use improvisational skills in role plays and simulations.

8. Create "daffynitions," "silly spoonerisms," "malapropisms," "puns," "tall tales," and so forth in language or creative writing.

9. Have students develop comical test items for your serious subject content.

10. Encourage students to organize and conduct a "Humor Festival."

11. Construct jokes using professional formulas (e.g., Steve Allen's [1992] *How to Be Funny*).

12. Teach the art of ad lib.

Humor as process stimulates specific types of mental activities and requires identifiable cognitive processes. It is the dimension of constructing humor that supports the intentional inclusion of humor as process in the learning experience. This reinforces the previous comments acknowledging that the teacher is not expected to become a clown, a jester, a stand-up comic, or an entertainer. The teacher facilitates the development of specific cognitive processes in students by structuring learning tasks that require the engagement of these processes.

Humor and Cognition

A sense of humor is basically intellectual. It is, in part, a sense of proportion and ability to differentiate comparisons and contrasts. Incongruities are especially enjoyed. (Baughman, 1974, p. 53)

People who are humorous are intelligent. It isn't that the humor is an indication of wisdom, thoughtfulness, or cleverness. Creating humor is a cognitive process. Laughter comes from the psychological surprise that occurs when an unexpected point of view or an alternate perspective is articulated. This flexibility in thinking is a manifestation of intelligence. Some psychologists suggest that flexibility in thought is the highest level of intelligent behavior.

Responding to humor cannot occur unless thinking is engaged. It requires specific mental processes to be appreciated. The momentary engagement of the intellect that is required for understanding why the situation (statement, joke, anecdote, etc.) is funny is automatically a learning activity. Understanding why something is funny or creating comedy is a cognitive process.

This also reminds us that humor is always contextual. The laughter comes from the circumstances surrounding the event—the context. Some humor is language specific and can be appreciated only in the language in which it is spoken. Some humor is culturally specific and is entertaining only to those who are thoroughly familiar with the nuances of the culture.

Some humor is related to character or persona. Jack Benny's humor revolved around his character. His humor was distinctly different from George Burns's or Phyllis Diller's humor, because George Burns and Phyllis Diller presented different characters. Robin Williams's humor is related to Robin Williams, and Bill Cosby's or Carol Burnett's comedy is significantly different from that of Robin Williams because Bill Cosby and Carol Burnett are different people and different characters. There is a fundamental need to intellectually comprehend the language, culture, or the character (or any of the other contextual variables) before the humor is evident.

Some brain theories based on a concept of hemisphericity suggest that the rational, linear, and linguistic functions are housed primarily in one hemisphere of the brain, whereas the emotional, nonlinear, abstract, conceptual, divergent capacities are located in the other hemisphere. The brain is most powerful in learning when both hemispheres of the brain are engaged. Reacting to humor is a whole-brain activity. The linear components are required to understand the logic and to establish the mind-set for a logical conclusion. The unexpected creative, divergent components that are interjected cause the laughter. The moment at which the brain comprehends the humor is one of the rare occasions when both hemispheres of the brain are working in perfectly balanced symmetry.

Steve Allen (1992) introduces another dimension of laughter that is not yet resolved. It is the obvious connection, but unexplainable relation, to the cognitive process of laughter and the physiological response of laughter.

> Laughter would appear to be a physical reflex, although even if it is, this still leaves unanswered the question why the human response to humor is a convulsive spasm of respiratory mechanism rather than a crossing of the eyes or a waving of the arms. . . . Laughter is reflexive because of its involuntary nature. We do not decide to laugh; we simply respond automatically in much the same way that we blink. . . . Blinking, ducking, and other motor reflexes have an obvious biological function: to save the organism from pain or injury. But it is not so easy to be certain how laughter protects us. Perhaps as Arthur Koestler suggests in *The Act of Creation*, it is from the danger of emotional pain. . . . A second factor separating laughter from the other motor responses is that all others involve the brain only secondarily and the consciousness practically not at all . . . but the response of laughter comes solely out of the brain, in response to thought. A third factor distinguishing the laughter response from all others is that the incoming message can be one of great complexity. Indeed in most cases, it will be multifaceted. . . . Laughter is produced out of a sort of minor nervous explosion in the brain, a kind of short-circuit spark in that portion of our "computer" that automatically attempts to deal logically with incoming information.
>
> The brain is constantly accepting messages, thousands each second—billions in a lifetime—and filing them away, in an incredibly rapid and orderly way, for future reference. In the case of incoming material that we would describe as humorous, the brain is automatically filing away the material according to what appears to be its face-value meaning, when suddenly—literally in a fraction of a second—our conscience perceives that there is more than one interpretation of the material. The brain is therefore momentarily startled, and its normal function interrupted. We suddenly face the fact that we have been tricked. (Allen, 1992, pp. 13-14)

Humor opens the mind to diversity and allows it to view things from a different perspective. Originality, divergent thinking, and creative problem solving require that individuals be flexible in their thinking. Encouragement to use humor results in individuals being more adaptable in their processing of information. As Joel Goodman says, "Humor prevents hardening of the attitudes" (cited in Klein, 1994, p. 89).

Current literature articulates the inevitable disappearances of corporations and businesses that do not understand the necessity of functioning as "adaptive organizations" to accommodate the changing nature of our global culture. When we extend the notion of humor as cognitive process, we can see a phenomenological link between humor, aesthetics, and adaptive organizations.

The link between humor, aesthetics, and adaptive thinking/learning is that humor requires a shift in perspective that is immediate and rapid. Aesthetics is a shift in perspective that takes place through time. It is the artist's ability to

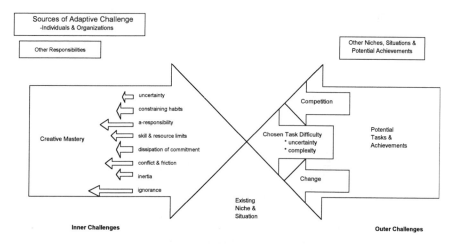

Every adaptive challenge has an inner and outer dimension, each with its own range of barriers to overcome.
The inner challenges are often not even recognized, so they are frequently the main cause of failure.

Figure 15.1. Sources of Adaptive Challenge: Individuals and Organizations
SOURCE: Action Studies Institute, Calgary, Alberta, Canada, 1994. Used with permission.

observe things from a totally different point of view and through the art form, to make that "point of view" observable to others. Flexibility in thinking, the ability to see things from a new and unusual perspective, is critical for both individuals and organizations that are to be adaptive.

The "inner" and "outer" sources of adaptive challenge are identified in Figure 15.1. Humans attempt to resolve the challenges through our conventional approaches and through those strategies that have been successful in the past. We limit our thinking to those perspectives with which we are most familiar. Sometimes we do not even recognize these challenges, although they can be the main cause of failure. We get trapped by the limitations of our own experience, positions, viewpoints, and perceptual filters.

Figure 15.2 emphasizes the pitfall of rigidity of thinking. We are so locked into the complexity of the task difficulty that we become obsessed with that outlook. This shackles our capacity to engage in original thinking, strategic flexibility, and, ultimately, effective mastery. The narrowness of perception results in myopic thinking and becomes a barrier to resolution or a fixation on inappropriate or ineffective solutions.

Perspective shifts that are stimulated in the search and development of humorous responses provide a fluidity to learn, to flow through and around problems instead of banging up against them through narrow channels of habitual thinking—our cognitive addictions. Humor is a powerful process for shifting our perspective. Historically, in medieval times, the jester was a hated member of the monarch's court. The jester sat by the monarch as the citizens presented their petitions. The role of the jester was to ridicule the petition—to point out through humor the weaknesses and fallibilities of the arguments and propositions as they were offered. Through humor, the jester advocated a

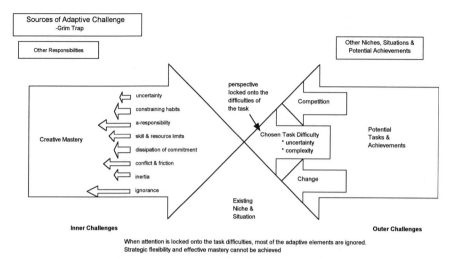

Figure 15.2. Sources of Adaptive Challenge: Grim Trap
SOURCE: Action Studies Institute, Calgary, Alberta, Canada, 1994. Used with permission.

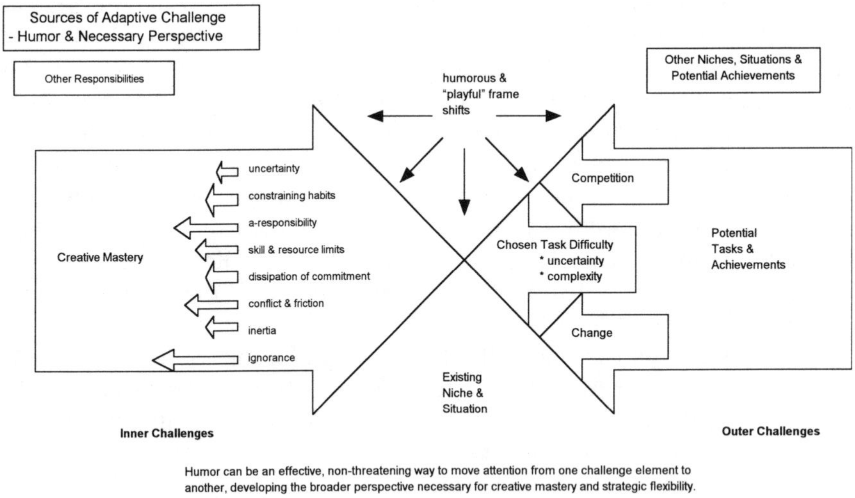

Figure 15.3. Sources of Adaptive Challenge: Humor and Necessary Perspective
SOURCE: Action Studies Institute, Calgary, Alberta, Canada, 1994. Used with permission.

different view that exposed the vulnerabilities and revealed the possibility of failure. Figure 15.3 suggests that humor and playful attitudes contribute to making the perceptual shifts that help individuals or organizations see the weaknesses of their thinking. Humor increases the capacity to think divergently and creatively. Humor contributes to the ability to be adaptive.

The intentional creation of humor or comedy is a unique and complex cognitive process that requires a high level of intellectual functioning in each of the five dispositions of mind identified by Costa and Garmston (1994).

Flexibility. The humorous mind is willing to examine every side of every issue and every side of every side. It is contingent on the capacity to see things from alternative perspectives. This flexibility in thought is supplemented by the notion of spontaneity—to leap from one mode of thought to another and see instant connections. These connections that may be seen so rapidly by others become the source of surprise and delight. These phenomena are also linked to the ability to break from conventionality and to perceive, process, and react beyond the bonds of conventional values of a particular place, time, and culture.

Craftsmanship. The construction of humor is a precise art. Humor in language necessitates infinite attention to elements such as choice of language, sequence of words, and resolution of cognitive dissonance. Visual humor requires detailed attention to such things as creation of context, the phenomenon of anticipation, and the intentional stimulation of imagination. Developing comedy not only is a complex creative process requiring a high level of divergent thinking but also is a demanding science that is successful only when it is executed with pristine exactness.

Interdependence. Much humor is created privately and expressed publicly. This interconnectedness between the individual and social context displays the interdependent nature of humor. Humor is about things, about experiences, about situations, and about life. It is delivered to the individuals who are aware and understand those things, experiences, and situations. There is a personal dimension of humor, but it is closely related to the public context of the humor.

Consciousness. Two elements of consciousness become prevalent in the development of humor. First, there is an understanding that some humor occurs spontaneously and without premeditation. As a learning process, however, we are intentionally focusing on humor as a "conscious" process so that we can develop it, refine it, use it, apply it, and increase those cognitive capacities that are used in the creative process of designing humor. Second, it is essential that individuals involved in the development of humor be conscious of the power and impact of its use and have a sensitivity to the potential destructive nature of insensitive laughter. It is important to recognize the repercussions of humor on others, to be consciously aware of why we find certain things funny, and to assess the appropriateness of that humor by anticipating the potential impact that it will have.

Efficacy. Each of us has the capability to increase our "humor quotient." It is a frame of mind, it is a skill, it is a technique, and it is a set of cognitive processes that can be enhanced and developed. No one else can do it for us; we have to make the decision that it is important, and we have to initiate the action that will help us accomplish it.

The humor-conscious teacher uses material resources that offer rich opportunities for the development of flexibility, craftspersonship, interdependence, consciousness, and efficacy—the characteristics essential to the humorous outlook or frame of mind.

Epilogue

I doubt whether the importance of humor has been fully appreciated, or the possibility of its use in changing the quality and character of our entire cultural life—the place of humor in politics, humor in scholarship, and humor in life. Because its function is chemical, rather than physical, it alters the basic texture of our thought and experience. . . . The tremendous importance of humor in politics can be realized only when we picture ourselves a world of joking rulers. Send, for instance, five or six of the world's best humorists to an international conference, and give them the plenipotentiary powers of autocrats, and the world will be saved. As humor necessarily goes with good sense and the reasonable spirit, plus some exceptionally subtle powers of the mind in detecting inconsistencies and follies and bad logic, and as this is the highest form of human intelligence, we may be sure that each nation will thus be represented at the conference by its sanest and soundest mind.

This I conceive to be the chemical function of humor: to change the character of our thought. I rather think that it goes to the very root of culture, and opens a way to the coming of the Reasonable Age in the future human world. For humanity I can visualize no greater ideal than that of the Reasonable Age. For that after all is the only important thing, the arrival of a race of men [people] imbued with a greater reasonable spirit, with greater prevalence of good sense, simple thinking, a peaceable temper and cultured outlook. The ideal world for mankind [humanity] will not be a rational world, nor a perfect world in any sense, but a world in which imperfections are readily perceived and quarrels reasonably settled. . . . This seems to imply several things: a simplicity of thinking, a gaiety in philosophy and a subtle common sense, which will make this reasonable culture possible. Now it happens that subtle common sense, gaiety of philosophy and simplicity of thinking are characteristic of humor and must arise from it.

The humorist indulges in flashes of common sense or wit, which show up the contradictions of our ideas with reality with lightening speed, thus greatly simplifying matters. Constant contact with reality gives the humorist a bounce and also a lightness and subtlety. All forms of prose, sham, learned nonsense, academic stupidity and social humbug are politely but effectively shown the door. Man [Humans] becomes wise because man [humans] becomes subtle and witty. All is simple. All is clear. It is for this reason that I believe a sane and reasonable spirit, characterized by simplicity of living and thinking, can be achieved only when there is a very much greater prevalence of humorous thinking. (Yutang, 1937, pp. 77-83)

References

Allen, S. (1992). *How to be funny.* Buffalo, NY: Prometheus.

Baughman, D. M. (1974). *Baughman's handbook of humor in education.* West Nyack, NY: Parker.

Costa, A. L., & Garmston, R. J. (1994). *Cognitive coaching: A foundation for renaissance schools.* Norwood, MA: Christopher-Gordon.

Klein, A. (1994). *Quotations to cheer you up when the world is getting you down.* Westminster, MD: Random House Value.

Neuliep, J. W. (1991, October). An examination of the content of high school teachers' humor in the classroom and the development of an inductively derived taxonomy of classroom humor. *Communication Education, 40,* 345-351.

Pelletier, K. R. (1992). *Executive health: Oxymoron or attainable goal?* Presentation at the 10th annual Power of Laughter and Play Conference, San Francisco.

Rogers, V. R. (1984, April). Laughing with children. *Educational Leadership, 41,* 45-50.

Sylwester, R. (1995). *A celebration of neurons: An educator's guide to the human brain.* Alexandria, VA: Association for Supervision and Curriculum Development.

Yutang, L. (1937). *The importance of living.* New York: Reynal & Hitchcock.

Zemke, R. (1991, August). Humor in training: Laugh and the world learns with you. *Training,* 26-29.

The Essence

Process as Content

Louis Rubin

The volumes in the *Process as Content* trilogy are rooted in the persuasive conviction that thought serves as the essence of the educational process. Because there are distinct modes of thinking for the accumulation, interpretation, and application of knowledge, each of these warrants due curricular emphasis. Moreover, because students can know without understanding—and understand without perceiving implication or use—good schooling must ensure that acquiring and exploring the powers of insight are significant by-products of learning. In short, learners must know things—know what they really mean—and know how they can be used.

Such arguments are of particular moment at a time of massive ferment and upheaval in the quest for effective reform. Federal initiatives such as Goals 2000: Educate America and the Elementary and Secondary Education Amendments (1969), for example, aim at high expectations for all students—measured by what they know and can do—and structured, presumably, by sensible conceptions of consequential teaching and worthy subject matter. Much depends, however, on what knowledge and capabilities are deemed worthy and what learning experiences are harnessed to their attainment. It is hardly surprising, therefore, that in the wake of ideological insecurity, an ambiguous curriculum spawns confusion.

Margaret Mead (personal communication, 1965) once noted that "the task confronting today's schools is to teach the young how to solve yet unborn problems, through still unknown solutions." Her point was that students now in school will face an inevitable and immense array of social problems. Without knowing the precise nature of these difficulties, however, we cannot teach their solutions. Our only viable option, then, is to teach youth *how* to solve problems. It is in this spirit, perhaps, that the editors saw fit to organize the volumes around the premise that teaching that (a) generates knowledge and understanding, (b) poses related problems, (c) demonstrates potential steps to their solutions, and (d) integrates direct practice in problem solving not only can increase comprehension and retention but—of even greater consequence—can enhance intellectual capability as well as the capacity to use acquired knowledge constructively. Knowledge is the most useful when it propagates intuition. The distinction between inert and active knowledge, in sum, lies in the degree of functionality.

Furthermore, a growing body of research-based theory suggests that connectivity is central to the construction of meaning and the sense of application. Too often, we tend to break down complex operations, assuming that learning is at its best when discrete conceptual components are taught separately. Psychologists contend, however, that only when the pieces are reconstructed into a workable entity are complete meaning and significance grasped. In the absence of such reconstruction, a disjointing of perception occurs. There are instances, for example, when an idea is best comprehended by contemplating the whole rather than the sum of the parts. In piecing together an unassembled table, to wit, some find it easier to form a mental picture of the end product rather than to insert peg A in slot B. Similarly, the child tinkering with the family computer may fathom its intricacies as fast—or faster—than the adult laboring through a manual. Put succinctly, the fracturing of reality has its liabilities.

We are once again, ironically, in the periodic cycle of debate over the relative merits of segregated and integrated curriculum. There are those who maintain that much is gained when concepts from different subject areas are coalesced into a holistic perspective, as well as those who contend that the discipline's unique methods of inquiry and knowledge structure are not lost in homogenization. Both views have their validity, and the error may lie in opting for one over the other—rather than exploiting the advantages of each. Generic and universal thinking modes clearly exist. For example, mathematical understanding, literary insight, and historical interpretation each require distinct cognitive operations that can be taught in conjunction with knowledge acquisition and use. "Knowing" and "using" are discrete—but corollary—dimensions of learning. The interplay between perception and use, moreover, can also serve as a unifying mechanism for integrating classroom and external experience.

Because human minds function in an interlocking sequence of networks through which we meld multiple sources of comprehension, formulate meaning, and grasp significance, events and encounters are meshed, juxtaposed, and counterbalanced in a continuing web of cognitive activity that eventually enables us to make sense of things. For this reason, the aims of education are assumed to be encapsulated in both the subject matter and experiences of schooling. Students are shaped, thus, by the range and complexity of whatever occurs in the classrooms and the consequent interplay with perceptions gained elsewhere. Yet the curriculum does little in the way of orchestrating and consolidating the emotional and intellectual activity such occurrences encompass. Perkins and Blythe (1994) and others repeatedly have reminded us that useful learning evolves when students assemble, analyze, and interpret diverse information and gradually create personal meaning that leads to conceptual applications. But our ways of choreographing learning and instruction typically assume that chunks of this and that can be added, subtracted, or combined willy-nilly.

It also is tempting to assume that if random efforts to raise standards, improve instruction, update content, and enhance curriculum organization are each managed competently, schools will benefit and students will be better served. It has now become plain, however, that such temptation is naive. Disjoined innovation, although advantageous in piecemeal ways, does not circumvent the need for connection and synergy. The degree to which such initiatives attend to linkage, congruence, and common cause is of consummate importance. Policymakers, nevertheless, often approach their task unilaterally; content specialists advocate revisions inspired by their subject matter; textbook manufacturers are guided by marketplace appeal; leadership is geared to one temporal fad of the moment or another; revisions are initiated in response to the clamoring assertions of vested interest groups; opportunists exploit the commercialization of learning; and intelligent cohesion in service of the strengthening of mind has become a lost cause.

Worse, because one aspect of restructuring frequently affects others, single-minded change invariably has a downside. Pedagogical innovations, as a case in point, are governed by the practitioner's adeptness in using them skillfully. Similarly, policy changes—placing greater emphasis on cultural diversity, for instance—necessitate coupling with compatible instructional methodology. Seemingly lacking, however, are viable ways to conceptualize and initiate reform in broad, carefully aligned patterns that overrun the miasma of the ordinary.

In the same vein, much attention during the last decade has been devoted to thoughtful curriculum implementation: using rational theory in a context and manner that enhances organizational cohesion, combining efficient instruction with discerning evaluation, and so on. The aftereffects have not been encouraging. In subsequent efforts to unravel the problem, three significant conclusions emerged: First, good curriculum constructs, used unintelligently, produce little good and sometimes considerable harm; second, disordered attempts to reform and restructure have a short life as well as limited advantage; and, third, implementation difficulties make it plain that good constructs can be perceptibly weakened by artless management. And, in the absence of de facto centric planning, some provision for effective coalescence is essential. The trilogy fashioned by the volumes' editors sets forth the compelling logic that a process curriculum can provide badly needed cohesion.

A variety of recent educational policies have sought to resolve current dilemmas by regulating minimum standards, toughening assessment procedures, and intensifying content criteria. Few of these, however, have achieved their intended effect. There is, in addition, a growing suspicion that even good improvement policies are difficult to actualize with any degree of success—first, because they are isolated and lack connection with other independent organizational provisions; and, second, because they frequently fail to make due allowance for the pragmatic problems schools confront.

Even when implemented effectively, moreover, they may not accomplish their intent because the reformers often decipher problems inaccurately, neglect to anticipate the barriers in prevailing practice, and ignore the lessons of historical analogy and precedent. Additional hurdles lie in the gulf between curriculum and reform strategies. If process as content is to affect teaching practices, it must addresss the broad spate of attendant factors involved. Preparation, licensing criteria, performance assessment, instructional objectives, and student evaluation must be tied to the nurture of process capability. A realignment of purpose and focus will also need to cope with vagaries of organizational change, competing concerns, and theoretical divisiveness. And more impediments exist in the possible fallout between means and ends—the aims of process curriculum and the necessary course of action. The restructuring literature provides little in the way of guidance or workable blueprints for dealing with the stumbling blocks of disparate policy, divergent implementation tactics, and the combined overload of excessive school obligations. All this suggests that our greatest need is a shrewder fix on the matters of greatest importance. A major challenge thus arises: How can we best establish new goals within the system, mount a coordinated thrust toward process-based education, and create collaborative forces to energize the changeover itself?

What sort of networking theory, for example, would enable schools to take advantage of existing models? How might school improvement programs evolve new teaching and learning procedures yielding symbiotic benefit? Can the necessary connective tissue be most effectively accomplished by the architects—or the users—of process-based innovations? Can concurrent attention be focused on a process curriculum *and* its corresponding need for pedagogical approaches?

The significance of these requirements is highlighted by problems stemming from recent reform endeavors. Emphasis has focused on three primary goals: (a) formulating better organizational approaches to professional development; (b) introducing intellectually more demanding content, wherein teachers guide students in constructing cumulative personal meaning as well as a sense of its use; and (c) eliminating restrictive controls that inhibit teachers and administrators from right-minded self-direction. Progress has been uneven. Some teachers, caught up in the promise of the intended reform, stay committed. Others, either out of disinterest or confusion, lose interest. Highly motivated at the outset, they gradually abandon a process approach and return to old patterns of pedestrian teaching and the lures of convenience. Hence, although newer texts reflect a conspicuous leaning toward cognitively oriented curricula, most instruction remains dominated by teacher-talk and didacticism.

What might constitute an optimum melding of subject matter and cognitive development? Skills developed through repetitive drill—such as rote memorization knowledge devoid of understanding—neither provoke thought nor enlarge the intellect. Conversely, skills developed through discerning practice—and comprehension evoked by inferring, interpreting, and organizing meaning that is applied in related problem solving—result in a richer, more functional, knowledge stockpile and a considerably expanded efficacy for productive thinking. The critical challenge confronting curriculum practitioners, consequently, is to sequence optimally useful subject matter, incorporate process-centered learning activities, integrate a variety of instructional formats in diverse contexts, ensure that all of these experiences extend mental proficiency, and devise assessment measures that verify the accomplishment of process and content objectives.

When teachers help students access information and ideas, cognitive processing can occur. But only when learners actually "get it"—relating new conceptual insight to previously acquired understanding—does knowledge becomes functional. It follows, therefore, that content and thinking are best taught and evaluated simultaneously.

New instructional materials and testing prototypes are beginning to embrace a conception of teaching and learning wherein functional knowledge is seen as a blend of knowing and using. The 1994 National Assessment of Educational Progress geography tests are illustrative. Subject mastery was construed not as naming world capitals and rivers but rather as the ability to interpret maps; describe significant physical and cultural features of regions; discuss political, social, and economic characteristics of world areas; and so on. The assessment, in turn, dealt not with simple recall but with the competence to analyze, compare, and generalize—to think.

In a sense, process education lends additional weight to Dewey's convictions regarding activity-centered curricula and what currently is referred to as constructivist learning theory. Reduced to its essence, the theory postulates that concepts within subject areas can be taught in a manner that encourages students to draw on their own social experience in constructing meaning. Such personally constructed understanding can also be used in classroom analysis of social phenomena to inject situated cognition—learning in actual contexts. Teaching that enables students to grasp meaning in their academic tasks, to correlate concepts from different subjects, and to fuse learning with the outside world creates an impressive repertoire of useful skills.

Viewed in the large, then, the volumes' implications are of considerable consequence—particularly in pointing the way to replace our present leaden approach with boldly invigorated curriculum designs. In this effort, however, we must not allow preemptive hostility to thwart significant advances—to do so would taunt an already concerned public. New frameworks can structure disciplinary concepts and process-linked instruction into a cognate nexus embracing texts, methodology, and evaluation. Teachers, obviously, will need to redefine goals and procedures, as well as adopt a broader range of intentions, but the advantages would be substantial. Once empowered and unfettered, intellectual processes develop a life of their own, cumulatively acquiring through repeated use strength, complexity, and applicability. Few reform efforts could make more of a difference.

References

Elementary and Secondary Education Amendments of 1969 (Public Law 100-297), 102 Stat. 302, 20 U.S.C. Sec. 1201 et seq.

Perkins, D., & Blythe, T. (1994, February). Teaching for understanding. *Educational Leadership, 51*(5).

Index

CORWIN
PRESS

The Corwin Press logo—a raven striding across an open book—represents the happy union of courage and learning. We are a professional-level publisher of books and journals for K-12 educators, and we are committed to creating and providing resources that embody these qualities. Corwin's motto is "Success for All Learners."